Popcorn Prozac!

Movies to Cure the
Recession Depression!

Popcorn Prozac!

Movies to Cure the Recession Depression!

edited by
Gary J. Svehla and Susan Svehla

Midnight Marquee Press, Inc.
Baltimore, Maryland, USA

Copyright © 2009 by Gary J. Svehla and Susan Svehla
Interior and Cover Design: Susan Svehla
Copy Editors: Barry Atkinson, Janet Atkinson

Without limiting the rights under copyright reserved above, no part of this publication may be reproduced, stored in or introduced into a retrieval system, or transmitted, in any form, or by any means (electronic, mechanical, photocopying, recording or otherwise), without the prior written permission of the copyright owner or the publishers of the book.

ISBN 13: 978-1-887664-94-3
ISBN 10: 1-887664-94-7
Library of Congress Catalog Card Number 2009932870
Manufactured in the United States of America

First Printing by Midnight Marquee Press, Inc., August 2009

Dedication

to all those
who have the gift of
making us laugh

TABLE OF CONTENTS

8 RANDOM GRUMPINESS ON THE STATE OF THE WORLD AND THE MOVIES THAT WILL CHEER US UP

10 MOVIES THAT MAKE ME HAPPY!!

41 MIDNIGHT MARQUEE'S TOP MOVIES TO FIGHT THE RECESSION DEPRESSION

79 AFI 100 TOP LAUGHS!

80 IT'S A LOVE STORY: OUR FAVORITE ROMANTIC SCENES

92 MOVIES WE MUST HAVE IF WE WERE LOST ON A DESERT ISLAND!

RANDOM GRUMPINESS ON THE STATE OF THE WORLD AND THE MOVIES THAT WILL CHEER US UP

Why do we feel the need to provide people with a list of movies to cheer them up?

Well let's see:
- The economy is in the toilet.
- Our soldiers are horrendously wounded and dying in wars we don't believe in or understand.
- Our beloved Congress can't seem to remember that they work for us, not their political party or lobbyists or big business.
- Doctors don't know one patient from another and keep shoving pricey pills into us and ordering expensive tests—mostly because those mysterious health chart statistics are revised every other day—if you have good blood pressure one day, the next day it's too high, so break out the meds.
- A visit to the supermarket requires a home equity loan, and if we don't buy expensive organic foods, we're dooming our families to cancer and other chemically induced ills.
- Any major purchase will fall apart immediately after the warranty expires.
- Customer service is a thing of the past—if you do find a human and they happen to speak English, chances are they are either mean, stupid or lazy and don't care about you or your problem—and don't even get me started on speaking to customer service in India or Guam on the telephone. I know there are people out there dedicated to doing their best, and there are many fine products being manufactured—we just can't seem to find any of them.
- Credit card companies keep cutting our credit limit, then rejecting charges—because we're too near our credit limit. Remember when bills were due in 30 days? No more, they give you only a few days from the time the bill is mailed until the payment is due. I've received statements that were late before I even opened them! Then they make the due date on a Sunday, so there is no way the payment will be received on time.
- In *Night of the Living Dead* and sequels the reason those guts-chomping zombies rose from the dead was, "when there is no more room in hell, the dead will walk the earth?" Well, it must be filling up pretty fast down there between those religious fanatics that think killing anyone who doesn't agree with them is okeydokey with God; those who approve torture and war for no reason except power and greed and oil rather than protecting the helpless and innocent from abuse and slavery and hunger and homelessness or people who hurt children or animals, etc., etc., etc.
- Schools are teaching kids how to pass tests that teach them nothing except what's on the test—it terrifies me to think that these future doctors, police, nurses, teachers, firemen, etc. can pass a test but can't do much else—except text each other. And those world-shaking texts consist mostly of asking each other what they are doing as they are texting. I'm sorry, but I don't think anyone's life is so interesting that they have to talk on the phone or text while driving, shopping, eating out or visiting friends.
- Fashionistas and Hollywood have us convinced that anyone over a size 2 is fat. In a survey taken a few years ago, women overwhelmingly felt that they would rather be hit by a bus than be fat. Do you realize that today Marilyn Monroe and Jane Russell probably couldn't get a job because they would be considered too fat!
- Is it just me or do most TV and movie stars all look the same? They are either generic blonde or brunette—I can't tell the good guys from the bad guys or the nice girls from the sluts. And what's with commercials that don't tell you what they're selling? And BTW, who are these reality TV people all over the cover of magazines and TV talk shows? That's NOT Entertainment.
- Torture porn and slasher films have desensitized people to the point that nothing shocks audiences—the news is constantly reporting teenagers or preteens involved in stabbings or shootings. Even the TV previews for the 2009 remakes of *Last House on*

An average guy wakes up 500 years in the future and the populace is so stupid that he's the most intelligent person alive in *Idiocracy* (2006)

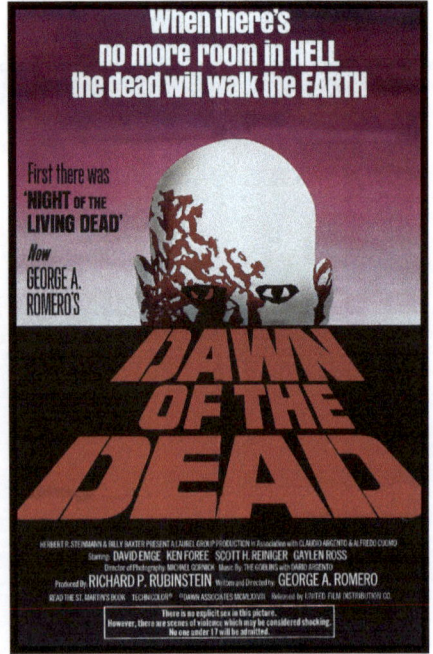

the Left and *Friday the 13th* have been too frightening for me. And seriously, calling those movies "re-imaginings" rather than remakes, how stupid do they think we are?

•Whatever happened to a nice 90-minute film? The last thing a depressed populace needs is another pain in the butt from sitting through a three-hour movie that would have been a better picture cut to 90 minutes.

And why are the only films shown at film festivals or considered for major awards pretentious, heavy, ponderous dramas? Even *Marley and Me* (2008), which was advertised as a sweet comedy, turns into the most gut-wrenching movie experience since *Old Yeller* (1957). I've always said if I want to be depressed, I'll call my family—I don't have to buy a ticket.

•Why are most comedies today filled with bodily function jokes and the quest to get laid? Once in a while a token women's film is made—some beautiful but silly marriage-mad girl meets the perfect man, they argue, their hate turns to love. This is the best they can do? Do they really believe women don't go to movies or control the purse strings? Think how much money Hollywood could make if they actually made movies for everybody, not just teenage boys.

But what is more annoying than bad writing and insipid jokes is the absurd theory that if a movie has even one miniscule chuckle it's a comedy. These modern films are all considered comedies: *Adaptation* (2006) *Bad Santa* (2003), *Big Fish* (2004), *Bowling for Columbine* (2002), *Cabin Fever* (2003), *Chicago* (2002), *The Darjeeling Limited* (2007), *Duplex* (2003), *Eternal Sunshine of the Spotless Min*d (2004), *Juno* (2007), *Little Miss Sunshine* (2006), *Lost in Translation* (2003), *The Royal Tenenbaums* (2001), *Rushmore* (1998)—comedies—seriously? I don't think so.

•Finally, don't turn on the news or you may as well just get out the noose. War; Economic Downfall; Death; Torture; Abuse; Illegal Immigrants; that idiotic, unemployed woman who had eight babies; Pandemics; Food Scares; Health Scares; Reality Television…

Oh my God, I'm so depressed! I'm going to have to either crawl into a fetal position in a dark closet or make some popcorn and cocoa, gather up my equally depressed husband and our never-depressed dog Buddy (he likes the popcorn), and have a cheer-ourselves-up movie marathon.

But what movies should we choose for our marathon? During the Great Depression, which is considered to have lasted from the stock market crash of 1929 through 1941, Hollywood turned out glitzy, bubbly light-hearted entertainment to bring a much needed smile to the face of audiences that could barely afford the 10-cent movie ticket. But people managed to spare that dime and turned out to the movie palaces in droves. Don't get me wrong, there were dramas, mysteries and horrors aplenty. But during those days, most movies ended on an upbeat note. Today, it's almost mandatory to have a downbeat ending; how many times is that dead villain going to come back for one

Today, Marilyn Monroe and Jane Russell would be considered too fat by Hollywood.

last murderous attack? In those days, a hero was a hero (not a whiny angst-ridden mess), the women were feisty (not snarky or abusive know-it-alls) and the endings were always happy.

• • • • •

We asked readers of our magazines, *Midnight Marquee* and *Mad About Movies,* and our website http://www.midmar.com to tell us what movies they viewed to cheer themselves up. The replies are quite interesting, not to mention intriguing (or kinda scary!). It's always fun to discover how other people think. Through the years we have also had our readers and writers tell us their favorite love scenes in movies and what three movies they'd take with them to a desert island. I've also included those lists—I find them fascinating, and hope the readers of this book will do so as well. And finally, Gary and I made up our top list of movies that make us happy. The selections are not all critically praised—some have been pretty well trashed by film critics, but we still love them. Gary tends to like darker movies—he says they make him feel better about his life. While I tend to like what he calls fluffy bunny movies, but I'm not ashamed—the more sappy, sugary happiness the better—but only if the story is decent and the acting is good. It really is true, one man's trash is another man's treasure.

> *First we're going to let our readers take it away!*
> *We've tried to keep the format of this book consistent, which is a real chore with a book of lists. For the sake of space (and laziness), we've only listed the year of the film's release the first time it is mentioned in the book.*

MOVIES THAT MAKE ME HAPPY!!

First up: Jeff Miller (author *Horror Spoofs of Abbott and Costello: A Critical Assessment of the Comedy Team's Monster Films*):

Recently, a Los Angeles-based family began publishing a free newspaper called *The Happy Times* devoted—obviously—to what makes people of all ages happy and content. I contributed an article to their second issue entitled, "Meeting My Heroes Makes Me Happy," a light-hearted telling of how, after all these years in Hollywood, I finally got to meet Robert Culp, one of my favorite actors.

As manager of Rocket Video, I am always asked for movie recommendations and the other night, an attractive young woman asked me what movies make me happy. She was looking solely for an evening of feel-good flicks and I gladly obliged with some of my personal favorites.

This theme of happiness is obviously on a lot of minds. It's no surprise—in today's economic climate, it is becoming more and more difficult to feel anything but despair. So I'm not surprised that I am once again discussing what movies and television shows make me happy.

While I find it easy to list the films and television episodes that make me happy, I find it difficult to explain why they do. Multiple factors play a part in how a movie will affect me—who am I viewing it with, what frame of mind I am in, where I am seeing it, etc. I do find that most of the flicks that make me happy inevitably end up on "my top 10-20 films of all time" lists, since these are the movies that I return to again and again for that warm, cuddly feeling of contentment.

I believe that many people actually do NOT compile their film favorite lists based on what makes them happy. I have encountered and known many film buffs, historians and students over the years, and more often than not, their favorite lists are more dependent on the quality of the pictures. I find that many of these people—let's just go ahead and call them film snobs—will compile a list of what they feel are the top-10 best movies ever made as their own top-10 favorite list, and not take into account movies that affect them on a more personal or emotional level. It makes me wonder—there's nothing wrong with putting the greatest films ever made on your personal top-10 list, but does one really stick in a DVD of something like *The Bicycle Thief, Battleship Potemkin* or even *Schindler's List* when one's spirits need lifting?

I also find that others view my favorite movies as "guilty pleasures." Now the folks at Midnight Marquee published two wonderful volumes of authors writing about their guilty pleasures from the horror genre, and I must say I loved these books (in fact, they were my first introduction to the world of MidMar and now I'm writing for them!). But I have to be honest—I don't like the term "guilty pleasure." Why should I feel guilty if a film such as *Sh! The Octopus* or *The Gorilla* makes me happy or brings me enjoyment? As long as you're not watching kiddie porn or snuff films, one should not feel guilty enjoying any movie if it brings personal satisfaction and fulfillment.

I guess what I am trying to say is that there are lots of films out there—some critically acclaimed, others abhorred—that delight me and make me happy from the beginning of their running time until the end. And most of the time, I don't know why they make me feel so good. Truthfully, I don't care. My favorite films need no defense and require no explanation. I simply connected with them at the right moment in time and space and they won a place in my heart. So here are five choices from my ever-expanding list of favorites that I turn to when I'm down. I'll even try to tell you a little bit about them:

ABBOTT AND COSTELLO MEET FRANKENSTEIN (1948)—When I was a kid, I used to get up on Sunday mornings, get the TV guide from the Sunday paper and see which Abbott and Costello film was going to be shown at 11:00 on the Sunday Morning Movie on WPIX Channel 11, out of New York. If it was an Abbott and Costello horror comedy, I was very happy. If it was **Abbott and Costello Meet Frankenstein**, I was ecstatic.

From the moment I first started comprehending the movies I was watching, I loved Abbott and Costello and old horror flicks. So it was magical to me that a film existed that featured my favorite comedy team matching wits with my favorite monsters. It made me wish that all my favorite fictional characters could cross over and meet one another. That's why I once wrote an episode of the Incredible Hulk where he travels to Cabot Cove, Maine and helps Jessica Fletcher solve a murder. It's also why my friend Sandy wrote an *X-Files* episode just for me where Mulder and Scully meet fellow agent Bill Maxwell and investigate reports of a man in a red suit performing superhuman feats. It's why I wish the programs *Monk* and *Psyche* would cross over before *Monk* ends its run.

It's difficult for me to understand how anyone can dislike this film. Most agree it is the greatest horror comedy of all time. The comedy side of the film features Bud and Lou at their best, and the horror side—played straight by the Universal monsters—can still frighten the youngsters. It is the perfect combination—the Reese's peanut butter cup of movies—two great tastes that taste great together.

I have had many long-lasting friendships over the years that started because the person was a fan of the film like me. I love sharing favorite lines and reciting dialogue with these people. Everyone has his/her favorite moments. I was once madly in love with a girl who loved the cute way Costello asks "Me?!?" after being accused by MacDougal of being "in on it." My friend Sean and I currently share a laugh over one simple Bud Abbott line from the flick: When Lawrence Talbot says, "You must be Chic Young," Bud replies, "So what?" Don't ask me why, but it tickles our funny bones.

This film is my all-time favorite. It tops the list. I've written about it over and over again and here I am writing about it again. I can't seem to escape it. But since it makes me so happy and continues to do, I don't really care!

FLY AWAY HOME (1996)—This is the film with Anna Paquin as a young girl who has just lost her mother in a car accident. Sent to live with her eccentric father (Jeff Daniels) in Canada, she has difficulty adjusting to her new life and surroundings. When she finds an abandoned nest of eggs, she cares for them until they hatch, revealing adorable little wild goslings that imprint themselves based on the girl they see as their mother.

Now Paquin must teach them how to survive. She must also teach them how to fly south for the winter, so her aviator father and his friends build two small planes that will lead the geese to a preserve in the United States. Their flight brings them national news coverage and little Anna becomes a heroine.

This feel-good film is shelved in the children's section of my video store, but it's a film anyone can enjoy. Just thinking about it makes me smile. I'm a sucker for this kind of story and I never seem to get tired of it. What I really like is that it's not just a story about a girl saving some geese; it's also a story about a father re-connecting with his daughter. I'll be brutally honest now, too—every time I watch this movie, I bawl. I'm not talking crying because I'm sad; I'm talking bona fide tears of pure joy. There's something about those damn birds and how the world embraces their plight—excuse me, for a moment, I'm starting to tear up just thinking about it.

The premise of the film is not that far-fetched, by the way. The film is based on a book called *Father Goose* about two men who experimented with imprinting wild birds using small aircrafts. The idea would be that eventually we could save species of birds on the verge of extinction by changing their migration patterns and leading them to safe refuges for the winter. Isn't that fantastic?

BABE (1995)—Everyone calls it "the pig movie" and it's another one that makes me cry with happiness every time I see it. I lose it at the end, just after Babe has led the sheep into the pen before the astonished eyes of the sheepdog competition's judges and audience. James Cromwell says, "That will do," the judges award top scores and the audience is on its feet cheering and screaming. But it's that one shot of Mrs. Hoggett crying, as she seems to fall in love with her husband all over again (and finally seeing in Babe what he has seen all along) that brings on the waterworks.

If you want to see a film that defines the word "charming," this is it. From the adorable mice who giggle as they read the titles to the song that Farmer Hoggett dances to when Babe is sick, the film is loaded with wonderful moments that win me over no matter what my mood. At the same time, the film inspires cultural and racial understanding, reinforces the belief that we can do great things no matter what everyone else says and gives us the satisfaction of seeing an underdog come out on top. Not bad for a movie about a talking pig.

THE FULL MONTY (1997)—Unemployed and broke, five British men in a dying town decide to earn money by putting on a strip show *a la* Chippendales. One of them is fat, one is old, one is skinny and suicidal, one is divorced—in other words, they're five unassuming, average, normal men. To sell tickets, they decide to go "the full monty," which means strip completely naked. The film follows them as they conquer their fears and actually regain their dignity by taking off their clothes in front of a packed house of friends and family.

Despite a plot that might put off some people, **The Full Monty** is a charming, classy pic. It was a star-making vehicle for at least three of its cast members and it launched a craze

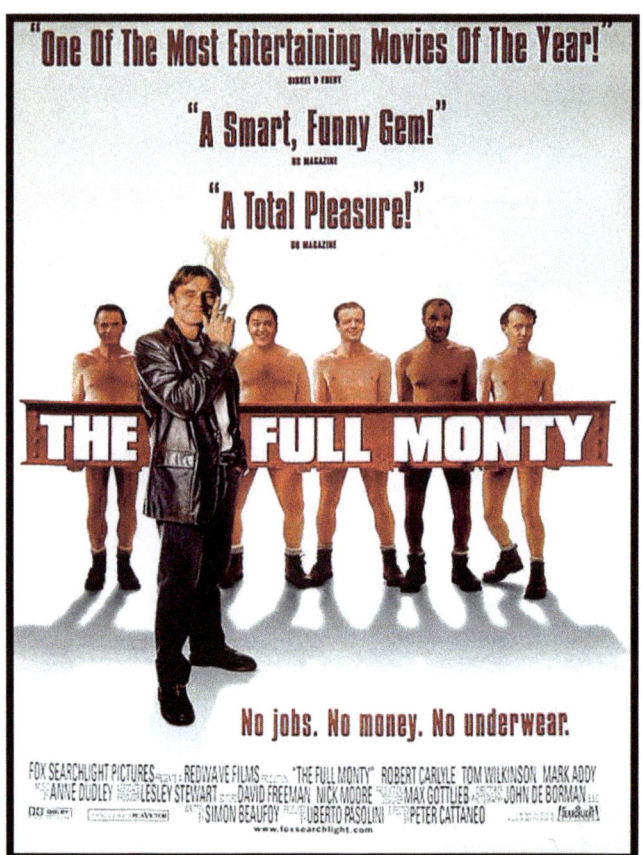

that led to a Broadway musical as well as imitations such as a take-off episode (no pun intended) of *The Drew Carey Show*. The film is funny and touching and designed to make you feel good. The ending gets me every time—what's magical about it is that the audience of women *and* men who come to see our heroes bare all aren't there to jeer or mock them. They are there to support them. They applaud their efforts to do something bold and beautiful. They applaud their efforts to regain their dignity and earn money. And I think they are applauding their efforts too, for one night, they bring some life and zest to a town that has curled up and died. This film is a modern day classic.

YOU'LL FIND OUT (1940)—This horror-comedy-musical is despised by almost everyone. Very few have anything kind to say about it. But I love it. I've watched it over and over because it always brings a smile to my face.

I was in college when I first read about the film in Greg Mank's classic book *Karloff and Lugosi*. After a childhood consuming every creature feature I could see, I could not believe I had never heard of this film before. Despite Mank's negative take on the film, it sounded intriguing to me, so I was delighted when I caught it a few weeks later at midnight on a Sunday evening on the local public television station. I was hooked. For me, the film works, because like **Abbott and Costello Meet Frankenstein**, it balances its horror and comedy sides so evenly.

On the horror side, the film manages a handful of moments that can still cause a chill to run up and down a spine. There's a séance sequence that features ghostly apparitions and frightening vocals and it ranks as one of the creepiest scenes from the horror genre flicks of the 1940s.

Plus the film boasts three great villains—Boris Karloff, Bela Lugosi and Peter Lorre—the only film in which the three horror greats appear together. Each man gets some choice dialogue and each one is given a great entrance into the film's action. (I remember sharing the film with a female acquaintance on a rainy afternoon, and after Lugosi appeared in the film, she remarked, "Bela Lugosi always knew how to make an entrance.")

On the comedy side, you've got the antics of Kay Kyser and his College of Musical Knowledge. Many of their jokes, especially those from the band's comic Ish Kabibble, are pure corn but my tastes happen to run to that kind of period humor. Kyser and his playmates come off as likable in the long run and they make the movie more of a party than anything else.

The songs are fun, some combining humor with catchy melodies. They mostly come in the first half of the film. Once the action starts and multiple murders are attempted, the cast puts aside its singing in order to chase ghosts.

Again, I can't explain it. This one just makes me happy.

The "assignment" to write a few words about the films that make us happy mentioned that we could also discuss our favorite television episodes. I'm going to list four of my favorite television shows (these series make me happy en masse) and name my favorite entries from each:

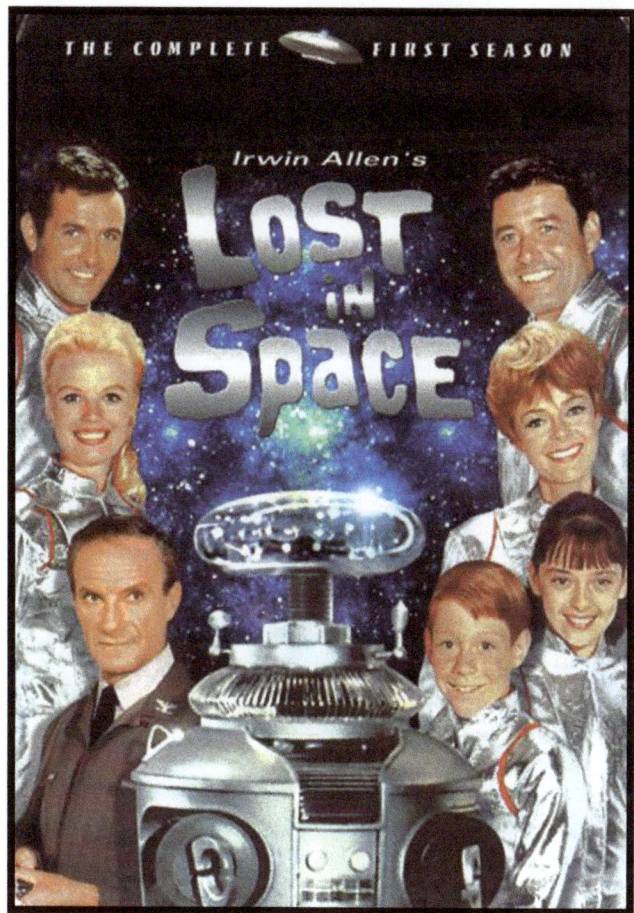

THE INCREDIBLE HULK (1978-1982)—Along with Abbott and Costello, the Hulk shaped my life and continues to do so. I still dream of being Bill Bixby, wandering the country and turning the tables on bad guys and bullies by transforming into a super strong juggernaut. The magic of the show, for me, is that when the Hulk makes one of his appearances, he becomes the ultimate center of attention—all eyes are on him and everything else that is going on comes to a complete standstill. At times, I wish I could have that affect on given situations; paradoxically I sometimes crave the anonymity that David Banner has, traveling under aliases and believed to be dead. My favorite episodes include the two-part "Prometheus," where Banner is stuck in mid-transformation and captured by a top secret military installation who believe him to be an alien; "The First," another two-parter where the Hulk battles an evil, murderous Hulk; "Metamorphosis" with the Hulk disrupting a punk rock concert and "747," where the Hulk lands a plane. Truthfully, however, when I'm feeling blue, I just stick in any random episode from the series and watch Bill Bixby turn into Lou Ferrigno. Those moments—complete with frenetic music and the shot of Banner's white eyes—still make me so excited I want to pee and still have me squirming with excitement like I remember when I was a kid—though now *not* followed by my frustrated father's exclamation, "Calm down! It's only a TV show!" If only, for me, it was…

THE GREATEST AMERICAN HERO (1981-1983)—All of us kids dreamt of having super powers, but the fun of this show is what happens when a guy who doesn't want super powers actually gets them. This show makes me laugh out loud while at the same time completely draws me into the action. I like everything about this series. I like William Katt and his hair. I like Connie Selleca—how can you not? I like the music. I like the suit (I have one of my own that I wear every Halloween). I like the fact that Ralph lost the instruction book which will always keep him on the defensive, because he's never quite sure what the suit can do. Finally, I like Robert Culp. Put simply, Bill Maxwell is one of the greatest television characters of all time. My favorite episodes include "The Beast in Black," a haunted house episode where Ralph enters the spirit world only to find his suit does not work there; "The Shock Will Kill You," where a magnetized Ralph must face a deadly space alien and "My Heroes Have Always Been Cowboys," where we see that being a hero can be difficult and learn that those who we see as heroes are often just as human as ourselves.

LOST IN SPACE (1965-1968)—Like Bill Maxwell, Dr. Smith is another of television's all-time greatest characters. Unlike most everyone else, I actually enjoy the later, campy color episodes where Smith is a buffoon more than the more serious black and white ones where Smith is cunning and evil. The friendship between Smith, Will Robinson and the Robot is classic and endearing to me, and I love this series because it's old-fashioned fun. My favorite episode is "The Time Merchant" where Dr. Smith goes back in time to a few hours before the launching of the Jupiter 2. The Robot is sent back to tell him that if he does not stowaway on the ship, the Robinsons will be killed. Will Smith sacrifice his newfound happiness? At one point Smith tells the Robot that he wishes he could be different and be a more courageous man, and this becomes a great moment. I also love "The Promised Planet" which features a planet full of teenagers who use the word "groovy" a lot trying to brainwash Will and Penny. See this one just to watch Jonathan Harris dance.

EVERYBODY LOVES RAYMOND (1996-2005)—I think this is one of the funniest sitcoms of all time. It's simple and basic but fueled by great writers and great actors. My favorite character is Brad Garritt's Robert Barone—he makes the show worth watching, hands down. The best episodes are "She's the One," where Robert's frog-obsessed girlfriend eats a fly; "Marie's Sculpture," one of the funniest half-hours of TV ever and "Lucky Suit," which throws in an incredibly touching moment in the middle of belly laughs that shows that Marie does love Robert just as much as Raymond.

Just thinking about all these wonderful movies and television shows makes me want to go back and watch them all over again. It also creates a chain reaction in my mind as I think of more and more films that also make me smile and feel good. There's actually enough out there to keep me happy forever. What more can a person ask for?

• • • • • • •

by Steven Thornton (*Midnight Marquee* contributor):

SAFETY LAST (1923)—The image is as outrageous as it is iconic—Harold Lloyd dangles precipitously from a skyscraper while the hustle and bustle of a busy metropolis passes by far below. **Safety Last** is the film, and while it may not be the most critically lauded comedy of the silent era, it is a movie that never fails to tickle my funny bone.

Like all classic silent comedies, **Safety Last** is a primer in the art of the sight gag. Lloyd's predicament, the absurd but logical climax of a series of little white lies and unforeseen complications, grows in scope and intensity until he is quite literally hanging by a fingertip. And despite the "primitive" cinematic techniques of decades past, the imagery is so breathtakingly real that even jaded viewers of today will be tempted to ask, "Just how in the hell did they do that?"

Lloyd may not have been able to generate the pathos of Charlie Chaplin nor could he channel the existential zaniness of Buster Keaton, but his crowd-pleasing comedies consistently hit the bull's-eye with audiences of the 1920s and still hold up solidly today. In times like these, when it feels like we are all about to fall off a ledge, a little laughter may be just what we need.

LAUREL AND HARDY COMEDIES (1930-1935)—Of all the different styles of entertainment, comedy is arguably the most transient. What is hilarious to one generation may hardly elicit a chuckle from the next. Fortunately a few comedic legends have overcome this barrier and managed to produce laughter that stands the test of time. In my book, no comedian or comedy team holds up as well as Laurel and Hardy.

The perfect venue for Laurel and Hardy were the short films that the duo made for Hal Roach Studios in the early 1930s. Watching these assorted two-and three-reelers, I am amazed at the precision of the formula by which the pair worked—set up the joke, build the tension, delay it with some pleasingly daft verbal interchange, then deliver the payoff, usually with an unexpected but inspired pratfall as an added punctuation mark. The personalities add as much to the hilarity as the gags do. In fact, I often find myself returning to these films just to spend some time in the company of Stan and Ollie. I can't think of a nicer compliment to pay any film performer.

THE ADVENTURES OF ROBIN HOOD (1938)—Did you ever dream of brandishing a sword, rescuing a fair maiden and vanquishing the forces of evil from your homeland? If so, sit back and watch this film bring that fantasy to life in vivid, glorious Technicolor.

Starring Errol Flynn in the role he was born to play, **The Adventures of Robin Hood** is a grand and glorious romp that spotlights all the best attributes of Hollywood's Golden Age. The cast is well nigh perfect, from the enchanting Oliva de Havilland to the villainous trio of Claude Rains, Basil Rathbone and Melville Cooper. Add to this mix a cadre of colorful and familiar character actors, an Oscar-winning score by Erich Wolfgang Korngold and the taunt direction of the legendary Michael Curtiz, and you've got an entertaining and action-packed spectacle that holds its own against the best films of all time. The world "classic" hardly does justice to this movie—they really don't make 'em like this anymore.

IT'S A MAD, MAD, MAD, MAD WORLD (1963)—Before adjectives like "subversive" and "cutting edge" became synonymous with popular entertainment, the world was amused and diverted by a generation of comics whose goal was to simply make people laugh. As those days were coming to a close, **It's A Mad, Mad, Mad, Mad World** captured the feeling of that gone but fondly remembered era in all its over-the-top glory.

Featuring a once-in-a-lifetime collection of Old School comic pros (Sid Caesar, Milton Berle, Ethel Merman, Jonathan Winters, Edie Adams, Phil Silvers, Buddy Hackett, Terry-Thomas and Mickey Rooney, just to name the principles!), **It's A Mad, Mad, Mad, Mad World** makes no pretense about any high-minded social significance. Spencer Tracy is on hand for the obligatory straight role in a loosely concocted story that, for those who need a moral, makes light of the folly of human greed. But it's the scene stealing by the comic stars and cameos from nearly all the living legends of classic screen comedy (the bit by Jerry Lewis is priceless!) that really makes this show come to life.

It's A Mad, Mad, Mad World is far from perfect—burdened with an elephantine structure (192 minutes in length, in its original Roadshow version), the film runs out of gas well before its finale. The endless barrage of stunts in the latter reels, expertly executed though they might be, only adds to the impression that the film is trying a little too hard for its own good. But as a window into the entertainment world of generations ago, **It's A Mad, Mad, Mad, Mad World** is a unique experience that is sure to help whenever you feel that you are starting to take life a little too seriously.

A HARD DAY'S NIGHT (1964)—The movie that legitimized the Beatles in the eyes of the adults, **A Hard Day's Night** is a joyful time capsule of the mid-1960s. Fresh, fun and oh so irreverent, it provided compelling evidence that the Fab Four was everything the hype machine proclaimed them to be.

For me, this movie also supplies the compelling tug of nostalgia. The pop music scene of the 1960s was such a heady, crazy experience to witness firsthand. Change was in the air and the new faces and compelling voices of the younger generation were leading the way. The Revolution, it would seem, was coming via vinyl 45s and transistor radios. Everyone was invited—all you had to do to participate was to follow the lead of four playful subversives who were phenomenally skilled at the joyful noise that was called rock and roll music.

Time would soon tarnish the memory of that naïve but hopeful dream. Even the Beatles eventually fell victim to "I,

Me, Mine" bitchiness that seems to be the eternal province of adults. But **A Hard Day's Night** is my ticket back to a time when the world was so much younger and dreams were in the air.

And, damn, those tunes were catchy too.

• • • • • • •

by Gary J. Svehla : In no particular order:

SONS OF THE DESERT (1933) with Laurel and Hardy. This film never fails to make me laugh, and even the stereotypical shrew wives and drunk party boys exist in a far more innocent era. The talents of Laurel and Hardy are here at their peak, demonstrating their talents in their finest sound feature. I can watch this film (and **WAY OUT WEST**) twice a year, and it never gets old. Just the manner in which our boys attempt to outsmart the wives, thinking their lie (shipwrecked on a health vacation cruise) is foolproof (while they were actually hooting it up at the annual Sons of the Desert convention) is classic. And when Stan finally cracks, crying his heart out, when his wife suddenly appears coming home from a hunting expedition, rifle in hand, is hilarious. And for his truthfulness, Stan gets rewarded, allowed to put on his smoking jacket and smoke a cigarette in the house. Ollie, on the other hand, gets a black eye from being pelted with a heavy metal assault of pots and pans.

Any **THREE STOOGES** two-reeler. As a kid I bought into the party line that The Three Stooges were second-rate hacks compared to Laurel and Hardy. Today, I think their shorts are comedy classics. Anything featuring Curly or Shemp is okay by me. In these short 20 minutes of comic insanity, I can forget all the tensions and problems and simply laugh out loud. Even though the shorts was formulaic and often repeated the same basic premises, the antics of the Stooges with their distinct comic personalities and physical antics never failed to make me laugh.

The best of the **SHIRLEY TEMPLE** features always offer emotional support. As a kid I would watch them all when they were shown on Sunday morning. I just enjoyed that perfect world where a child could reunite feuding parents or stowaway at sea to heal all wounds. Add to her cute antics the singing and dancing, and we have perfect escapist cinema. **HEIDI** (1937) was always my favorite, and as a child, always made me cry. **THE LITTLE PRINCESS** (1939) was a close second. The persona of young Temple was every kid's best friend, and she demonstrated the goodness that exists in all of us.

Even though Sue never understood why, **IT'S A WONDERFUL LIFE** (1946) always makes me feel good about the human condition. The world of Bedford Falls where even the local slut comes off as almost virtuous is a revelation. Everyone always rises to the occasion and does the right thing, and even if we are forced to live a life of constant sacrifice, in the end we are glad we lived the life we did.

All of the classic and not so classic **Republic, Universal and Columbia Serials** always give me a pleasant thrill. The ultimate battles between good and evil, told via stereotypical scientists, heroines, heroes and villains never fail to comfort me and remind me of a world I never knew. I enjoy the stilted

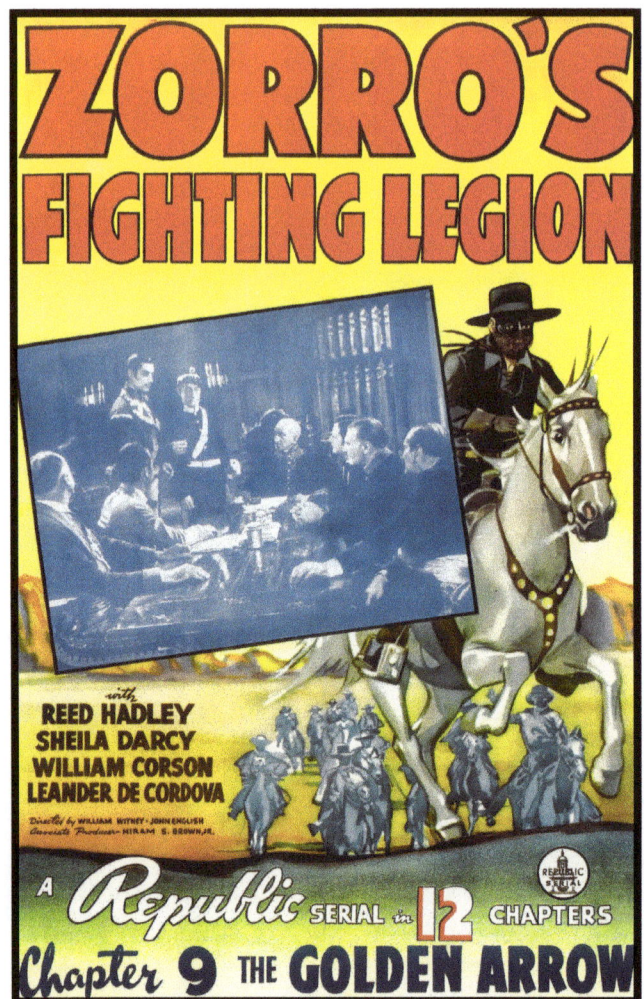

dialogue, the fantastic science fiction and horror elements (including death rays that might destroy the world) and those wonderful Republic free-for-all fights.

• • • • • • • •

by Allen Kretschmar: Here's an odd assortment, but they all fit the category for me:

STAR TREK IV: THE VOYAGE HOME (1986)—Offers hope for the future of we silly humans, punctuated with lots of humor, but never too goofy; featuring a wonderful and audacious time-travel plot; and as an extra bonus for us *Trek* fans, the movie does the best job of any *Star Trek* film of giving every member of the crew something meaningful to do.

RIO BRAVO (1959)—Reinforces the triumph of good over evil, love over hate, and redemption over oblivion. A great feel-good Western.

APOLLO 13 (1995)—Shows what individuals can accomplish when they truly work as a team toward a common goal, even against all odds. Gotta love Ed Harris as Gene Kranz! Where was the best supporting Oscar?

THE WORLD'S FASTEST INDIAN (2005)—"based on a true story"—Inspirational tales are often forced and stodgy, but Anthony Hopkins' absolutely spot-on perfect performance—and a great screenplay—elevates this one into the stratosphere.

A LITTLE ROMANCE (1979)—Chuckle if you will, and honestly I've never been able to quite pin down why I love this little George Roy Hill picture as much as I do, but I do. It's got a great score, a beguiling innocence, and a delightfully hammy Laurence Olivier (and a debuting Diane Lane). It also features some inside references for movie buffs, and Broderick Crawford appears as himself!

• • • • • • •

by Mark F. Berry:

THE COURT JESTER (1955)—Best comedy swashbuckler ever! Danny Kaye plays a meek and mild type who masquerades as the titular character and ends up saving a kingdom from the evil machinations of Basil Rathbone. Delightful songs, that wonderful trademark Danny Kaye patter, brilliant swordplay, a wonderful supporting cast featuring John Carradine, Angela Lansbury, Glynis Johns, Robert Middleton and Cecil Parker. Also a great message: Danny doesn't need pecs and biceps to save the day, just a caring heart, kindness and a little strategic hypnosis to bring out the hero within! "The pellet with the poison's in the vessel with the pestle!"

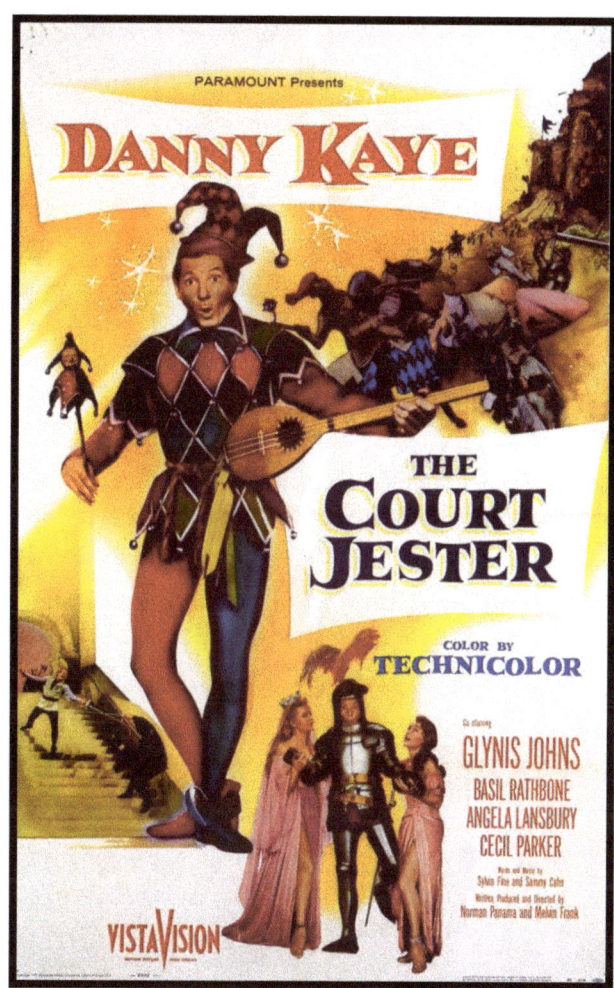

THE ADVENTURES OF ROBIN HOOD—The greatest swashbuckler of all time. The perfect cast, Errol Flynn in his signature role, fighting for truth and justice in a medieval once-upon-a-time world that never existed but should have. The film features a perfect supporting cast, perfect action scenes, gorgeous 3-strip Technicolor. The perfect film! Hasn't aged an iota since 1938, and never will. Its message is timeless.

THE FLYING DEUCES (1939)—The gospel according to Laurel and Hardy is childlike faith, loyalty, friendship, unconditional love and the ability to remain uncorrupted by the world. Stan joins the Foreign Legion with Ollie to help him forget an unhappy infatuation. Try this one and **CHUMP AT OXFORD** on the same theme.

CITY LIGHTS (1931)—The poignant uplifting story of the Little Tramp's love for a blind flower girl—and the sacrifices he makes to help her see. An unforgettable conclusion—one that James Agee said was the highest moment in movies. No argument here! Chaplin's pinnacle, and the film becomes his truest evocation of his immortal creation.

THE STRONG MAN (1926)—Very early Frank Capra film featuring legendary silent comedian Harry Langdon. Langdon plays a Belgian soldier who comes to America as the valet of the titular character, in search of the female pen-pal he has fallen in love with, but has never met. Along the way he has a hilarious encounter with a femme fatale, and cleans up a wicked saloon town before settling down with the girl—who turns out to be blind. The meek shall inherit the earth!!

• • • • • • •

by Cadaverino:

GODSPELL (1973)—A disparate group of young people gather for a modern-day Jesus, and re-enact the gospel parables. David Greene's joyous film adaptation of the long-running stage musical by John-Michael Tebelak uses New York City as a playground for an Indian summer of '60s flower power. Stephen Schwartz's bright song score ranges from folk to gospel, vaudeville, and rock. Victor Garber and Lynn Thigpen make their screen debuts among a talented ensemble cast.

RUGGLES OF RED GAP (1935)—An English butler (Charles Laughton) is brought to the American west by a couple who have won him in a poker game. A Lubitsch-worthy comedy of manners, directed by Leo McCarey, that's also a valentine to American self-definition.

THOROUGHLY MODERN MILLIE (1967)—Screwball musical set in 1920s NYC, with new gals in town Julie Andrews and Mary Tyler Moore mixing it up with charmers John Gavin and James Fox and dragon lady Beatrice Lillie. Toss in Chinatown hijinks, a chase climax, and Carol Channing fired out of a cannon. Fizzy fun on a big budget.

MIRACLE IN MILAN (1951)—An unsinkable Chaplinesque innocent inspires his shantytown neighbors in their confrontations with authorities.

POCKETFUL OF MIRACLES (1961)—Alcoholic street vendor Apple Annie (Bette Davis) gets a respectable makeover from a Damon Runyon cast of characters when she learns her daughter (Ann-Margret) will be visiting her. Heart-warming comedy directed by Frank Capra shows the importance of community and looking out for one other.

• • • • • • •

by Dick Klemensen (editor *Little Shoppe of Horrors*):

THE GOODBYE GIRL (1977)—You come away believing there are some good people in the world, and a man can love and be loyal to a woman (who has been dumped so many times) and her suspicious child. Love this movie!!

MASK (1985)—I always cry at the end, but the strength of this young man who was dealt a bad hand makes me feel very good.

MIRACLE OF MORGAN'S CREEK (1944)—Man, Norval Jones (aka "Ignatz Ratskywatsky") and his total love for Gertrude—to go to jail for her and take on her children. Great warm hearted movie, and it's a very funny comedy.

• • • • • • •

by John Wooley (co-author *Forgotten Horrors 4*):

Well, I'm game. Here are five movies that never fail to lift my spirits, all for various reasons. As you can see, it's a pretty eclectic group, but I suspect you could say the same about a lot of the other lists you're receiving. Here they are, in no particular order:

WHITE CHRISTMAS (1954)—Yes, it's a beautiful picture with some great (and a couple of not-so-great) Irving Berlin tunes, swell production numbers and amusing repartee between Crosby and Kaye. I was lucky enough to see it in a real theater a few years ago, when Paramount gave it a seasonal reissue, and the VistaVision presentation is still breathtaking.

But what I like most about **White Christma**s is the fact that it's all about selflessness. Doing something for someone else, in fact, is the axis on which this picture spins. Everybody's trying to do some good and help one another out, and while this impulse gets everyone involved into trouble (lending credence to the cynic's pronouncement about how no good deed goes unpunished), each character comes out fine in the end, when one joyously sentimental moment gets piled onto another.

That ending, in fact, is one of the two parts of the film that never fail to choke me up. The other is the moment when Dean Jagger, as the general, walks across that stage in his uniform and hears one of his old soldiers bark out: "Ten-hut!" Cheap emotion? You bet. But when you get caught up in the stresses and predicaments of your own life, it's good to think about the joys of helping someone else out, and **White Christmas** reinforces those thoughts in a consistent and very sweet way.

FREAKS (1932)—The ultimate revenge of the nerds, this peerless little picture still has the power to shock, disturb and stick in your head. I show it in a class I teach on horror movies at Oklahoma State University's Tulsa campus, and even students hardened by the over-the-top splatter of the *Saw* and *Hostel* movies often seem shell-shocked when the lights go up. It's never hard to get them to talk about it, either. Some see it as a film about greed, others as a commentary on outward vs. inward beauty, and still others as an example of social-class barriers right up there with *The Outsiders* (which remains highly popular in these parts because it was filmed by Coppola in Tulsa and written by the city's Susie Hinton). One guy even saw the famous wedding banquet ("one of us...one of us...") as a form of Holy Communion.

Freaks really is the kind of film you want to talk about, because it's hard for those encountering it for the first time to believe what they've just seen. Sure, it flopped big and horrified MGM when it originally came out, but as a musician friend of mine says, you can starve to death just as easily being ahead of your time as you can being behind it. This may indeed have been the picture that derailed Tod Browning's career, but he does a brilliant job of illuminating (as well as casting shadows across) the subterranean world of the 1930s sideshow and making it into a kind of weird funhouse-mirror version of our own.

I became a fan of Wallace Ford because of this film; to this day, I hope I'm a little like his character Phroso, a reasonably "normal" guy who has plenty of compassion and empathy for anyone who needs either, and who lifts the people around him up without making them think he's doing them any favors. His character is nothing less than noble, and the little romance between him and Leila Hyams' scrappy Venus, as well as their interactions with the "freaks," never fails to warm my heart.

ROCK 'N' ROLL HIGH SCHOOL (1979)—P.J. Soles gets the role of her career, as Riff Randell, a kind of punked-out Betty Boop, constantly in motion, always grooving to the music in her head. Dey Young is sweet and beautiful, a just-right foil for Soles' character, and the Ramones are, well, the Ramones, the objects of Riff's affection. Just as good are the authority figures, played by three of my favorite character actors of all time: Paul Bartel (as a teacher), Dick Miller (the police chief) and Mary Woronov (Principal Togar).

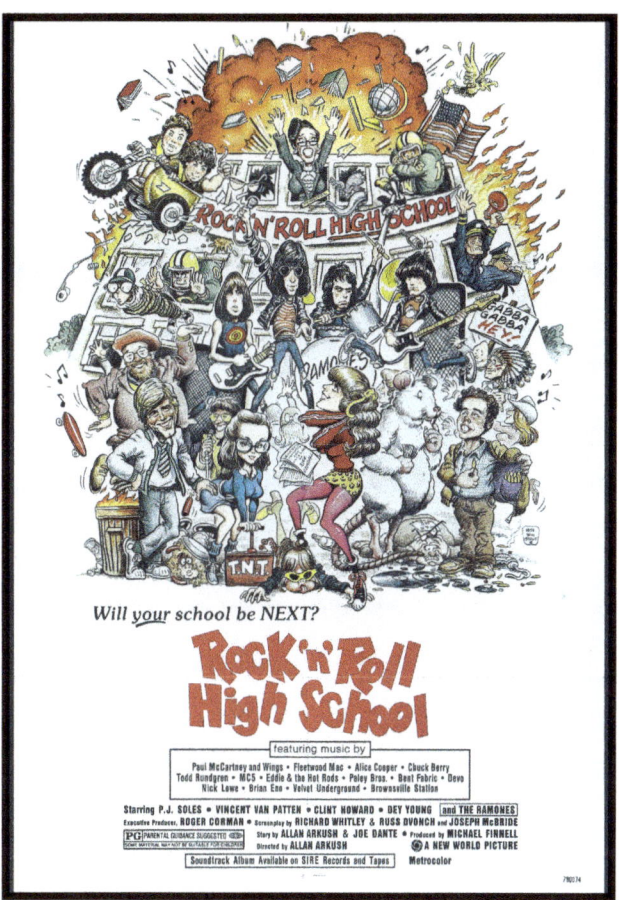

The picture's full of wonderful scenes, from the brief but hilarious throwaway discussion of the Ramones between Miller and Woronov, to the performance of the title cut by Soles and her gym-class pals, a colorful (if low-tech) production number that's as close as a movie can get to bringing certain male high-school fantasies to life. Somehow, Allan Arkush and his pal Joe Dante managed to combine the innocence of a '50s rock 'n' roll movie with the anarchic punk sensibilities of the late '70s and make it all work. You can lay a lot of that success on the shapely shoulders of Ms. Soles, too, who does herself proud here.

HOW DOOOO YOU DO!!! (1945)—My great pal and writing partner Michael H. Price turned me on to this picture years ago, and we ended up writing about it in *Forgotten Horrors 3*. The copy Mike sent me was taped off some one-lung UHF station and threatened to fade out at any time—which only added to its appeal.

Essentially, **How Dooo You Do!!!** is a film made up almost entirely of sidekicks, second bananas and supporting actors, all thrown together in a bizarre murder story with a crazy self-referential ending. It's from the beloved Poverty Row outfit PRC, which of course couldn't afford major stars or even radio headliners like Fibber McGee and Molly and Eddie Cantor. So what we get right at the start is a sit-down conversation between the announcers of those two programs, Harlow Wilcox and Harry von Zell, establishing a strangely compelling and near-documentary feeling of being inside Hollywood show biz, albeit not on the top rung. This is intensified when von Zell addresses us, the audience, and introduces several other cast members, who stand and smile like they're on a runway, while von Zell notes that "technically, these people are known as supporting players."

In **How Dooo You Do!!!** they support Bert Gordon—who's the name above the title (which is taken from one of his catch phrases) as the Mad Russian, Cantor's radio sidekick at the time—and von Zell, as the two of them head off to get some rest at a resort lodge. Soon, they're joined by "supporting players" Claire Windsor and singers Cheryl Walker and Ella Mae Morse, all playing themselves, and complications ensue. When a guest is found dead, still more actors show up at the place, guys like Keye Luke and Matt McHugh, all summoned by Gordon because of their experiences playing second bananas in crime pictures.

I have long been fascinated by the idea of being backstage in the B-movie world, and in the lives of the second string during Hollywood's Golden Age. This one doles all of that out in spades, and while the big cast of secondary players is probably just a ploy from the threadbare studio to get as many quasi-familiar names into the film as it can afford, **How Dooo You Do!!!** ends up as a kind of massive in-joke that the cast lets us in on from the beginning. There's simply not another film like it, and it never fails to bring a smile to my face, and to catalyze that achingly beautiful but hard-to-define little feeling that combines nostalgia, joy and wonder.

OUT OF SIGHT (1966)—Another oddball film not available on home video at this writing, **Out of Sight** sends up beach-party movies, secret-agent pictures, the British Invasion and even the Cold War, as a bumbling butler named Homer (Jonathan Daly), employed by a currently incapacitated British spy named John Stamp (John Lodge), invades the world of the beach bunnies to thwart a Russky agent (John Lawrence) intent on derailing a big music festival featuring a mop-topped foursome from England. We're of course supposed to think the quartet is the Beatles, and dialogue throughout the film reinforces that notion without ever actually saying it—there's even a scene where they're supposed to be in the dressing room of the theater.

The closest we get to seeing the Fab Four, however, are the moderately goofy Brits Freddie and the Dreamers, who perform in the finale along with Dobie Gray, both acts on a multi-level set studded with go-go dancers (one of whom was reportedly Terri Garr). Out of Sight's other rock groups, including Gary Lewis & the Playboys, the Turtles, the Astronauts (with one of the whitest versions of "Baby, Please Don't Go" you'll ever hear), and the Knickerbockers (who give the Tom Jones hit "It's Not Unusual" a good try) appear in various other places to do a tune each.

Daly, in his film debut, makes a good comic hero, the music is swell and the girls are beautiful and intriguing. Maybe it's because I have this film on 16mm, which always enhances the viewing experience, but **Out of Sight** never fails to take me to a sweet Neverland where the sun always shines, the girls are all perfect and major rock 'n' roll acts hang around everywhere you look, supplying the soundtrack to this sweet golden life.

• • • • • • •

by Mark Evan Walker (graphic artist *Ellery Queen's Mystery Magazine*):

Immediately after 9/11, I was so sobered and depressed, I was not able to watch any "entertainment" for about a week—only news. But then I had a craving for the essence of my country, for pure Americana. I was a bit surprised that those turned out to be episodes of **THE HONEYMOONERS** (1955-1956) and several Hopalong Cassidy movies I'd taped off of TV.

Otherwise, when I need to cheer up, there's nothing like an episode of:

I LOVE LUCY (1951-1957)
FRASIER (1993-2004) usually.
YOU BET YOUR LIFE (1950-1961)—Groucho is priceless!

Movies include:
THE THIN MAN series
THE PINK PANTHER (1963)—the first, not the series, and original only!
IT'S A MAD, MAD, MAD, MAD WORLD (and gosh isn't it!)
THE GREAT RACE (1965)
BRINGING UP BABY (1938)
HIS GIRL FRIDAY (1940)
Also, any Fred Astaire and Ginger Rogers musical
The Marx Brothers
Jack Benny—**TO BE OR NOT TO BE** (1942), **ARTISTS AND MODELS** (1955) and Bob Hope—my favorite...**GHOST BREAKERS** (1940).

Have they made any good movies after 1980???? Just kidding, but I'm old fashioned, and the new style of mean-spirited, raunchy, bathroom humor doesn't much appeal to me. I probably left out several, but that's more than five!

• • • • • • •

by Roger Hurlburt:

As to a "cheer up" motion picture(s)—I know I sound corny, but I brighten up after **MY MAN GODFREY** (1936, Eugene Paulette slays me in that one) and **YANKEE DOODLE DANDY** (1942) braces me via Jimmy Cagney's energy and the upswing of the whole affair. Kudos also to dear Mel Brooks with **YOUNG FRANKENSTEIN** (1974)—Marty Feldman attacking Madeline Kahn's mink stole gets me every time—just the anticipation of it...Ever see the out-take reel? It took Brooks about 40 takes to get the shot between Feldman's mugging and Kahn's continual cracking up.

Gene Wilder, Marty Feldman and Terri Garr are depressed in *Young Frankenstein*, but they'll soon be "Puttin' on the Ritz!"

• • • • • • •

by Linda Walter and Mike Augustis in no special order:

MONTY PYTHON AND THE HOLY GRAIL (1975), an all-time favorite
BLAZING SADDLES (1974) and **YOUNG FRANKENSTEIN**
MONTY PYTHON'S THE MEANING OF LIFE (1983)
LIFE OF BRIAN (1979)
AIRPLANE! (1980) and **THE NAKED GUN** movies, for sheer silliness & puns.
The Peter Sellers **PINK PANTHER** movies
Woody Allen's earlier movies; **SLEEPER** (1973) is one of the funniest. And **LOVE AND DEATH** (1975) and **ANNIE HALL** (1977), although that's less slapstick—they still have great lines, and heart.
THIS IS SPINAL TAP (1984)
BEST IN SHOW (2000)
For cheer, can't go wrong with **SINGIN' IN THE RAIN** (1952).
If we are in the right mood for old movies, the Marx Bros. and Laurel & Hardy do the trick. I (not Mike so much) love Kevin Smith movies—especially the ones with Jay & Silent Bob, even in small roles, from **CLERKS** (1994) on. Great dialogue, much of it filthy but smart, observant and real-sounding.
RAISING ARIZONA (1987)
The Baz Luhrmann musical **MOULIN ROUGE!** (2001) with Nicole Kidman/Ewan McGregor—not entirely a comedy, but full of life, some humor, whimsy and color, costumes and dancing.
Old cult movie **HAROLD & MAUDE** (1971)
SAY ANYTHING (1989), because it's so young love/earnest romantic, and I adore John Cusack.
Charlie Kaufman-written movies—especially his first big hit—weird of course—Cusack, Cameron Diaz, Catherine Keener—in **BEING JOHN MALKOVICH** (1999). He also did **HUMAN NATURE** (2001), which no one saw, but it's funny.
THE SIMPSONS MOVIE (2007).
SOUTH PARK: BIGGER, LONGER & UNCUT (1999)
THERE'S SOMETHING ABOUT MARY (1998) and **THE 40 YEAR OLD VIRGIN** (2005) **SUPERBAD** (2007) **HAROLD AND KUMAR GO TO WHITE CASTLE** (2004)
DR. STRANGELOVE (1964)
PRIMARY COLORS (1998)
WAG THE DOG (1997)
BULWORTH (1998)
Also, any Monty Python TV episodes and their compilation movies such as **AND NOW FOR SOMETHING COMPLETELY DIFFERENT** (1971).
On TV at Xmas—**A CHRISTMAS STORY** (1983), **A CHARLIE BROWN CHRISTMAS** (1965), and **HOW THE GRINCH STOLE CHRISTMAS** (1966)
Plus **WINNIE THE POOH** cartoon shows

Spanish poster for *Once Upon a Time*

• • • • • • •

by Deborah Painter (author *Hollywood's Top Dogs*):

ONCE UPON A TIME (1944)—Once upon a time, there was a suavely handsome New York theater owner and producer by the name of Jerry Flynn (Cary Grant), who enjoyed one Broadway hit after another for eight years. For some reason, that changed after 1942. Through no fault of World War II, he suddenly lost his Muse. Now the patrons complain about his dumb musicals and the bank is giving him no more extensions on his 100 grand back payments on his theater. One week and that is it.

Jerry's one true friend, The Moke (James Gleason), still tries to encourage him to go ahead with his current idea of a show about the Pyramids and man's struggles for the expression of beauty. "How will I do it with one nickel in my pocket?" Jerry moans. Standing outside the entrance to what will soon no longer be the Flynn Theater, he tosses the nickel over his shoulder as part of a superstitious move. Two boys happen to be right behind him on the sidewalk. They ask him if it is his and he says they can have it. "He bought his chance to look, Fatso," one kid tells the other.

They wave a shoebox with a cardboard top and a small pinhole on one end. "Look inside, mister," they tell him, and Curly (Ted Donaldson) plays "Yes Sir, That's My Baby" on his harmonica. Flynn's dour look changes to a smile when he sees a caterpillar that dances to this one song!

He realizes that this little larva has the potential to save his theater if he can persuade someone to buy it. But at first, no other adult will even look in the box. Newspaper reporters treat it like some sort of insult to their intelligence. Popular broadcaster Gabriel Heatter (played by himself), hears about it and mentions it on that night's broadcast. The nation goes Curly crazy. One reporter who knows how unscrupulous Flynn has been in the past decides to discredit him by having lepidopterists pronounce the whole thing a hoax. It backfires when these learned men find that Curly is not only real, he really dances. Pinkie Thompson is becoming increasingly disillusioned by the guy, but older sister and guardian Jeannie (Janet Blair) is beginning to warm to him. Flynn assures Pinky and Jeannie that he is not going to sell their little miracle; he'll just be partners with them. He turns right around and sells him behind their backs for the 100 grand to a representative of the Disney Studios. Just as Flynn comes to collect the caterpillar, however, Curly suddenly goes missing! Flynn feels like a real heel, and helpless to find the athletic little bug, which at this point he would gladly return to its owner.

But never fear, there is a happy ending. The end scene in this picture is genuinely charming. A true family movie with talented acting and none of the schmaltz we typically associate with such films, *Once Upon a Time* is a hidden gem that used to be on television all the time and then vanished and was not even released on DVD until 2007.

FRANKENSTEIN (1931)—What is it about this film concerning a scientist who pieces together a man out of fresh corpses and animates it using "that great ray that first brought life into the world"? Why would I like to watch this film over and over again during good times and bad? Why should that be? Do I have ambitions of creating a monster? Have I already created a monster and am secretly reveling in the similarities Dr. Frankenstein and I share? Have I given away too much information?

Many have called this film a classic. But why is it such a classic? Gosh, there are so many things wrong with it, we are told by Modern-Viewers-Who-Know-So-Much. For one thing, the sky backdrop in some of the sets such as the beginning cemetery set and the climactic confrontation of creator and creation has some wrinkles in it! There is no music in the film except in the opening and closing credits. Precisely! Why should that be a hindrance? The actors, the mood and the photography more than make up for a lack of music whose function presumably is to tell us what emotions to have.

The film is a grim one. Young Dr. Henry Frankenstein (Colin Clive) is in a grim profession. Medical doctors in his time and place (Germany, 1930s) still have to steal corpses for research, because they are not allowed to obtain them through any other means. Moreover, Dr. Frankenstein is taking his research into odd realms. He wants to create life. He asks his old professor at the University, Dr. Waldman (Edward van Sloan), for help, but the Professor warns against his plan of bringing life to the dead. He refuses to help Frankenstein, so he is forced to rely on the assistance of Fritz the hunchback (Dwight Frye), who has been helping him get bodies

Triumphant in this effort to animate a stitched together man, he shows Dr. Waldman his handiwork (Boris Karloff, in his most famous performance). Waldman is impressed, all right. "You have created a monster and it will destroy you!" Fritz breaks up this meeting with a flaming torch, which terrifies and infuriates the creature. The Monster kills Fritz and then Waldman when he has him on the dissecting table in a later scene. The creature then runs off into the countryside. In just the space of a week Dr. Frankenstein has cut off all contact with the being he was so eager to create. In many ways he is like a father who was so proud to have a son until the son showed signs of being a burden. Now he is eager to cast him off, but the creature is his responsibility. The film works wonderfully as an analogy for neglectful parents. It also works as a cautionary tale about hurrying along scientific breakthroughs into the marketplace without regard for their potential negative impacts. Watching **Frankenstein** is like seeing a magnificent work of architecture, which combines structural integrity with artistic excellence, and the pleasure I gain is derived from sheer enjoyment of seeing art done right.

ON A CLEAR DAY YOU CAN SEE FOREVER (1970)—Barbra Streisand is not by any stretch of the imagination one of my favorite actresses, but she is amusing and in fine voice here in this lush musical that juxtaposes so-called "New Age" metaphysics with an old fashioned style. Daisy Gamble (Streisand) is a ditzy, fashionable college girl who has a tiny New York apartment with a rooftop garden. Her psychic communications with plants help them bloom faster than normal. Jack Nicholson is her rather spastic boyfriend. Daisy wants to stop smoking and he puts her in touch with a professor at the local University who hypnotizes people so they can stop the nicotine habit. Yves Montand is Dr. Chabot, the older professor, who becomes fascinated when he hypnotically regresses Daisy back to childhood…and beyond, to a past life as Melinda, a slinky, sexy member of the British aristocracy of the 1800s. In that past life she was really a poor girl who gained the position through mistaken identity and sheer subterfuge. The Professor also finds that he is starting to feel psychically in tune with her and is falling in love too. But is Dr. Chabot falling in love with Daisy or with Melinda? "Come Back to Me!" is the most popular song from the Broadway version of this musical. Bob Newhart is in the movie and he has some of the best lines in the picture, approaching the University staff with a proposal from his client who sees commercial and financial potential in controlling and directing reincarnation! I appreciate the way reincarnation is treated humorously without ridiculing the notion. Do we live many lives? Do we have a chance to fix our bad behavior by learning from it and not repeating it in the centuries (and lives) to come? Daisy is not the adulterous person she was in her 19th-century past life. Maybe, on a clear day when love and life is revealed to be a continuum, we really can see forever.

FLYING SAUCERS OVER HOLLYWOOD: THE PLAN NINE COMPANION (1992)—Director Edward D. Wood, Jr.'s immortal statement on man, his relationship to the cosmos and his tendency for self destruction, 1956's **Plan 9 from Outer Space** cried out for decades for a documentary to be created on its history. And in 1992 we film aficionados got our wish. We are bringing you all the evidence, based only on the secret testimony, of the miserable souls who survived this terrifying ordeal. The incidents, the places. My friend, we cannot keep this a secret any longer. Let us punish the guilty. Let us reward the innocent. My friend, can your heart stand the shocking facts of the people who produced what was originally titled **Grave Robbers from Outer Space**?

Watch the delightfully inept **Plan 9 From Outer Space** first if you have not seen it, and then watch Atomic Pictures' documentary which interviews every surviving cast member to share his or her memories of making this unfortunate career move...er, I mean, participating in this classic. In addition we get a visit by Conrad Brooks, who played Patrolman Jamie, to the old Quality Studio where **Plan 9** was filmed in 1956. Film professors discuss why it is important to know this film, because it helps us understand what goes on in the mind of a filmmaker who does not know he or she is making an unintentionally funny movie. Narrator Lee Harris does an exceptional job of keeping the various threads of the documentary together. It is fun from beginning to end.

HOT TO TROT (1988)—Why did I ever watch this movie? Answer: I watched it because I wanted to see for myself if it is as bad as everyone claimed. And you know what? I found it hilarious! It opens with a montage of Cro-Magnon cave paintings of horses and explains that throughout the ages there have been a few "chosen" horses which can talk and think as well as (make that better than) humans. They pass this trait to their offspring.

Bobcat Goldthwait's movie career has been undeservedly underrated. He is Fred P. Chaney, the put-upon loser with good intentions. In **Hot to Trot** Fred's mom has just died and his evil stepfather Walter Sawyer (Dabney Coleman) is co-owner of the family fortune. Sawyer makes no secret that he hates his guts and wants to trick him out of his inheritance. For now, they have to share the family horse farm. Okay, so Fred is a dork and he has a weirdly high squeaky voice, but it's more pathetic than annoying. Enter Don the horse, who speaks, sounding a little like actor John Candy. No, wait, he sounds a lot like John Candy. The horse is the only inheritance that Sawyer does not fight Fred over. He tricks Fred out of the farm. The two men divide their investment firm office in half, and Sawyer tries to ruin Fred's chances of making any money, so he will go away.

Fortunately, Don knows about stocks. He hears the rich guys talking about them when they sneak off with their mistresses for a little clandestine roll in the hay over at the horse farm! Then he shares the tips with Fred and he starts raking in the dough! Fred gets a penthouse apartment and Don moves in with him, much to his dismay. Fred has a hard time impressing girls as it is, and he has a harder time impressing the pretty secretary Allison (Virginia Madsen) when she finds out he has a live horse as a room mate. She likes him, though, and she comes to his aid when he has to win a horse race against Sawyer's filly, where the stakes are the entire farm! Doesn't practically every horse movie ever made have this sort of climatic horse race in it? Look for the things that set this one apart from all the others.

I visit this film again and again because I spend a lot of time around horses, and for some reason I imagine them thinking the sorts of things Don says!

THE BLACK STALLION (1979)—From silly talking horses I switch gears to expound the virtues of this beautifully photographed film. Not only is it one of the best horse films of all time, it is one of the best adventure films of all time. Francis Ford Coppola shows that he is indeed a perceptive producer here, fresh from his success as director of *The Godfather*.

It's a well-acted period piece set in the time period of the early 1940s when Walter Farley, then just a youth himself, wrote the first **Black Stallion** juvenile novel. Kelly Reno is Alec Ramsay, a kid heading home to New York from Saudi Arabia with his father (Hoyt Axton). Their ship is attacked by a Nazi submarine and the boy thinks to release a beautiful stallion he had seen on board the vessel earlier. In a nail bitting scene that gives goose bumps, they are nearly caught up in the ship's propeller. Alec looks about for his father, but in the midst of all the flames and the screaming, all he can think to do is to hang on to the lead rope attached to the horse's neck as it pulls him steadily onward.

Alex awakens on a beach wearing only pajamas. There is not a single person on the island and he finds the horse all tangled up in the harnesses he was wearing on the ship. He frees him and the horse runs off and then stops and stares at him.

The story develops to show how a high-bred Arabian stallion which mostly hates and fears man because of abuse, begins to rely upon a boy for companionship on the sun drenched island. For a while things are touch and go for both of them as survival becomes more difficult. Their amazing relationship continues when the two of them are rescued and the horse, called "The Black" or simply "Black" by Alec, is willing to sacrifice its total freedom to stay with the boy and protect him. Clarence Muse has a memorable role as "Snoe," the driver of a vegetable wagon who keeps his old horse in a pasture and barn by a railroad track. Mickey Rooney turns in a fine performance as an aged jockey who owns the barn and who grooms The Black and the young boy for the glamour and high stakes of the racing life. Teri Garr is Alec's mom, who understands his love for the horse but is not happy about the whole idea of racing! The racing sequences are amazing, but the true appeal of this picture is the way the cinematography, music and animal action wordlessly convey the love the boy has for the magnificent black horse and the love it has for him.

THE CREEPING TERROR (1964)—This is it. This is the one you have heard so much about but never got around to seeing. Well, I am here to tell you that you should see it. You will laugh until you cry at the antics of the carpet monster, which escapes from a spaceship from another planet and spreads destruction across a rural California county. The filmmakers tried to be serious. However, as you will see, that intention went out the window. You will marvel at how the director managed to cover up, or try to cover up, the fact that there was not enough money for a soundtrack. He worked around this by having most of the movie narrated by a voice-over. The narrator is a news reporter from a local radio station who did it all in post production. The terror of the title is a creature that looks like about five big pieces of shag carpet sewed together with segments of vacuum cleaner hoses, to form its face, and animated by several boys underneath. I have to admit the effect of having someone make the hoses move around was pretty good. The film is utterly terrible and I mean that in a good way. There is actually some dialogue and it is all ludicrous. The carpet monster at the exciting climax crashes a dance party at the school auditorium and manages to inhale some of the buxom gals, while taking care not to knock any furniture over. During the dance fistfight between two greasers erupts, proving in a comforting way that even when a menace from outer space is in the vicinity, life as we know it goes on.

AELITA, QUEEN OF MARS (1924)—Without giving away the climax, I will say that if you like early Soviet propaganda, this is the film for you! It starts out rather slowly, with a Soviet engineer, Chief Engineer Los (Nikolai Tsereteli), being puzzled over radio messages that are heard bursting in on several stations. These messages consist of just the words "Anta Odeli Uta." Some people theorize they are coming from Mars. Los is having marital troubles with his wife Natasha because she is spending a lot of time working at the rations center day care center for female employee's children. Natasha has a hard enough life as it is, having to beg the guys who run the rations department to set aside an extra bag of flour or a box of chocolate bars for her every once in a while, and now, her husband does not like the fact that she puts in long hours. He thinks her overtime hours are being spent with a man. The poor gal cannot win. And to top all that, the Soviet government tells Los that he must give up the extra apartment he has been renting so he could work on plans for a rocket to Mars to solve the mystery of the radio transmissions. You would think that such a great and glorious scheme would merit him some consideration. But no, he has to ask his friend Yusev (Nikolai Batalov) to let him use his hangar.

He then shoots his wife for what he thinks is an indiscretion and then flees to the hangar to finish the rocket and fly to Mars. Meanwhile the haughty and beautiful Aelita, Queen of Mars (Yulia Solntseva), has been observing life in general on Earth, and handsome Los in particular, through a super powerful telescope. Los and his friend fly to Mars and find an abstract Art Deco architectural paradise. Aelita rescues them from the guards and shows them around. The Earthmen are aghast that the workers must toil underground (a foreshadowing of the 1925 German epic *Metropolis*) and that the planet is ruled by an aristocracy that is threatening to divide into two factions; one led by Aelita and the other led by Tuskub, the Guardian of the planet's energy supply (Konstantin Eggert). Los and Yusev find themselves heading up an insurrection that Aelita has promised will lead to a socialist-style government. Little do they know that she has ideas for her power and is not going to let anyone get in her way!

I don't know about you, but the prospect of severe chocolate shortages as in the USSR, where Natasha will practically kill for a candy bar, frightens me more than the carpet monster in **The Creeping Terror**. For that reason alone I am glad to live in a country where we can eat all the chocolate and have all the flour and eggs we want.

KING KONG (1933)—In 1933 the United States was in the worst year of a serious economic Depression. Despite that, **King Kong** brought in a very tidy profit wherever it played. Aside from the fact that it is one of those rare films where the pacing, the score, the performances and the special effects come together perfectly, it also provides one heckuva compelling fantasy escape. When you watch **King Kong** you really feel like you are on the steamer *Venture* traveling to a mysterious island in the Micronesias with the enthusiastic filmmaker Carl Denham (Robert Armstrong) and his leading lady Ann Darrow (Fay Wray). When you get to the island and encounter the less than thrilled natives and see the towering timber wall separating their village from the rest of "Skull Island," you feel the tension. "Something monstrous, all powerful, still living, still holding that island in the grip of deadly fear" is behind that wall, according to what Denham has heard from the skipper of a Norwegian barque. What could that something be?

The natives were right in the middle of a ceremony for Kong and the intruders disrupted it. So they try to get Denham and the skipper of the Venture to sell Ann to them, because she is unusual and they are sure Kong will like her. Denham and Captain Englehorn (Frank Reicher) decline the offer. At anchor that night near the island, Denham and Englehorn wait until morning when the party can try again to make friends with the native folk. The inhabitants are impatient. They abduct Ann and make her the latest sacrifice to Kong, a giant ape about 30 feet tall! The sailors open the huge gate in the wall and run out with rifles and gas bombs to find Ann. Denham has decided to give them one day. The ship leaves the next dawn, even if his first mate and the sailors don't return, and they are not expected to return.

Skull Island is a paleontologist's dream, or nightmare, if you prefer. The island is teeming with Pteranodons, Stegosauri, giant lizards, Tyrannosauri and Apatosauri, all aggressive and deadly. Ann almost becomes a meal for a Tyrannosaurus but her protector shows her that his status as King is not hyperbole. He kills the biggest land predator that ever walked the earth. All the sailors but First Mate Driscoll (Bruce Cabot) get slaughtered by the local fauna. Driscoll eludes the scaly juggernauts of this island and manages to get Ann away from the amorous Kong. Kong, however, is not going to take this sitting down, and tries to rescue and be near Ann all the way to the incredible showdown between him and the biplanes, in New York City, at the Empire State Building.

If you have not seen the original **King Kong**, you are missing a cinematic treat and an experience that still provides as many thrills as it did to moviegoers during the Great Depression.

• • • • • • •

by Barry Atkinson (author *You're Not Old Enough Son*):

CALAMITY JANE (1953)—In urgent need of a bit of light entertainment to put a smile on your face? Stick on Warner Bros.' 1953 **Calamity Jane** and let Doris Day and company work their magic, with great songs ("The Deadwood Stage," "Windy City," "Secret Love") and scatty situations, bolstered by Day's scenery-chewing star turn, and boy, could she sing! From the days when Hollywood knew how to make fantastic musicals and put on a family show, this is guaranteed to induce a feel-good factor in the most downcast of audiences, as tomboy-turned-wholesome-gal Day wins the heart of Wild Bill Hickok (Howard Keel), after numerous romantic misunderstandings. A movie full of good heart, running 101 minutes, that makes you forget the bad old world we live in.

KEEP YOUR SEATS PLEASE (1936)—George Formby's fourth film, released in 1936, and one of his funniest. The lad from Wigan with the mile-wide toothy grin is after £90,000 hidden in one of six antique chairs owned by his recently deceased aunt, which involves him becoming embroiled in one crazy stunt after another as he tries to locate the chair containing the fortune, aided by a criminal accomplice. Formby was Britain's biggest male attraction in the 1930s and, unbelievable as it may now seem, the fifth highest paid film star in the world. Feted by royalty, his near-the-knuckle songs, crammed full of *double entendres,* banned from the radio but still selling millions, and he was a mean ukulele player to boot, Formby couldn't put a foot wrong, his engaging charisma, pathos and natural tomfoolery making for box office gold. Ironically in Britain, most of the comedian's movies (he made 20) were A-rated because of their (sometimes) lewd content and highly convoluted plots which youngsters couldn't figure out. **Keep Your Seats Please** presents Formby at his scatterbrained best, 82 minutes of lighthearted fun with a happy ending, as Formby gets the money *and* the girl. Such endearing fare from a lost age of innocence in the cinema is tough to find!

POPEYE THE SAILOR—You can keep your goody-goody Mickey Mouse! Rough old Popeye does it for me any time! Created as a comic strip by Elzie Segar in 1929 and brought to the big screen by Max Fleischer in 1933, the Bolshie sailor with a penchant for spinach went on to star in over 700 cartoons, which also featured Olive Oyl, Pappy, Bluto, Swee' Pea, Wimpey, the Jeep and other weird and wonderful characters. Many of the earlier cartoons were fantasy-based (Popeye meeting Sinbad and Ali Baba) and it's the black and white 1930s animated features that I enjoy the most rather than the colored, sketchy versions that appeared in the 1950s. The artwork in the 1930s classics is beautifully rendered, with amazing detail and depth. This black and white animation lovingly crafted the action in more inventive ways as well. Recently released to DVD after years of contractual hassles, re-watching these Popeye classics transports us back to Popeye's anarchistic world, where every episode climaxes with the hero gulping down spinach to regain his strength, followed by one almighty punch-up.

THE SEARCHERS (1956)—No, it's not a comedy, but if modern-day moviemaking techniques leave me cold and disheartened, I put on John Ford's classic saga of the West just to reaffirm my long-held belief that the 1950s was a golden age in film production, especially for the Western. Released in 1956 (A-rated in Britain), the opening 50 minutes of Ford's

undisputed sagebrush masterpiece is rock-solid perfect cinema; in direction, script, acting, locations (Utah's Monument Valley), cinematography, music, pace, the handling of complex themes and in John Wayne's towering performance as embittered, Indian-hating Ethan Edwards, **The Searchers** doesn't falter for a single second. After that outstanding first half, the movie settles down as Wayne and Jeffrey Hunter begin their five year search for Natalie Wood, kidnapped by a Comanche raiding party, but for all students of film, that initial 50 minutes, from the first sight of Wayne slowly approaching his brother's house, to Wayne and Hunter reflecting on the task ahead, is a blueprint of how a movie, *any* movie, should be constructed—note that all the scenes are short and snappy, played out like operettas, punctuated by swift bursts of Max Steiner's magnificent score and Wayne's terse delivery, the sandstone bluffs and cliffs a stunning, monolithic backdrop dominating the tragedy taking place. Wayne's eyeball-to-eyeball confrontation with Chief Scar counts as one of celluloid's greatest stand-offs and the final shot as Wayne, framed in a dark doorway, turns and ambles off with that famous gait into the glaring desert wilderness, his job completed, alone once more, is iconic cinema at its most moving and memorable. It makes you realize what a powerful medium film can be and this is one of the reasons I go back to **The Searchers** time and time again; it was also my father's all-time favorite picture, another fond reason for watching it. And let's not forget Wayne's unforgettable rejoinder: "That'll be the day!"

UP IN THE WORLD (1956)—Norman Wisdom was almost a natural successor to George Formby (John Paddy Carstairs directed movies starring both comedians in his career) and was one of Britain's top entertainers in the 1950s, both in the cinema and on television. **Up in the World** dates from 1956; Wisdom is a much put-upon window cleaner who becomes friendly with a boy millionaire. Wisdom, who has been employed to spruce up hundreds of windows at a huge country mansion, comes to the rescue when the youth is kidnapped and Wisdom saves the day by foiling the gang of kidnappers in the hilarious finale, which nosedives sharply into slapstick farce. Not everybody was a fan of Wisdom's trademark knockabout humor, but one peculiar talent the comedian had up his sleeve was a highly infectious laugh, so infectious that he could have a staid audience in stitches just by standing at the mike (or rolling all over the stage) and laughing hysterically. He does it in this movie when the snooty lad traps him in a window and tickles his feet, Wisdom howling and hooting until the kid stops. It creases me up every time I see it; yes, it's childish and stupid, but it sure gets me going to the point where I have tears running down my cheeks, much to the bewilderment of my wife!

Let's make it favorite 10!

AUF WIEDERSEHEN, PET (1983-2004) Series 2, episode 5—The first series of **Auf Wiedersehen, Pet** burst upon British TV screens in 1983 and became a colossal hit across the nation. Charting the gritty misadventures of a gang of seven English laborers working on a building site in Germany, not only did it reflect the climate of social unrest in Thatcher's Britain (class division, the need to travel abroad to seek work) but the quirky leading characters embedded themselves into the public psyche—Oz, Dennis, Barry, Neville, Bomber, Wayne and Moxey; not without reason were they termed "The Magnificent Seven." Series two, broadcast in 1986, had the lads refurbishing derelict Thornley Manor, a vast Gothic-style country mansion, to be converted into an old people's home. My favorite episode is number five, *A Home From Home*, in which the lads, after being turned away from every guesthouse in the area, are forced to bunk down in the uncomfortable and creepy surrounds of the manor. Banned from the local pub because Londoner Wayne has bedded

The lads of *Auf Wiedersehen, Pet*: Timothy Spall, Jimmy Nail, Tim Healy, Kevin Whately, Christopher Fairbank, Pat Roach and Gary Holton

the publican's daughter (and hence has become ostracized by the other six), boredom creeps in, Brummie Barry content to do a bit of brass rubbing in the nearby church where he learns that the manor may be haunted. If you're not from the U.K., the thick Birmingham and Newcastle accents would need subtitling, especially Jimmy Nail's Oz, spouting off obscenities in almost unintelligible Geordie as he curses Wayne for preventing them from popping down the pub after a hard day's graft (only someone like Oz, who has a complete disregard for authority, would walk around a supermarket and drink from a can of beer before it has gone through the checkout, an offence in Britain). Wayne redeems himself in the end, discovering a videotape containing footage of an orgy taking place at the manor in which the loathsome publican ("Call me tiger," he leers at a half-naked blonde bimbo, drooling all over her breasts) is a chief participant. The seven then drive straight down to the pub where a little case of bribery works wonders as Wayne presents the tape to the enraged landlord, holding it as a police threat if they are not served with drinks. It's the interaction between the players that captivates: Dennis the exasperated boss, Bomber the giant, good-natured builder, skirt-chasing Wayne, fussy, mother-hen Barry, ex-jailbird Moxey, worrier Neville and couldn't-give-a-shit Oz, a once-in-a-TV-lifetime gathering of disparate souls that gel together to form their own group solidarity (them against the world), fighting against the 1980s malaise of greed, self-interest and shallow relationships (and, in some cases, law and order). A big "two fingers" at British society in the class-ridden 1980s, **Auf Wiedersehen, Pet** has to be one of the greatest series, both in wit, human observation and writing, ever foisted onto a TV audience, and Nail's O3 (one tooth missing, lanky, scruffy, with his "f—k you lot" attitude) is now part of television folklore, almost a mythical, working-class figure that a whole generation of British males identified with at the time.

HANCOCK: THE BLOOD DONOR (1961)—First televised on BBC-TV in June 1961, **The Blood Donor** has entered the annals of British television history as the funniest 25 minutes ever broadcast to an audience of millions. Anthony (Tony) Aloysius St. John Hancock, with his raincoat, pork-pie hat and lugubrious features, was the embodiment of the downtrodden working class man forever ranting against the establishment and society's ills. Big-headed, vain, self-opinionated, insensitive, pompous, obnoxious and a coward at heart, Hancock was a doomed genius, committing suicide in 1968 at the age of 44 through a complete lack of self-worth. Prior to **The Blood Donor** being broadcast to a live studio audience, the comedian had been involved in a minor car accident and had only run through the script twice, so teleprompters were used which is why Hancock's eyes tend to wander during the transmission and he trips over his lines once. No matter, the tragic legend demonstrated his unparalleled gift in comic timing by pulling off the performance of a lifetime, Alan Simpson and Ray Galton's script, crammed full of comedic gems, delivered to perfection. Basically, "the lad from Railway Cuttings, East Cheam" turns up at a hospital to give blood ("A body full of good British blood and raring to go"), harangues the nurse on duty (June Whitfield), gives blood and then becomes the recipient of his own corpuscles when he cuts himself badly at the end. "British, undiluted for 12 generations. 100% Anglo Saxon with perhaps just a dash of Viking," he brags before going on, in answer to Whitfield's question of whether he has given blood before: "Given, no. Spilt, yes!" Whitfield later asks him whether injections bother him at all. Naturally, they don't: "Got arms like pincushions. Needles the size of drainpipes. You name it, I've had it!" "Do you get a badge for doing this?" he enquires, putting his own selfish interest before duty. The classic line is, of course, "But a pint? That's very nearly an armful! I'm sorry, I'm not walking around with an empty arm for anybody" when he realizes that a pin-prick doesn't constitute donating blood, labeling the doctor (Patrick Cargill) a "legalized vampire." Very much of its age, with references to pop stars Cliff Richard and Adam Faith and the then-current advertising slogans ("Drinka Pinta Milka Day," "Coughs and Sneezes Spread Diseases"), this remains magic and timeless entertainment, as rib-tickling today as it was all those years ago, a tonic to bring out and savor and put a broad smile on your face.

A HARD DAY'S NIGHT—Being English, I count myself well and truly privileged at having experienced "Beatlemania" first-hand, in all of its insurgent glory. I turned 16 in January 1963 as the Fab Four burst upon the British pop scene, a much-needed breath of fresh air revitalizing a stagnant and talentless showbiz chasm, the group spearheading not only a musical but a cultural revolution on a scale never seen before, or since. The Beatles' first feature film proved that not only were they capable of producing brilliant, everlasting music but their monumental charisma could successfully be transferred to the big screen ("We didn't want to make a crappy pop movie like anybody else," John Lennon said succinctly). Blessed with a witty script by Alun Owen and enhanced by Richard Lester's dazzling, innovative camerawork, **A Hard Day's Night**, filmed at a helter-skelter pace, triumphantly encapsulated the sheer exuberance of the times and of the Fabs themselves—John the master of the sarcastic put-down, George dry and cynical, Ringo's droll humor and Paul perhaps coming off fourth best in the dialogue stakes, content to be eye candy for millions of pubescent teenage girls. The music for the soundtrack captured the group on an artistic high and at their effervescent best, their most upbeat album and upbeat is the word to describe the movie, a joyful, uplifting experience that was a direct forerunner of the music video industry to come. On summer break from college in July 1964, I was working in a hotel in Newquay when the picture was first released and caught it at a midnight showing at the Astoria cinema. Needless to say, I couldn't hear one word of that cracking script or the fabulous music—one thousand screaming teenagers put paid to all that! But happiness is often linked to nostalgia, and those were heady days in England if you were aged 20 and under—watching **A Hard Day's Night** brings it all back, a sure guarantee to chase away those winter blues and get the feet tapping at the same time.

PLAY FOR TODAY: NUTS IN MAY (1976)—Screened on BBC-TV in 1976, writer/director Mike Leigh's 85-minute tale relating the adventures of an eccentric couple at loose in the wilds of Dorset is an absolute scream, although incorporating in its scenario an almost tragic undercurrent. Keith Pratt and wife Candice Marie (wonderful performances from Roger Sloman and Alison Steadman) drive down into Dorset in their Morris Minor convertible and pitch tent near Lulworth Cove. Sloman is an obsessive, nit-picking, pretentious, dominating vegetarian know-it-all ruled by schedules and timetables; his wife a pseudo-hippie composing ghastly, two-chord folk tunes, played on guitar and banjo. However, despite Sloman continually barking at his wife ("Come along, Candice Marie." "Don't do that." "What are you doing?") and the down-trodden Steadman biting back on occasions, these early eco-warriors have their hearts in the right places, although Sloman cannot abide other human beings, as when Welshman Ray turns up, infuriating Sloman when Steadman takes a platonic shine to him (the scene where the couple coerce the unfortunate Ray into joining in on one of their self-penned ditties, "I Want to See the Zoo," is a classic of mirth and embarrassment). Paced leisurely at first, Leigh's camera takes full advantage of Dorset's splendid scenery—the ruins of Corfe Castle, Old Harry rocks, the fossiliferous limestone cliffs, the green rolling hills, Lulworth

Cove and Stair Hole Cliff before darkening the tone as a couple from Birmingham (Finger, dressed in awful 1970s flairs, and Honky, tottering around on stacked heels) arrive on their noisy motorbike, disrupting the peace of the campsite ("Look at all them bleedin' bluebells"), clowning around and, against regulations, lighting a fire. This releases a kind of perverted violence in the emotionally repressed Sloman who chases the uncouth Brummie with a stick before breaking down, crying and fleeing into the woods. At the end of their tether, the "odd couple" pack up their tent and belongings and drive off, eventually ending up in a farmer's field, Steadman warbling away on guitar about pollution as, pointedly, her husband, spade and toilet roll in hand, is seen clambering over a fence to perform his ablutions. Dorset holds fond recollections as one of Southern England's most beautiful counties, it's where my wife and I used to explore the rugged coastline for a number of years, so again, **Nuts in May** becomes a nostalgia trip, like a travelogue down memory lane and this, combined with Leigh's marvelous insight into human behavior, snobbery and class divide, elevates it to essential viewing in my case, bringing forth a rosy glow every time I watch it.

ROAD TO MOROCCO (1942)—The funniest of the *Road* movies, this 1942 Bing Crosby/Bob Hope vehicle is 83 minutes of no-holds-barred lunacy, an explosion of witty one-liners and sight gags that many of today's so-called comedies could look and learn from. Hope and Crosby, the two biggest box office draws of that period, were off-screen friends when they collaborated on the *Road* pictures and it shows onscreen, their natural *bonhomie* lighting up the production, the pair loosely sticking to Frank Butler and Don Hartman's sizzling script but allowed free reign by ad-libbing their way furiously through a lot of the episodes to hilarious effect (as when the camel turns and spits at Hope, unintentional but retained in the print). Stowaways Hope and Crosby get washed ashore on the North African coast when their liner blows up,

Hope (Orville "Turkey" Jackson) becomes engaged to princess Dorothy Lamour but is destined to die as foretold in the stars, Crosby (just plain Jeff) is then earmarked to be the hapless first husband, sheik Anthony Quinn (betrothed to Lamour) captures and dumps the pair in the desert and eventually, after a great deal of clowning, our heroes rescue Lamour from the clutches of oily Quinn in his wedding tent. Lamour gets it together with Crosby, Hope hitching up with another beauty. All this plus talking camels, Hope's guardian angel, Aunt Lucy (Hope in drag wearing a wig), the famous "nodding heads" scene in the palace, Hope turned into a monkey and great melodies by Johnny Burke and Jimmy Van Heusen ("Moonlight Becomes You," "Constantly," "Ho Hum" and the title theme). What more could a depressive want to cheer himself up! From Hope's opening line, "Look at us, two on a raft, sunnyside up!" to his last, "I might have won an academy award!" **Road to Morocco** is one great big hoot with so many rapid-fire wisecracks and zany situations that everything merges into a dizzying, madcap whole:

Hope: You can't sell me. I'm not a horse, it's just the way I comb my hair.
Crosby: Now kiss him on the nose. See if you can straighten that out.
Camel: This is the screwiest picture I was ever in.

Priceless stuff, even though Lamour was once quoted as saying that acting with Hope and Crosby was akin to being a "sandwich between two hams." I never tire of wallowing in **Road to Morocco** or appreciating the good-natured silliness, enthusiasm and boundless energy of the leading stars radiating from the screen—it's all good innocent fun without resorting to crudity and bad language to raise the laughs, a real pick-me-up if ever there was one!

• • • • • • •

by David Langford, Atlanta, GA:

1. The earliest Curly-starring **Three Stooges**. By the way, I think that the sound effects person is an unsung fourth Stooge. I crack up when I hear the sound of a lead pipe meet Curley's head. Also, did you ever notice that whenever something happens to Moe, Larry laughs his head off. I know that's not scripted.

2. **THE EXORCIST** (1973)—The greatest movie ever filmed about faith lost and found.

3. **ABBOTT AND COSTELLO MEET FRANKENSTEIN**— Abbot and Costello aren't particularly funny, but watching this movie never fails to be a wonderful experience.

4. **ANIMAL CRACKERS** (1930)—To me, Groucho at his best.

• • • • • • •

by Janet Atkinson:

CAST AWAY (2000)—If it cheers you up to forget your troubles for a while, then escape with Tom Hanks to a deserted Pacific island. You will be spellbound for the whole 143 minutes as you survive a plane crash with Hanks and end up alone on this island for four long years, your only friend being Wilson, an American volleyball, discovered among the packages washed ashore from the crash. Hanks' relationship with Wilson is overwhelming, as is his acting, carrying much of the film in splendid isolation and with very little dialogue. Wilson heroically bears the brunt of Hanks' frustrations and his bloodied smile never falters. Hank's eventual reunion with his once fiancée, Helen Hunt, now married with a child, will break your heart. **Cast Away** is a truly emotive story in which you feel for Hanks every step of the way. Superb.

THE FULL MONTY—There is nothing like a good laugh to cheer me up; add to that a touch of nostalgia and the recipe is even more rewarding! (The film takes place in Sheffield, close to my mother's birthplace). I first watched **The Full Monty** with my heavily pregnant daughter, and oh how we laughed.

The story is of a group of young men made redundant from the steel works, and the affect this has on their lives. Each character is different—a broken marriage with a child to support; spiraling debt with the wife unaware that her husband no longer has a job; sexual leanings making one feel suicidal; erectile problems and weight issues—but they all need to make some money and thus it is that they decide to put on a strip show at a local venue. The result is one side-splitting scene after another, yet with an underlying poignancy as they bond and we are treated to a look at their private lives away from the group.

The famous scene, of course, is when they are queuing in the Job Center and Hot Chocolate's "You Sexy Thing" comes across on the piped music, the number that they have chosen to strip to, and they all start performing their moves as they wait in line. Hilarious, even Prince Charles was later broadcast to

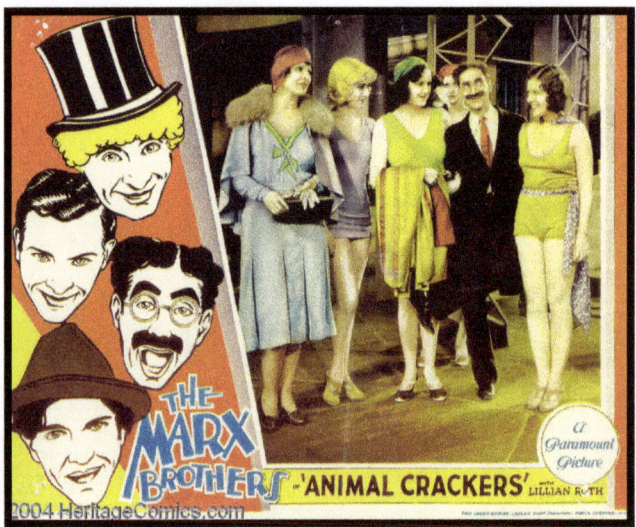

the nation, at one of his engagements, emulating the scene when he heard this music! A definite "cheer me up" with a royal seal of approval.

RANDOM HARVEST (1942)—No film listing would be complete without a good old black-and-white movie, and so I've chosen **Random Harvest**—what a lovely, tender, romantic film this is. I do enjoy a sad picture with a happy ending, and you can have a good weep right throughout this film as it tells the tragic story of loves lost and found.

Ronald Colman, a fine English gentleman, and Greer Garson, with those beautiful eyes that reflect such emotion, admirably play the main characters.

Colman, shell-shocked from the First World War, loses his memory and his speech, wanders out of the asylum where he is being held and meets up with Garson who takes pity on him and helps him to get away. They fall in love and marry but after an accident in which Colman suffers a nasty bump to the head, he comes to and remembers his pre-war past, but now forgets his three years with Garson. After seeing Colman's picture in the paper (it turns out that he's the head of a large family business), Garson takes a job as his secretary in the hope that she can restore his memory, alas to no avail. Finally reporting him as having been missing for seven years, their marriage is annulled, freeing him for another woman that he is betrothed to, but over time he never marries. However it all works out well in the end when Colman, bothered by a key he still retains from the past, tries to retrace his steps back from the day of the accident. He finds that the key is to a cottage that he rented with Garson years ago, and with it the realization that she is the one he truly loves. The film closes with them back in each other's arms and with me all misty eyed.

SHIRLEY VALENTINE (1989)—As a Grecophile and a romantic, **Shirley Valentine** never fails to cheer me up. Pauline Collins plays a middle-aged housewife and mother, with a son who has left home, a teenage daughter prone to temper tantrums and a husband who treats her as a skivvy (maid or servant); she feels trapped in a life that revolves solely around her family day in and day out. When a friend wins a couple of tickets for a Greek holiday, Collins, after much soul searching, eventually agrees to accompany her, leaving a note for her husband as she knows he would not have let her go if she had told him about her plans.

Humor abounds in the scenes building up to the time when she leaves for her holiday—Collins talking to the walls and choosing sexy underwear and skimpy bikinis. Then there is the island of Mykonos, the sunshine, blue seas, beautiful scenery, breath-taking sunsets and, to top it all, an affair with Greek taverna owner Tom Conti, which convinces her that she isn't

just a down-trodden housewife. When her husband turns up in the final scene to take her home, she knows for sure that she is a changed woman.

The open-ended finale leaves it to the viewer to decide on the best course of action; should she, or should she not, return to England—with or without her husband? I know what I would do!

SOMETHING'S GOTTA GIVE (2003)—I do love a Jack Nicholson film. I think he's great with those devilish eyes and that wicked grin, and those adjectives well describe Nicholson's character in this splendid, serio-comic love story.

Nicholson is an older man who seeks only the company of younger women, but things start to change for him when Diane Keaton, the mother of his latest girlfriend, appears on the scene and he slowly falls in love with her. There are many touching moments throughout the picture but also a lot of laughs—Keaton and her sister arriving home unexpectedly to find a strange man (Nicholson) at the refrigerator in just his boxer shorts; Nicholson's face when he sees Keaton bearing down on him, about to give him the kiss of life as he suffers a mild heart attack; Nicholson in the hospital denying that he has taken Viagra, then pulling the tube from his arm when the dishy doc, Keanu Reeves, tells him the drip contains nitroglycerine which could be fatal if mixed with Viagra—but the best for me is Nicholson, still in the hospital, going loopy due to the effect of what the doctor has given him to help him sleep. Wearing just socks and a hospital gown, loosely tied at the back, he staggers into the corridor and a glimpse of that barenaked posterior is guaranteed to have me rolling about in stitches. That bare backside makes up for Keaton's awful wailing scene that is yet to come! A real pick-me-up, and they must have had so much fun making it.
Editors note: I agree with Janet, sometimes a good old-fashioned tearjerker makes me happy, weird as that sounds.

• • • • • • •

by Margaret Anez:

BROADWAY DANNY ROSE (1984)
NATIONAL LAMPOON'S CHRISTMAS VACATION (1989)
ONE, TWO, THREE (1961)
SMALL TIME CROOKS (2000)
TWENTIETH CENTURY (1934)

Comedian1701 (from the CHFB):

A GOOD YEAR (2006)—Marvelous movie about slowing down life. And about living life how it should be lived. Not chasing down money wherever you can, but finding happiness instead.

GO (1999)—Hilarious stories intercepting each other. The Las Vegas ride by Simon and the boys is truly brilliant and makes you want to go to Las Vegas yourself. Heck, I did, and I practically lived in the Riviera room in which the characters of this movie check in.

BONNIE SCOTLAND (1935)—Probably not the boys' most liked movie, but my personal favorite of Laurel and Hardy. But pretty much every other L&H movie is just as good. If things look dire, look to L&H to cheer you up like nothing else in the world.

FRIED GREEN TOMATOES (1991)—Even better than the disjointed feeling book. This movie is so rich in subtext that you can watch it over and over again. And here's a movie that makes you feel that family and friends are the only important thing in life.

VAN HELSING (2004)—Not a good movie by any means, but one that is truly awesome, for all the wrong reasons. Richard Roxburgh is a God. He interprets Dracula in such a ludicrous way that we can only watch, wonder and cheer. Here is overacting at its best. For the rest? The dialogue is atrociously bad and therefore fun without end.

• • • • • • •

by Nick Anez (author *Celluloid Adventures: Good Movies, Bad Timing*):

A FUNNY THING HAPPENED ON THE WAY TO THE FORUM (1966)
A SHOT IN THE DARK (1964)
DUCK SOUP
IT'S A MAD MAD MAD MAD WORLD
THE GREAT RACE (1965)
Runner-up: **HARRY AND WALTER GO TO NEW YORK** (1976)

• • • • • • •

by Sam Borowski (*Creature Feature: 50 Years of the Gill-Man*):

IT'S A WONDERFUL LIFE—To me, this is the *classic* Cheer-Me-Up Movie—there is *no other* in its league. May sound silly, but to this day, it *still* brings tears to my eyes. I will slip the DVD in when I am feeling down and possibly even a bit overwhelmed, and I can just relate with George Bailey. The ending never fails to touch me. And who can't relate with being "discouraged," as "the voice"—presumably God—points out to Clarence Oddbody, angel second-class. And what a dream cast; Jimmy Stewart, everyone's All-American, Donna Reed, the sweetheart wife from next door, everyone's favorite tiny

We asked one of our younger friends to give us a list of cheer-up films for the Twitter Generation. Her choices were interesting, and, weirdly, they were also some of Gary's favorite films.
by Rachel H. Ellis
1. **TRAINSPOTTING** (1996)
2. **MEAN GIRLS** (2004)
3. **SCHOOL OF ROCK** (2003)—surprisingly cheerful
4. **WET HOT AMERICAN SUMMER** (2001)
5. **RUSHMORE** (1998)
6. **SAVED!** (2004)
7. **SUPERBAD** (2007)
8. **DARJEELING LIMITED** (2007)
9. **AMERICAN BEAUTY** (1999)
10. **DAZED AND CONFUSE**d (1993)
11. **BILLY ELLIOT** (2000)
12. **TWO DAYS IN PARIS** (2007)

daughter with a name beginning with Z—ZuZu, played by Karolyn Grimes—and even Lionel Barrymore gets into the act. How could this *not* be the *classic* Cheer-Me-Up-Movie?

ROCKY (1976)—Hey, what can I say—I am an American Male that grew up watching Stallone chase his celluloid dreams with this movie! It's a close second for me...and as soon as I hear "Gonna Fly Now," my spirits rise and I am on the path to being cheery. And there is nothing to criticize in Stallone's Oscar-worthy performance, or his Oscar-winning film, for which he penned the screenplay. Talia Shire is wonderfully convincing as Adrian, and who among us can't relate with getting a second-chance on our dream...and life.

NIGHT SHIFT (1982)—That's right, Ron Howard's second directorial effort to me is *still* one of his best and certainly most underrated. This film always cheers me up and makes me laugh at life. Perhaps it's Michael Keaton in his rookie starring role, or Henry Winkler's hysterical performance as a man too timid to stand up for himself. The line, "This is *Chuck* telling *Bill* to *shut up...shut up...shut up!*" Perhaps it's Keaton's explanation about how he got kicked out of a casino for being "too good," though admittedly he was several hundred down at the time? A standout cameo is the blink-you-miss appearance by future Oscar-winner Kevin Costner—his first-ever movie appearance—as a Frat Boy partying in the morgue. Or an even easier to miss cameo by the young director himself....you mean you missed that redheaded guy making out against a building? Or the feel-good ending that featured a Rod Stewart version of "That's What Friends Are For," that most people aren't even aware of. Bottom line, who among us can't relate with Keaton's high jinks?

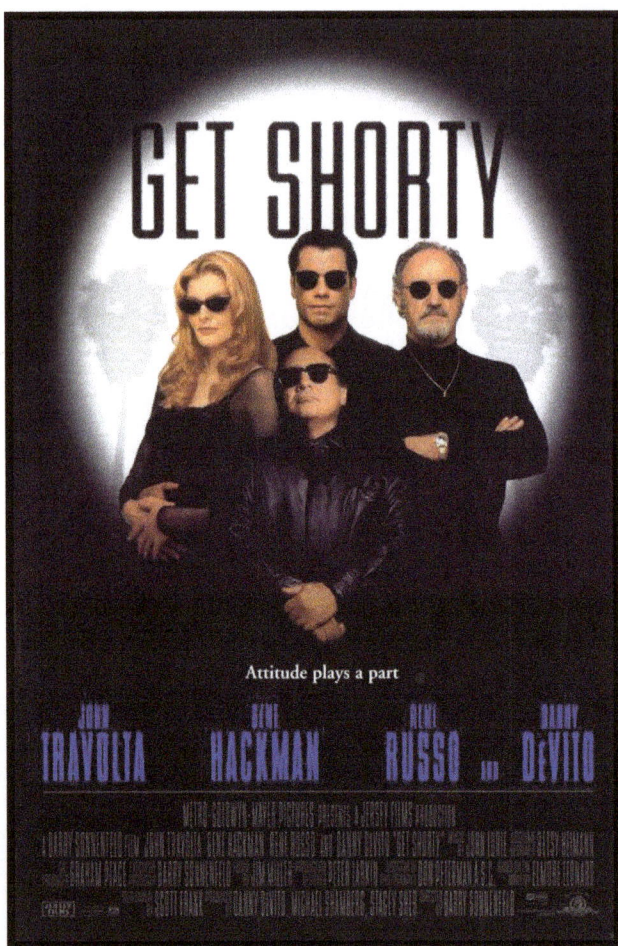

relate with the Creature, a classic character who is persecuted from his homeland, and who in the grand scheme of things, just wanted a lady....and *oh*, what a lady in Julie Adams!! And what child can't remember the first time they heard the horns and oboes blaring, signaling the arrival of the lovelorn green guy on screen. And hey, the Gill-Man's a lot *more lovable* than Bruce the Shark from *Jaws*, who Kevin Smith confesses could be played by Ben Affleck...But could Ben pull off the Creature? I don't think so. Not a knock on Ben, but hey, it took a special person—who just happened to also be named Ben—to don the Gills...Goodnight Ben Chapman, wherever you are...

• • • • • • •

by Dan Graffeo:

ARMY OF DARKNESS (1992)—Woe to any poor soul who sees Bruce Campbell and doesn't cheer up. **Army of Darkness** is the third entry in the *Evil Dead* series, but seeing the previous installments isn't necessary to follow it. Despite bombing in theatres in 1992, it has become not only a cult phenomenon, but is almost mandatory for every 14- to 35-year-old guy to see. Zombies, chainsaws, boomsticks, beautiful wenches, cheesy dialogue, Three Stooges-like action and horror's greatest hero: What's not to love?

Most would agree that Bruce Campbell is one of the few actors working today who can take a lousy film and make it entertaining simply by being in it. If you don't believe me, see

GET SHORTY (1995)—Anyone that knows me, knows how much I *love* this film. Perhaps it's not as *feel-good* as the top two, but hey, it makes *me* feel good! John Travolta in a vintage JT performance. And I still love the line, "Well, I don't know about the mixing with celebrities part—that's something new that was just added?" Or how about when Travolta's shylock, Chili Palmer—in a sense my producing mentor—sits down with Delroy Lindo's coke-dealer, who tries to convince Palmer just how "easy" it is to write a movie script? How about Dennis Farina's Ray Barbone-character, who likely would have the MidMar crew washing his mouth out with soap? "No, no, bleep you bleep-ball—L.A.'s an open city and I don't need permission from *nobody* for *nothin'*?" Or when Travolta talks down a depressed henchman in James Gandolfini—asking him about what movies he performed stunts in? And Gandolfini's Bear character actually starts to feel good about himself? Just as I do when I watch this hysterical satire, with a bowl of buttered popcorn. And who among us can't relate with John Travolta, who has been more resiliant than Rasputin!!

CREATURE FROM THE BLACK LAGOON (1954)—Yes, again, not a traditional top cheer-me-up movie, but any of you who are familiar with my film, *Creature Feature: 50 Years of the Gill-Man*, know that this has been a fave film since my childhood, so of course, it would cheer me up! Do I really need to explain? He's the Creature? And, who among us, cannot

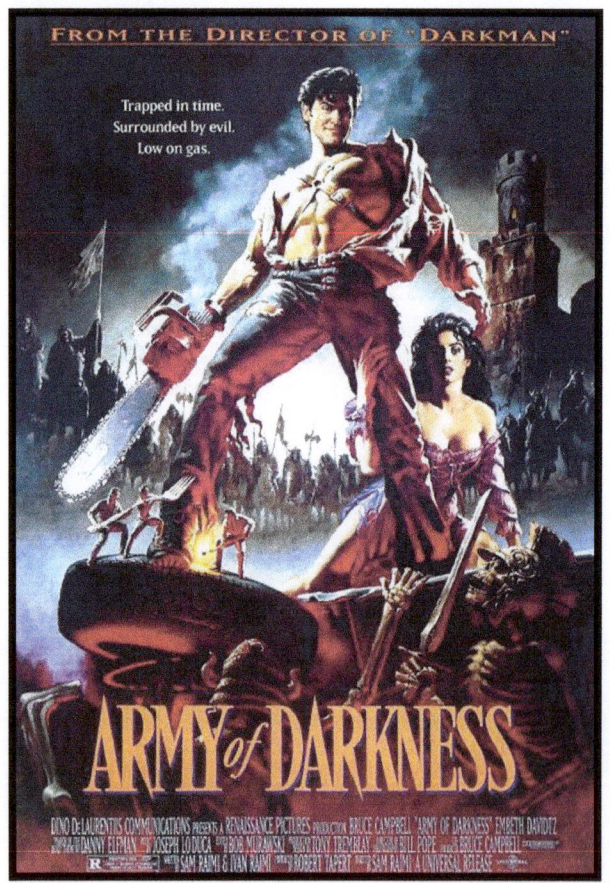

Alien Apocalypse or *Terminal Invasion*. His character, Ash, has left such an impression that for almost two decades horror fans have been pleading for an *Evil Dead 4* or the once-proposed crossover idea, Freddy vs. Jason vs. Ash. Campbell's plight is almost unique in Hollywood. There is no demand for Peter Weller to play *Robocop*, or Wesley Snipes to play *Blade*, or Mel Gibson to play *Mad Max*. There is good reason behind it. The viewers can relate to Ash because he isn't a Navy SEAL or a cop with an attitude. He's a clerk at S-Mart, which gives him a blue-collar magnetism that Jackie Chan or Vin Diesel could never have. Ash is the kind of hero that can kill the monster, kiss the girl, then accidentally fall off a cliff. When Ash fights, he gets his clock cleaned, especially by possessed women like the witch who interrupted his female pampering and his medieval love interest, Sheila. Yet, somehow those scenes are more sincere to the common fan that can't identify with Jason Statham, who always hits his target or Jet Li's smooth martial arts. We also love that Ash isn't that bright and that most of his troubles he brings upon himself. Who can forget the scene where he assures the Wiseman that he knows the proper words to speak before grabbing the Necronomicon, only to forget them at the most crucial time? There is also the alternative ending where Ash can't keep track of how many drops of time-traveling juice he is suppose to consume, only to wind up in a post-apocalyptic future. **Army of Darkness** is a fun movie that doesn't apologize for its silliness and fans wouldn't want it any other way.

Editors Note: We are also Bruce Campbell fans. Check out Bubba Ho-Tep *for his turn as Elvis, who winds up in a nursing home and must take on a mummy with the help of JFK, another resident, who is now an old black man. But our favorite Campbell work is the TV show* Brisco County, Jr. *and his new gig,* Burn Notice. *Campbell's role as Sam in* Burn Notice *fits him like a glove and he's never been better.* **Brisco County** *was just rollicking good fun that was cancelled much too soon.*

SOUTH PARK (1997-)—This is the show that put Comedy Central on the map. After 12 years, the four kids made from construction paper continue to be Comedy Central's highest rated show, and along the way has collected Emmys, a Cable Ace Award and a Peabody. At its core, **South Park** is a sentimental look back for those of us who grew up in the suburbs. Many boys have played robot ("Awesom-O") and all-powerful ninjas ("Good Times with Weapons.") Many girls have made lists on popular culture ("The List") and possess the knowledge on how to make a cootie catcher ("Marjorine.")

Like any sitcom, **South Park** isn't always drop-dead funny. What was the deal with that Towlie-Oprah Winfrey episode anyway? What **South Park** has always done, however, is nail the subject that is the episode's focal point. Examples of this are: "The Return of the Fellowship of the Ring to the Two Towers" where the gang is dressed like *Lord of the Rings'* characters in the quest to return a pornography tape (representing the dangerous ring) to the video store. Their mission is a perfect parallel to the Tolkien trilogy, which includes running into Ringwraiths, represented as sixth graders, and the twisted Smeagol eager to possess the ring, represented by Butters and his obsession with the pornography tape. Anyone who played minor-league baseball and hated it can relate to the "Losing Edge," where the gang, who play baseball only to satisfy their parents, is trying to break their winning streak so their season can end and they can enjoy the rest of the summer. The problem is the rest of the teams in the league are doing the same with even more determination, as they've trained themselves to be incompetent. There is also the "Fantastic Easter Special," which not only lives up to its name, but may be the best Easter special ever made. Satirizing Dan Brown's *DaVinci Code*, Stan finds out that his father is a member of the Hare Club for Men and a protector of Saint Peter's descendent—who's actually a rabbit. Soon, the Vatican discovers the secret that could crumble their organization and are willing to do anything to kill the rabbit. Jesus himself gets imprisoned when he attempts to stop them.

South Park continues to be on the cutting edge, more so than the *Simpsons* and the *Family Guy*. All of these shows at one point made fun of senior citizen driving, homosexuality, religion, and drugs. The last eight years have also been one George W. Bush joke after another, yet **South Park** hardly participated in it. This isn't because creators Trey Parker and Matt Stone are hardcore conservatives. It's because everyone else was doing it. Parker and Stone went in the opposite direc-

tion. They made fun of things "we're not suppose to": Native Americans ("Red Man's Greed"), Al Gore ("Manbearpig"), 9/11 conspiracy theorists ("Mystery of the Urinal Deuce"), Global Warming ("Two Days Before the Day After Tomorrow"), Police set-ups ("Jefferson's") and the Homeless ("Night of the Living Homeless.") Remember in the old days when the homeless characters on TV shows and movies were educated, dignified, hard-working, sober individuals who just caught a tough break? No more! They also praised the organizations "we're suppose to hate": Big corporations ("Gnomes"), Tobacco companies ("Butt Out") and land developers who destroy the rain forest ("Rainforest, Schmainforest.") On a side note, they also went to the other end of the spectrum on film. While modern action movies seem to be all about special effects, Parker and Stone created a puppet movie—the underappreciated *Team America:*

World Police. Their unique outlooks and refusal to jump on bandwagons have put **South Park** in Time's "100 Best TV Shows of all Time."

THE LONE RANGER (1949-1957)—In an age where almost all superheroes wear black and talk like Clint Eastwood, it's recommended that in order to see something fresh, one may wish to go back to the days of early television. **The Lone Ranger** probably strikes Generation Y and Z as too dated, but his history is just as rich as any other popular hero. It's also just as enjoyable. As John Reid, he and his brother Dan were part of a team of Texas Rangers who fell victim to an ambush from the Butch Cavendish gang. Although wounded, Reid was the only survivor or the "lone ranger," when Tonto found him. Tonto recognized Reid as an old friend who had saved his life when they were children, which is why Tonto calls him "Ke-mo sah-bee" or "faithful friend." After Tonto nursed him back to health, Reid carved a mask out of his brother's leather vest and vowed, that for every Texas Ranger killed in the ambush, he would bring a hundred criminals to justice. He used his family's silver mine for money and to make silver bullets. The silver bullet's purpose was to remind him that life was precious and every time he shot his gun, it had to be for a good reason, or it would be a waste of his wealth.

Hi ho Silver, Away! The Lone Ranger starred Clayton Moore and Jay Silverheels.

Some may feel that **The Lone Ranger** is too goody-goody, but I think today this symbolism is needed more than ever. Much like the Wild West, we are living in uncertain times. Society is suspicious of any potential role model and some modern "anti-heroes" have become too violent for general audiences (*Spawn, the Punisher, Watchmen, Hellboy*). It may be time to re-introduce ourselves and our children to the masked rider, who was not only dedicated to justice, but valued life, didn't drink, didn't smoke, didn't swear and practiced what he preached. In the **Lone Ranger** series, we knew who the good guys and bad guys were and there is nothing wrong with that. If we're willing to suspend disbelief with almost every modern action movie (see Michael Bay's films), we can do the same here. There must be something special about the Lone Ranger because Clayton Moore, the actor who played him, also made a conscious effort to live by the **Lone Ranger** Creed in his own life. The public adored Clayton Moore's dedication so much that there was an outcry when producer Jack Wrather forbade Moore from making public appearances as the **Lone Ranger** in 1981. Wrather was trying to promote the new *Lone Ranger* feature movie, which Moore wasn't involved in. It also didn't help that the new Lone Ranger, Klinton Spilsbury, acted un-Ranger-like during filming, which included getting into a fistfight. *The Legend of the Lone Ranger* was a critical and box-office flop, despite heavy promotion. Producer Jerry Bruckheimer, however, also sees potential with the character because he's planning a 2010 remake. Johnny Depp is playing Tonto, but many fans online are hoping that the new Lone Ranger will be someone known for his integrity. That's how powerful this character has become.

THE IN-LAWS (1979)—Michael Douglas and Albert Brooks remade this film in 2003 with disastrous results. It is a reminder that messing with classics is a bad idea. The original **In-Laws** starred Peter Falk and Alan Arkin, and it works today just as it did thirty years ago. Alan Arkin plays Sheldon Kornpett, a mild-mannered dentist whose daughter is marrying the son of Peter's Falk's Vince Ricardo, a CIA agent whose credibility and sanity is in constant question. The Bay of Pigs was his idea: "You win some, you lose some." The weekend their children are to be married, Vince walks into Sheldon's office and says, "I need a hand for maybe five minutes." From this one act, Vince drags Sheldon almost halfway around the world to perform a sting operation on a psychotic dictator, while thugs and mercenaries are shooting at them. In one of the funniest scenes, Vince is telling Sheldon, while dodging bullets, "Next time we're in Tijada, Shell, don't let me forget. They make a chicken sandwich here, they serve it on a hard roll, they eat it up with orange juice, you know, grande, a big one, or pineapple juice. And coffee, do you take coffee, Shell?"

The film is a pleasure to watch, not only because of its funny premise, but because of Peter Falk and Alan Arkin's chemistry. We identify with Sheldon because of the dangerous predicament he's been conned into. Throughout the film, Alan Arkin often makes silent, but hilarious, facial expressions that will remind audiences of Jack Benny. The expression screams, "How did I get into this mess?" Vince constantly assures Sheldon that from "here on in, it's strictly routine," only to be shot at again minutes later. Yet, Sheldon sees something about Vince that makes Vince trustworthy, despite all the lying and unexpected obstacles. The viewer will see it too. You'll be so entangled in their adventure; you'll almost forget that the main characters still have their children's wedding to go to.

CAMPFIRE TALES (1997)—I've been talking about this movie for over 10 years to anyone who would listen. **Campfire Tales** (not to be confused with David Johansen's horrible *Campfire Stories*) is the most underrated horror movie of all time. It went direct-to-video in 1998, when it should have been

widely released. The anthology premise has been done before. It's a series of horror stories with one wraparound tale, where a central character introduces them much like *Tales from the Hood* or *Tales From the Darkside*. The title says it all. The screenplay reenacts famous urban legends. The tales are simple as they are meant to be. Screenwriters Martin Kunert, Eric Manes, and Matt Cooper, however, did an outstanding job spackling plot holes that existed in the original folklore and making the urban legends believable.

"The Hook" was done in black and white to give a 1950s feel. This alone is refreshing because many filmmakers feel the need to give old stories an update, as if modern viewers can't appreciate a story that originated from a different era. The remakes of *Carrie* and *Salem's Lot* prove this. James Marsden of *X-Men* fame and Amy Smart of *Just Friends* play the couple whose make-out session is interrupted by a psychopath who wears a hook. "The Boyfriend's Death" stars Ron Livingston, of the cult classic *Office Space*. He plays the title role as he and his new wife's recreational vehicle runs out of gas and he is forced to walk in the dark to the nearest filling station. Once more, the screenwriters honor the legend and follow a rule in good horror: Don't show more of the monster than you have to. The next story, "The Licked Hand," is a revamp of an urban myth often called, "People Can Lick Too." I realize that I'm contradicting myself from my "Hook" critique when complaining about updating old stories, but in this case, it's justified. A plot hole in the original tale explains why a stalker would choose a random girl as his target. The script needed to provide an answer and Internet chat rooms made sense. Most of us have heard news stories over the years of impressionable youths talking online to molesters and perverts, masquerading as teenagers. As a result, this story could be the scariest one in the anthology. The final tale, "The Locket," isn't an urban legend, but a classic ghost story. It involves a drifter (the late Glenn Quinn of TV's *Roseanne*) who falls in love with a mute maiden (Jacinda Barrett), who always wears a choker necklace. Their romance is put in danger when the girl's cowboy father comes home and wants to punish the drifter for supposedly ruining his daughter's innocence. The drifter discovers a chilling pattern of events as the cowboy father repeatedly comes into the house, utters the same words, commits murder, then takes his own life when his temporary insanity dissolves. The drifter manages to escape the house, taking his new love with him, only to get a startling surprise when he removes the girl's necklace. Jacinda Barrett gives the best performance in the entire film, as she has to rely on facial and body language instead of dialogue. The wraparound tale involves four teens, which include Christine Taylor (*Brady Bunch*, *Dodge Ball*, *Zoolander*) and Christopher Masterson of TV's *Malcolm in the Middle*, waiting for a tow truck to pick them up after crashing their car. The film's ending is both unsettling and worthy of comparison to Rod Serling or M. Night Shyamalan's work.

Unlike most direct-to-videos, **Campfire Tales** is special because the cast gives each scene the respect it deserves. There is no trace of anyone hamming it up because they're in a B horror movie. Although none of them are headlining any blockbusters, most of the cast have gone on to have successful careers as shown above. How many direct-to-video casts can say the same?

• • • • • • •

by Vince DiLeonardi, Pasadena, MD:

NIGHT OF THE DEMON (1957, **CURSE OF THE DEMON** U.S. Title)—A genre masterpiece in all respects (music, cinematography, acting, storyline etc.). You name it, it's there.

FRANKENSTEIN—Another masterpiece in all respects, particularly in the portrayal of a human morality enigma (knowledge versus parameters of right and wrong).

CARNIVAL OF SOULS (1962)—A classic venture into the psyche and ethereal. Very haunting.

THE GORGON (1964)—Something about the tone and cinematography of this movie that fascinates me—mythical becoming reality.

THE UNTOUCHABLES (1959-1963)—1960's—early episodes mainly. "The Genna Brothers" episode is still a favorite. Marc Lawrence and whole cast turn in realistic performances. No wonder the Italians were getting nervous about this show.

Editor's Note: Ooookay Vince, whatever works for you!

• • • • • • •

by Brett Taylor:

Some Ramblings That May or Not Make You Feel Better

It's hard to say what makes people feel good. Look at the biggest money-making films of all time and you will see titles like *E.T., Gone with the Wind, Titanic, The Godfather*. In other words, a lot of sad endings occur. Women, at least, seem to enjoy sadness on the screen. Many men too, though they might not admit it.

It's commonly said that people during the Depression forgot their troubles with screwball comedies and Busby Berkeley musicals. Well, they did, but they were also watching George Raft and Jimmy Cagney blasting mugs with tommy guns. Even a lot of the lighthearted movies of the time addressed class struggle in one way or the other. Dialogue showed the class consciousness of the characters in a way movie dialogue today rarely does.

"Feel good" is subject to the whims of time, like everything else. At one time I thought Billy Wilder's *One, Two, Three* was one of the funniest things I'd ever seen, but the last time I saw it I thought it was forced. War propaganda movies can rouse people to cheer in the aisles, until the war drags on too long and people want to forget it. Then war movies no longer make anybody feel good. In its day *Birth of a Nation* was a real rouser, made a lot of people feel good. It suggested peace could prevail between North and South, in spite of that bloody civil war. However, it also made a large portion of the population pretty mad. Mainly black people and the people who thought they should have civil rights.

Deep Throat. Here's a movie that must have made people feel good. Why else would they spend half a billion dollars going to see it?

It's obvious why people enjoy films that make them feel good. The question is, why do people go to see films that don't make them feel good? Yet we do. *Night of the Living Dead* was a hit, but did it make anybody feel good? I would say it did, in the inner cities. Movies that had people cheering and waving their fists in the more rundown theaters, movies like that one and *Street Fighter*, weren't necessarily movies a respectable middle class audience would have considered feel good, although plenty of them still felt good about watching Charles Bronson blow away street punks in *Death Wish*. Generally speaking, though, mainstream feel-good films in the U.S. are about affirmation, not catharsis.

Offhand, I can't think of many things I like that would be considered "feel good." I'm not what you call a "feel good" kind of guy. Tell me how much you enjoyed *Mamma Mia!*, I'm likely to vomit on you.

Here's a few things that I think would make anyone feel better:

ANY THREE STOOGES SHORT. For that matter, any great comedy—W.C. Fields, Marx Bros., et cetera et cetera. The older you get, the harder it is to find anything funny. So why not get laughs where you can?

Any Japanese monster movie. Who wouldn't feel better after watching **GODZILLA** (1954) level Tokyo? It's nice to know that if when we humans get too big for our britches, Godzilla and his ilk will be there to reduce our armies to rubble and remind us how puny we really are. Makes your problems seem less important somehow. The beer helps too. I recommend you drink beer when you watch these, you'll feel better in no time.

ANY REAL KUNG FU movie: Real ones, from Hong Kong, not bad Hollywood imitations. To see a great Kung Fu athlete in action is to believe the human body can defy anything. Watching these guys defy gravity, jumping and flipping through the air, is to feel that human beings can do anything.

I'm not going to tell you what kind of porno does or doesn't make me feel good. Some things are private, so don't ask, you perverts!

• • • • • • •

by Pat Shields:

I'm happy to provide a list, but as far as explaining my choices... well, that's a whole 'nother matter. Why does someone prefer one shirt over another, the lobster over the filet, or Dean Martin over Frank Sinatra? What I'm saying is that my choices are based on gut feelings and decades of familiarity. Yes, there's drama, humor, wonderful writing, etc. But that's as far as I can go (perhaps I'm simply inarticulate!)—which probably ruins my eligibility. But here they are anyhow.

GUNSMOKE (1955-1975)
THE ROCKFORD FILES (1974-1980)
THE LOONEY TUNES VOLS. 1 – 4
THE DEAN MARTIN COMEDY HOUR (1965-1974)
THE LONE RANGER

Editor's Note: As any typical loving daughter, I worshiped my dad, and Pat lists several of his favorite shows. He loved **Gunsmoke** *and never missed it. Now* **Gunsmoke** *was on for years [1955-1975]. My mom once told me of how she would sit on my dad's lap and try to get him to turn off* **Gunsmoke**. *I was too young at the time to know what she meant, but since she was pregnant nine times, I think it likely he missed more than a few episodes! Like my husband Gary, my dad didn't laugh out loud much, but he always laughed at the* **Looney Tunes Road Runner** *cartoons. I never did figure those out, but I think they might be in the same category of the* Three Stooges, *another thing I never found funny. After I reached the age of 15, I was allowed to watch* **The Dean Martin Comedy Hour** *with my Dad. Every week we'd wait for Dean Martin to hop onto the piano—I still remember the day that piano crashed to the floor.*

• • • • • • •

Dean Martin and Ken Lane on *The Dean Martin Comedy Hour*

by Walt Hendricks, Baltimore, MD:

THE WILD BUNCH (1969)
YEAR OF THE DRAGON (1985)
THE PARALLAX VIEW (1974)
ROMEO IS BLEEDING (1993)
ALIEN AVENGERS (1996)

Though some hyperbole and violence here, all contain plot twists that can hold interest and keep one guessing...plus add a sharp moral conflict within one or more of the characters. Of these, only **Alien Avengers** is a comedy (dark, but hilarious none the less).

As for TV:
BOSTON LEGAL (2004-2008)
TWO AND A HALF MEN (2003-)
CHEERS (1982-1993)
TAXI (1978-1983)
MARRIED WITH CHILDREN (1987-1997), especially

These are comedies well written and individualistic in nature. Any in the list has (by reason of laughter or plain old-fashioned attention-grabbing) the power to take the sting out of reality for a while.

Editor's Note: Walt is an old-fashioned Renaissance Man, and his feel good movie choices are as esoteric as he is!

• • • • • • •

by Scott Essman (producer/director *Jack Pierce: The Man Behind the Monsters*, 2002):

ABBOTT AND COSTELLO MEET FRANKENSTEIN—A great horror romp all around, but nothing beats the moment where the Monster sees Wilbur (Costello) and becomes frightened of him!

YOUNG FRANKENSTEIN (1974)—A loving homage to the first three Frankenstein films in period detail with hilarity all over the place...Mel Brooks at his spoofing best.

WILLY WONKA AND THE CHOCOLATE FACTORY (1971)—If for only Gene Wilder's performance alone, **Willy Wonka** is an all-time classic, as sardonic and fantastical as any movie ever made.

THE WIZARD OF OZ (1939)—What else can you say about a Depression-era film that is so gleefully colorful and mesmerizing that it can be watched an infinite number of times with no amount of personal dissatisfaction at any moment throughout the joyous fantasy?

CHITTY CHITTY BANG BANG (1968)—A wholly underappreciated fantasy about a flying car, a mad inventor, his eccentric father, an evil king, a kindly toymaker and a menacing child catcher. Musical numbers abound, all of which add to the pure delight... more than a guilty pleasure!

Also:
THE GHOST BREAKERS (1940) with Bob Hope
TOPPER RETURNS (1941) with Roland Young, Joan Blondell, Eddie Rochester Anderson & the great George Zucco
THE CAT AND THE CANARY (1939) with Bob Hope
and The Disney college fantasies:
ABSENT MINDED PROFESSOR (1961)
SON OF FLUBBER (1963)
THE MISADVENTURES OF MERLIN JONES (1964)
THE MONKEY'S UNCLE (1965)
THE COMPUTER WORE TENNIS SHOES (1969)
STRONGEST MAN IN THE WORLD (1975)
NOW YOU SEE HIM, NOW YOU DON'T (1972)
and of course
THE THREE STOOGES mad scientist/haunted house shorts.

• • • • • • •

by Bob Bloom, Lafayette, IN:

FIELD OF DREAMS (1989)—I am a big baseball fan. During the winter months, my soul leaves my body and does not return until players report for spring training. Sometimes when I am blue I will just watch James Earl Jones' magnificent speech about what baseball has done for the country. I always watch the end when Kevin Costner says, "Dad... wanna have a catch?" Yes, it brings tears to my eyes, but they are tears of joy.

A serial chapter. Sorry, I cannot be more specific here, but I am a member of the Serial Squadron and love the old chapterplays. I usually watch something from Republic, usually a Zorro serial such as **ZORRO RIDES AGAIN** (1937) or **ZORRO'S FIGHTING LEGION** (1939). They bring a smile to my face and make me feel like a kid again.

ADVENTURES OF ROBIN HOOD—Who could stay sad while romping through the green of Sherwood Forest with Errol Flynn?

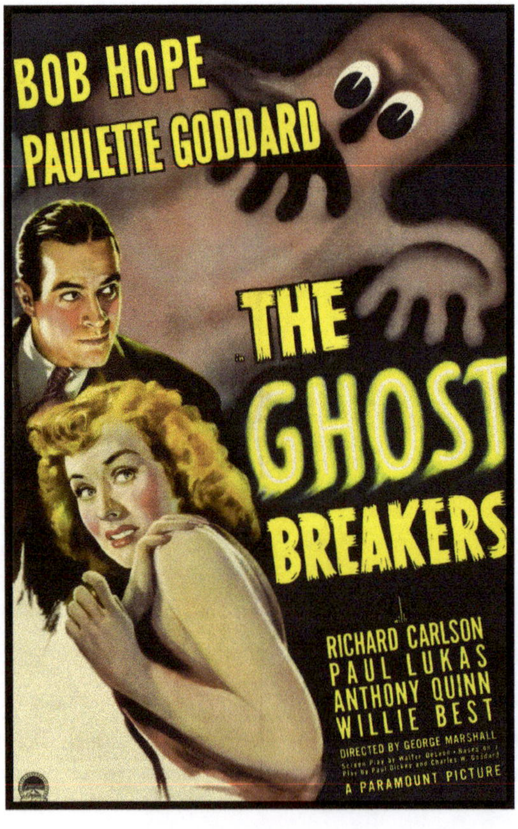

THE PRISONER OF ZENDA (1937)—The Ronald Coleman version. A great romantic adventure story and Coleman's soothing and melodious voice can lift the spirits of even the most die-hard grouch.

SINGIN' IN THE RAIN—The greatest musical ever made. If listening to Gene Kelly sing and dance the title song doesn't cheer you up, then you have no pulse.

• • • • • • •

by Kevin Shinnick (editor *Scarlet*):

MIDWINTER'S TALE (1995)
DUCK SOUP (Marx Brothers) (1933)
THE PRODUCERS (1968)—(the original not the recent version)
ARSENIC AND OLD LACE (1944)—just a delight
CITY LIGHTS (1931)—I laugh, I cry—perfection in filmmaking.

• • • • • • •

by Steve Haberman (author *Silent Screams*, writer *Dracula: Dead and Loving It*, 1995):

When I want to cheer myself up, I like to fantasize taking revenge on those who have misunderstood, wronged or just inconvenienced me. What better role model in tough times than Vincent Price at his most crazed and clever? What filmgoer would not want to identify with Vinnie as he channels his frustrations into something positive, like killing those he thinks, sometimes rightfully, have done him wrong? Just imagine members of Congress as the victims as you enjoy:

HOUSE OF WAX (1953)
MASQUE OF THE RED DEATH (1964)
WITCHFINDER GENERAL (1968)
THE ABOMINABLE DR. PHIBES (1971)
THEATRE OF BLOOD (1973)

I hope these orgies of retribution can put a laugh in your heart or at least a smile on your face, as you endure your own tough times.

Editor's Note: That Steve, he's such a fun guy!

• • • • • • •

In naming our top funny films, we don't claim to have the experience or the credentials of the AFI, but we do feel strongly about some of their choices. Therefore we offer our top choices, followed by their top 100 comedies!

MIDNIGHT MARQUEE'S TOP MOVIES TO FIGHT THE RECESSION DEPRESSION
(in no special order)

COMEDIES

ANIMAL HOUSE (1978) will always be a step above the typical frat-boy comedy. True its characters are worthless, but the beer flows, the skirts are chased and **Animal House** does it with such panache. John Belushi as Bluto can make us laugh, just by sneaking into the Dean's office. That poor horse! The food fight is the best ever, the toga party rocked, the music swings, the Delta House gets the best of the evil Omegas. I wouldn't like to be in the middle of that, but it's fun peeping into the windows of **Animal House.**

BARBERSHOP (2002)—Ice Cube made the crossover from rap star to major actor and **Barbershop** is one of his best efforts. His characters manage to remain calm while chaos

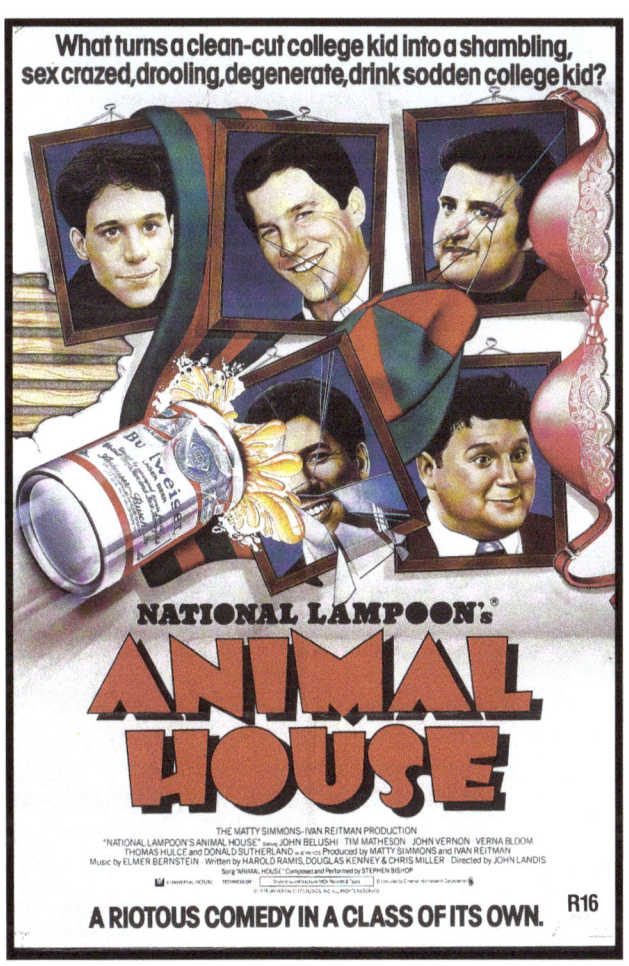

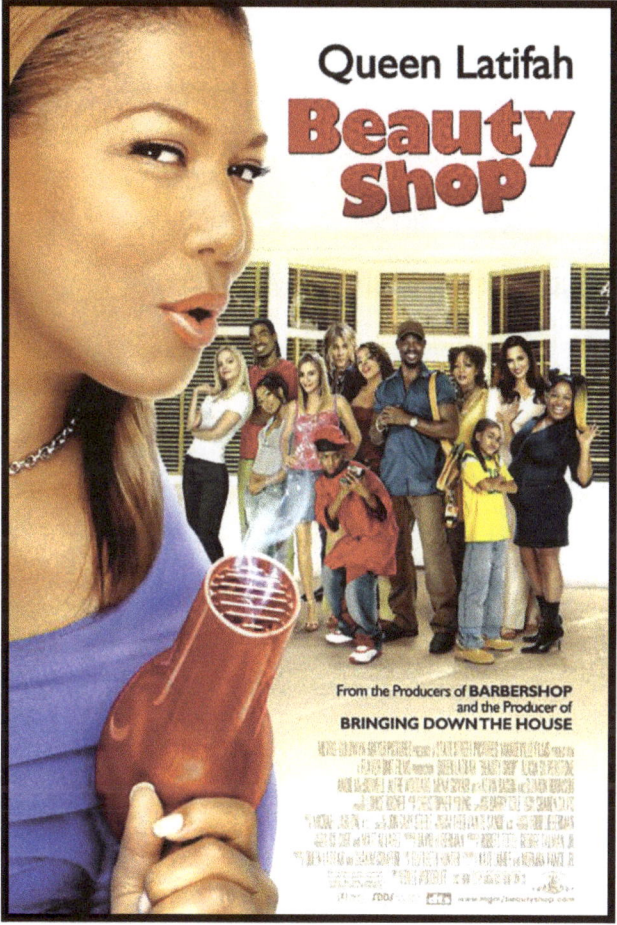

invades his world. Anthony Anderson and the always-funny Cedric the Entertainer help Calvin save his shop from loan sharks. Ice Cube is an appealing actor and has added quite a few comedies, as well as several family films, to his résumé. The popular **Friday** series follows the misadventures of Craig Jones and his rowdy friends and neighbors. The series includes **Friday** (1995, with Chris Tucker), **Next Friday** (2000, with Mike Epps) and the Christmas-themed **Friday After Next** (2002). On the family front, Ice Cube met his match when he decided to take his girlfriend's kids on a road trip to see their mother (Nia Long), in **Are We There Yet?** (2005).

BEAUTY SHOP (2005)—I think Queen Latifah is amazing and beautiful and most of her movies are fun, but **Beauty Shop**, with a cast that includes Alfre Woodward and Alicia Silverstone, is one of her best. Hunky Djimon Hounsou provides

41

the romance and Kevin Bacon turns in a hilarious performance as her business rival. Queen Latifah is simply one fabulous woman. For more laughs from the Queen, check out **Bringing Down the House** (2003) with Steve Martin, **Chicago** (2002), **Scary Movie 3** (2003), **Barbershop 2** (2004) and **Last Holiday** (2006). If you are an Alicia Silverstone fan, of course you have to check out Amy Heckerling's updating of Jane Austen's **Emma**, 1995's **Clueless**.

BLUES BROTHERS (1980) — I don't know what it is, but John Belushi just makes me laugh — the car chases, the music, the outrageous story, the fear of nuns (I can relate to that) — the movie's a smile inducer. The toe-tapping musical numbers will have you bopping in your recliner, and the BB rendition of the *Rawhide* theme at a redneck honky tonk is priceless — broken beer bottles spraying the band that performs behind a protective wire mesh fence.

BOWERY BOYS SERIES — from 1946 through the late 1950s, the boys, led by Huntz Hall and Leo Gorcey, starred in a series of low-budget comedies such as **Spook Busters** (1946) and **Master Minds** (1949). Their mangling of the English language, the comic situations they managed to get themselves into, their pretense of superiority and their good hearts make these tough-guy wannabes good company on a blue day.

A CHRISTMAS STORY (1983) — It's difficult to believe that the man who gave us **Porky's** (1981) and *Black Christmas* (1974), Bob Clark, also directed the film that has overtaken **It's A Wonderful Life** as the must see holiday movie. Every comic scene reminded Gary and me of our childhood — from the impossible-to-move-in snowsuits, to the typical

neighborhood bully, to the quest for the perfect Christmas gift. It's almost impossible to watch this without smiling. Since Gary and I wrote the book on Christmas movies (really, it's called *It's Christmas Time at the Movies*), we're major fans of holiday films. So if you want to celebrate Christmas in July, check out **Christmas Vacation** (1989), **Home Alone** (1990), **Mixed Nuts** (1994) and **The Santa Clause** (1994).

HEAVYWEIGHTS (1995) — A great underdog movie, **Heavyweights** concerns overweight teenage boys sent to a camp run by a kindly husband and wife. The boys can spend a summer free from insults and teasing and get some exercise while having fun. But the camp is going bankrupt and the owners are forced to sell it to a psychotic fitness guru (Ben Stiller), who proceeds to torture the kids with his diet quackery, all the while documenting their humiliation. But the kids and a sympathetic counselor capture the nutcase and save the camp. Today's hot property Judd Apatow co-wrote the screenplay. Fans of Apatow should also check out **The-40-Year-Old Virgin** (2005), **Talladega Nights** (2006), **Knocked Up** (2007) and **Pineapple Express** (2008). Ben Stiller is another major player in today's Tinseltown and has a huge fan base. Stiller is always good for a sly grin, so check out **There's Something About Mary** (1998), **Zoolander** (2001), **Dodgeball: A True Underdog Story** (2004) and **Night at the Museum** (2006).

GEORGE OF THE JUNGLE (1997) — I didn't expect to like this film, although I'm a Brendan Fraser fan. But I have to say, this movie made me laugh out loud. And I don't laugh out loud at a lot of movies. There are some brilliantly stupid bits in the film, although sometimes the time between the laughs seems a little long, but the wait will be worth it. Other Brendan Fraser titles that will cheer you up include **Airheads** (1994), **Bedazzled** (2000), **Looney Tunes: Back in Action** (2003), which is a must for cartoon and 1950s sci-fi fans.

IT'S A GIFT (1934) is considered by many to be W.C. Fields' best film. It was based on a story Fields wrote under his pen name Charles Bogle and is based on many of his classic Vaudeville routines. Fields plays a grocer battling with all the annoyances of life including children, a nagging wife, destructive customers and bothersome salesmen. Fields' character's name is the pretentious Bissonette, and he constantly corrects the pronunciation "Bee-so-nay." I have to wonder if the creators of the British sitcom **Keeping Up Appearances** were fans of **It's a Gift**. In every episode, their main character, Hyacinth Bucket, screws her face up with annoyance as she corrects the poor devil, "that's Boo-kay."

THE GREAT RACE (1965) and its cast alone can make a film fan grin with pleasure: Jack Lemmon as Professor Fate, Tony Curtis as The Great Leslie, Natalie Wood as Maggie Dubois, Peter Falk as Max, Keenan Wynn as Hezekiah and a supporting cast that includes Vivian Vance, Dorothy Provine, Larry Storch, Ross Martin and Denver Pyle. The hilarious Jack Lemmon steals the movie from Curtis and the interplay between Lemmon and Falk is priceless. It's hard to decide which character is funnier, Professor Fate or his lookalike, the idiot sovereign of Potzdorf, Prince Hapnik. The film could have used some judicious editing, but the good bits make it worth the wait. The piefight scene remains one of the best ever.

HAROLD AND KUMAR GO TO WHITE CASTLE (2004) is the silly story of two stoners, Harold (John Cho) and Kumar (Kal Penn), who are on a desperate search for White Castle burgers when a night of partying gives them a severe case of munchies. This movie will make you laugh, and also make you want a good hamburger! Neil Patrick Harris appears as an over-the-top hedonistic version of himself. Harold and Kumar returned in 2008 when they manage to become terrorist suspects and land in Guantanamo Bay. Once again Harris makes a hilarious appearance.

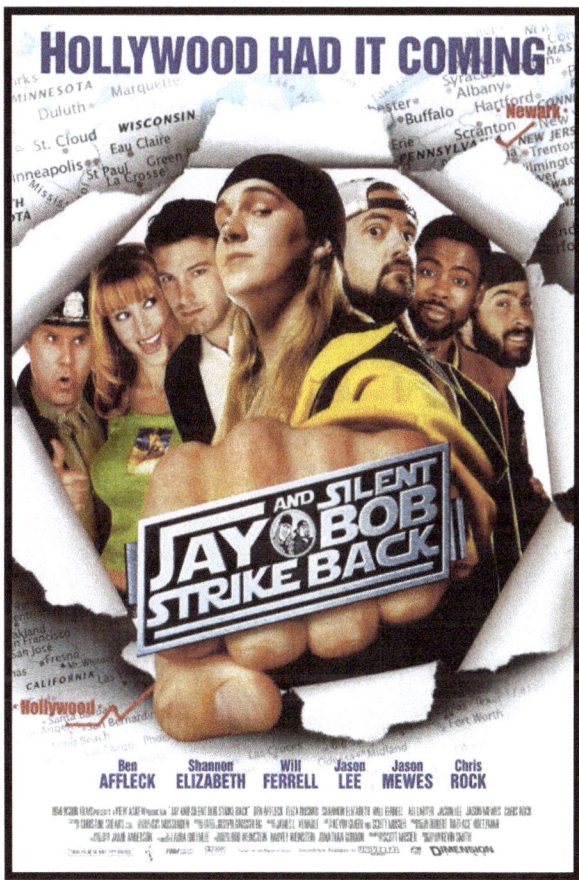

IT'S A MAD, MAD MAD MAD WORLD—This movie really did have a cast of thousands; it seems every comedian who ever worked in Hollywood has a part. It's a slapstick homage to silent film stars with ever increasing wackiness. Ethel Merman is especially funny as the mother-in-law from hell, and Dick Shawn as her drugged out mama's boy is another standout. But in this cast, everyone is a gem—Milton Berle, Sid Caesar, Mickey Rooney, Phil Silvers, Jonathan Winters, Eddie Anderson, Terry-Thomas, The Three Stooges and even Spencer Tracy.

JAY AND SILENT BOB STRIKE BACK (2001) contains typical Kevin Smith absurdities and ridiculous exploits of his endearing constant characters, Jay (Kevin Mewes) and Silent Bob (Kevin Smith). Smith never fails to amuse, but this movie has a finale that every artist has fantasized—be it writer, filmmakers, painter, etc. and evokes maniacal laughter. Whenever I see a bad review, I think of this movie and bless Kevin Smith for doing what I can't.

MR. HOBBS TAKES A VACATION (1962) stars that American treasure Jimmy Stewart. By the early '60s Stewart was mostly working in Westerns, in fact, that same year as **Mr. Hobbs**, Stewart starred with John Wayne in *The Man Who Shot Liberty Valance*, one of the greatest Westerns ever made. He also appeared in *How the West Was Won* with Hollywood legends Gregory Peck, Henry Fonda, John Wayne, Richard Widmark and Walter Brennan. No one could work wry dialogue like Stewart, and his over-worked, over-stressed, under-appreciated Mr. Hobbs offers Stewart some great material. Of course Hobbs' life couldn't be too bad—the lovely Maureen O'Hara played his wife. While Hobbs wants to get away for a romantic vacation with just his wife, she makes them spend a month-long vacation in a rented beach house that is in desperate need of some DIY, and she fills it to the roof with relatives, including two married daughters and their spouses and children.

OCEAN'S 11 (2001) (and **12** [2004] and **13** [2007]) is much more than merely a remake of the iconic 1960 "Rat Pack" movie, which starred Frank Sinatra, Dean Martin and Sammy Davis, Jr., among others. The original film was a minimalist shell allowing those ultra-cool show biz giants to have some

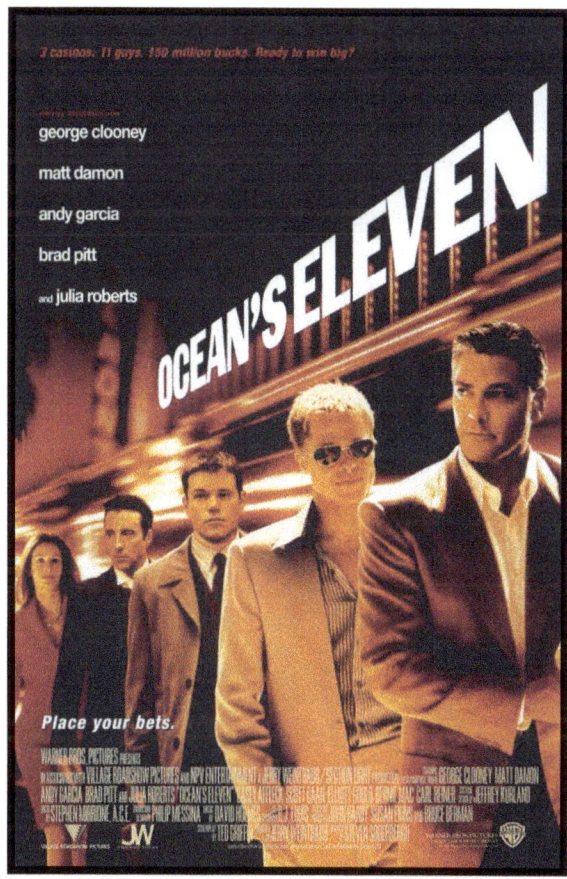

cinematic fun, with their star personalities overwhelming every other aspect of the film. Here, in 2001, director Steven Soderbergh, working with a script by Ted Griffin, which was loosely based on the 1960 original, again assembled the coolest stars currently working in Hollywood—George Clooney, Julia Roberts, Matt Damon, Brad Pitt, etc.—but this time, the movie's screenplay and direction rival the star power. Soderbergh wanted to create the ultimate hip heist film, one that is multi-layered and contains surprising twist after twist. Just when the audience thinks it has the surprises figured out, well, another topper appears to confuse everyone. But that's the ultimate fun this movie provides. The audience is forced to go along for the ride, enjoying the glitzy Las Vegas backdrops of hedonistic pleasure palaces, with a team of 11 criminal professionals trying to invade the vault of three gambling casinos. Why? Because the slimy owner (Andy Garcia) of the casinos stole Danny Ocean's (Clooney) woman, and besides wanting her back (we are talking Julia Roberts here!), Ocean wants revenge and desires to prove his mental superiority. Surprisingly, the crisp dialogue reminds me more than a little of the equally well-honed dialogue from the best film noirs of 1940s Hollywood, and for a film that seems so transparent and superficial, the screenplay oozes equal amounts intelligence and fun. When our movie-loving friends are over and the ladies get together, the ladies remark that this is the ultimate female eye-candy movie, and who cares about the plot—I suppose turnabout really is fair play. The sequels are more involved and lose a little of the charm of the first, but each offers entertaining escapism.

THE ODD COUPLE (1968) has become so famous that fussy, sinus-suffering OCD people are called Felix by their friends. The film stars Jack Lemmon as Felix the neatnik and Walter Matthau as slob Oscar. While the film as a whole never seems to work, there are moments when it's impossible not to laugh at Lemmon. Of course, the TV series with Tony Randall and Jack Klugman will give you more bang for your buck. And this may be sacrilege, but I think Klugman makes a better Oscar Madison and Penny Marshall, as his secretary, is equally funny.

OH BROTHER, WHERE ART THOU? (2000)—Thank heavens the Coen brothers are as odd as we are and manage to turn Hollywood upside down, shake it up and still make money. I can't even begin to tell you how much the KKK scene, an obvious **Wizard of Oz** homage, in **Oh Brother, Where Art Thou?** cracks me up. I actually get tears in my eyes from laughing. I love George Clooney, John Turturro, Tim Blake Nelson and Charles Durning as Pappy, and I never grow tired of listening to the music courtesy of T Bone Burnett. Several other Coen brothers' titles provide

biting satiric wit, including **The Big Lebowski** (1989), which has acquired such a cult following that it inspired a convention at a bowling alley. The film stars Jeff Bridges as The Dude and John Goodman, plus a slew of Coen regulars. I've always been more a fan of **The Hudsucker Proxy** (1994), not for any big laughs it brings, or because it is so beautifully shot and makes intriguing commentary about society, but because, in every frame, we can see that Joel and Ethan Coen love movies, and they revere the old classics as much as we do. Of course, if you're more in the murder-can-be-fun mood, there is always **Barton Fink** (1991) and **Fargo** (1996).

PLAY IT AGAIN SAM (1972) was one of Gary's top picks. And I have to agree. Forget **Annie Hall**, I think this is Allen's best film (of course, Allen did not direct this one)—maybe because it's about a film critic, or maybe because Allen gets advice from the great "man's man" Humphrey Bogart. Perhaps the apartment covered with film posters sucked us in, or it could be because we know so many movie geeks who are afraid of women. And you're not human if you can resist the **Casablanca** ending. Whatever the case, this movie makes us smile. Another Allen film I like (and I'm pretty much alone in this one) is **A Midsummer Night's Sex Comedy** (1982) with Mia Farrow, Jose Ferrer, Tony Roberts and Mary Steenburgen.

THE PRODUCERS (1968)—You only need to say the names Gene Wilder and Zero Mostel to know this movie is going to make you smile. And like poor old Max (Mostel), who is forced to seduce elderly women for investments, I know in my heart that if Gary and I tried to do something that would fail on purpose—and thereby make us rich—that would be the project that becomes a hugh success, no matter how much it stinks. There are so many laughs in this movie that it's difficult to even pick a favorite scene. But as a musical fan, the production number "Springtime for Hitler: is a black comedy goldmine. Who would think a movie containing the line, "Don't be stupid, be a smarty, come and join, the Nazi party," would be comedy gold and win an Academy Award for the screenplay written by Mel Brooks.

PURE LUCK (1991)—I know, you're thinking, how can we like a movie with a review from Roger Ebert that reads, "This is not a bad idea for a movie. But **Pure Luck** is a bad movie, all right—with leaden timing, a disorganized screenplay, and stretches where nothing much of interest seems to be happening."? Well, the first time I saw this movie, I didn't like it either. But for some reason, it keeps popping up on some cable channel we have and I always watch it. And it makes me laugh, not consistently, but enough to make me watch it whenever it's on.

Maybe I just enjoy Danny Glover's reactions to Martin Short's cursed character and the happy ending.

RAISING ARIZONA (1987) was the third film of the Coen brothers, Joel and Ethan, and stars Nicolas Cage and Holly Hunter, as a genial but pretty stupid ex-con and a police-booking officer who fall in love. Hunter's character, Ed, short for Edwina, wants a baby so bad, the couple decide to kidnap one of the babies from a rich man's quintuplets. Now these two aren't the brightest bulbs, they figure the rich guy and his wife won't miss one little baby. You'll either love the movie or it will annoy you, but either way, there are moments of comic hilarity.

RAT RACE (2001) is this generation's **It's a Mad, Mad Mad Mad World** for the TV generation. The huge cast is more familiar for their TV than film work and includes Breckin Meyer, Cuba Gooding, Jr., Seth Green, Whoopi Goldberg, Jon Lovitz, Kathy Najimy, Rowan Atkinson and John Cleese. We figured we'd hate it, but the film has moments that were stupidly funny, for instance when Jon Lovitz, through a series of slapstick accidents, winds up driving Hitler's car and getting something on his face that resembles Hitler's mustache. He then crashes into a Nazi rally, with hilarious results. The film loses a little steam at the end, but overall **Rat Race** is worth the trip.

SISTER ACT (1992) stars Whoopi Goldberg as Deloris, a Vegas entertainer, who must go into hiding after she witnesses a mob hit. The police hide her in a rundown convent that is ruled by a stern Mother Superior (Maggie Smith), who, not knowing what to do with the feisty Deloris, orders her to join the choir. Before long Deloris, posing as a nun, has the other sisters rockin' for Jesus. Kathy Najimy and crusty, but loveable, old pro Mary Wickes help turn the sleepy choir into a media sensation, bringing crowds back to church and saving the neighborhood. Many of the cast returned for **Sister Act 2: Back in the Habit** (1993).  While the plots are nothing new, Whoopi is always fun and the music will have audiences tapping their toes and grinning with delight. The prolific Goldberg manages to make even the worst scripts watchable. Whoopi fans looking for laughs should also check out **Jumpin' Jack Flash** (1986), **Ghost** (1990, for which she won an Academy Award), and **Soapdish** (1991).

SOME LIKE IT HOT (1959)—Jack Lemmon, Tony Curtis and Marilyn Monroe. What's not to like? Out of work musicians Lemmon and Curtis accidentally witness the St. Valentine's Day Massacre and have to get out of town fast. They

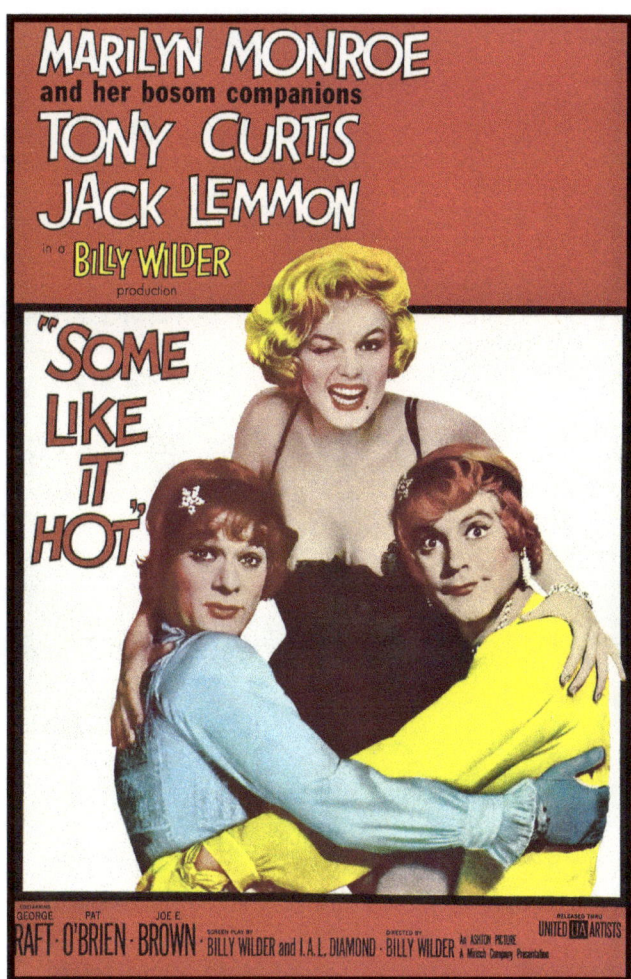

take a job in an all girl band, as "Daphne" and "Josephine." Of course this gives them ample opportunity for risqué one-liners and exaggerated expressions. Curtis impersonates Cary Grant as he woos Monroe—when he's not playing Josephine. And Monroe, as Sugar Kane, steals the show. All our characters are lying and using one other, but never in a reality show way. It's all good dirty fun, and if this movie doesn't make you laugh, you'd better take your pulse. My favorite Monroe films include the Technicolor dazzler **Gentlemen Prefer Blondes** (1953) with Jane Russell and the infamous "Diamonds Are a Girl's Best Friend" number; **How to Marry a Millionaire** (1953), with Lauren Bacall and Betty Grable as three models who spend all their money trying to land millionaires (I think it's one of Monroe's best performances and love the romance between her and David Wayne); and **There's No Business Like Show Business** (1954), an Irving Berlin musical that stars Ethel Merman, Dan Daily, Mitzi Gaynor and Donald O'Connor.

SONS OF THE DESERT has Laurel and Hardy up to their old tricks as they try to put one over on the wives so they can attend a Sons of the Desert convention. But like all men, they never learn—they'll always get caught. The boys tell the wives that they must take a sea cruise for Ollie's health, but, just their luck, the ship they were supposed to be on sinks. So now they have to figure out how to explain being alive and well. But the

45

wives are on to them the whole time—they saw them whooping it up in a newsreel. This is Gary's favorite Laurel and Hardy film, so pretty much any guy think it's funny. For women, it's sort of like the Three Stooges. Even if you don't get it, there are still some laughs for you. Gary also recommends **Way Out West** (1937), **Block-Heads** (1938), **Saps at Sea** (1940) and **Pack Up Your Troubles** (1932).

SOUTH PARK: BIGGER, LONGER AND UNCUT (1999)—Gary and I saw a press sneak of this film on our anniversary. We thought we'd hate it and expected to leave early. Who would have guessed we would love it. Parker and Stone put their foul-mouthed quartet into an old-fashioned big-screen musical with great songs and musical arrangements,—even if the titles of the songs are "Uncle Fucka," "Kyle's Mom's a Bitch" and "What Would Brian Boitano Do?" The movie is vulgar in the extreme and homophobes will choke at the scenes between Sadam Hussain and Satan. Every wicked moment is laugh out loud funny. Not really for Born Again Christians or avid churchgoers, but everyone else will have a great time.

THE THREE STOOGES were our must-see TV when we were kids. My five brothers and sisters and I were so smug since our six cousins weren't allowed to watch the Stooges. They really tried to use the Stooges' moves on each other—but we were allowed to watch them. In fact, we watched them with our dad, who laughed as much as we did. But as I got older, the Stooges seemed to be mostly mean and annoying. I think it's the Mars-Venus thing. Most men think The Three Stooges are geniuses and most women just don't get it. There are exceptions—so don't start raving yet. In our home theatre, I find the Stooges are much funnier on the big screen. But Gary and his movie buddies will laugh whether their heroes are on a 13-inch screen or a 9-foot screen. They particularly recommend: "A Plumbing We Will Go," "Micro-phonies," "Pain in the Pullman," "An Ache in Every Stake," "Men in Black" (which was nominated for an Academy Award for Short Subject), "Pop Goes the Easel," "You Natzy Spy" and "Spook Louder,"

TRADING PLACES (1983) can't miss with some great bits and a stellar cast that includes Eddie Murphy, Dan Aykroyd, and Jamie Lee Curtis. Also starring are two great old pros, Don Ameche and Ralph Bellamy, who play The Duke brothers—two jaded millionaires, who are so self indulgent that they ruin the life of one of their best employees (Aykroyd), over a one dollar bet. Their little experiment takes everything away from Aykroyd and gives it to con man Murphy. Their ultimate revenge on the Dukes inspires cheers for the underdog, and involves silly costumes and accents on a train, oranges and a love struck gorilla. How can that be bad?

YOU CAN'T TAKE IT WITH YOU (1938), directed by Frank Capra and based on the Pulitzer Prize-winning play by Moss Hart and George S. Kaufman, won the Academy Award for Best Picture of 1938. I don't think it was the best picture, and it's a little slow in parts, but in this heart-warming screwball comedy there are moments of brilliant lunacy by an incredible cast of Hollywood legends: Lionel Atwill, Jimmy Stewart, Jean Arthur, Edward Arnold, Ann Miller, Spring Byington and Eddie Anderson. Anyone with a typical dysfunctional family will think they're not so bad after watching this bunch of happy-go-lucky free thinkers.

ROMANTIC COMEDIES

ADAM'S RIB (1949) — Spencer Tracy and Katharine Hepburn star as battling attorneys who face each other in court when Hepburn defends a woman (the vivacious Judy Holiday) who shot her cheating husband (Tom Ewell) — while Tracy tries to prosecute her. The film was written by married (at the time) writers Ruth Gordon and Garson Kanin, who knew a little bit about the battle of the sexes. Hepburn and Tracy traded barbs in sure fire laughers including **Woman of the Year** (1942) and **Pat and Mike** (1952), with the infamous Tracy line, "Not much meat on her, but what's there is cherce."

ALL OF ME (1984) — A wealthy woman that is dying (Lily Tomlin) decides to have her soul transferred to a beautiful (but evil) blonde (Victoria Tennant). But something goes wrong and she ends up in her lawyer's body (Steve Martin). Sounds nutty, but it's funny and heart-warming. I've always found that many of Steve Martin's movies have a sweetness and warmth to them. **The Man with Two Brains** (1983) is an underrated comedy whose moral is that it's what's inside a person that counts, In **Parenthood** (1989) and **Father of the Bride** (1991) he gets to be the zany, put-upon dad, and in **Little Shop of Horrors** (1986) and **Dirty Rotten Scoundrels** (1988), he's just plain hilarious. But really, all he has to do to make me laugh 'til I cry is put that stupid arrow on his head and I'm gone.

THE AWFUL TRUTH (1937) is another great screwball comedy, with Cary Grant and Irene Dunne as a married couple who annoy each other so much that they decide to divorce. But secretly they are still in love and go to extraordinary methods to sabotage each other's romantic entanglements.

BABY BOOM (1987) stars Diane Keaton as a hard-nosed businesswoman, who is shocked to discover that she is the only living relative of a darling baby girl. The corporate killer panics and proceeds with putting the baby up for adoption, but when she meets the grim Midwestern farmers who are adopting a worker, not a child, she grabs the adorable baby and flees. Of course she's demoted at work and decides to leave the rat race for a more simple life in Vermont. All ends happily. Of course it's a fantasy, and things are never that easy in real life. But who cares, it makes me smile.

BRINGING UP BABY (1938) — A ditzy Katharine Hepburn sets her sights on equally ditzy professor Cary Grant, and with the help of a leopard named Baby and a dog named George, who steals Grant's dinosaur bone, lots of silly slapstick occurs before she finally gets her man. George is played by Skippy, who also starred as Asta in **The Thin Man** and Mr. Smith in **The Awful Truth**. The film bombed at theaters and Hepburn was considered box office poison — of course Kate recovered, and today the film is considered a classic.

DOUBLE WEDDING (1937) is the seventh film teaming William Powell (as Charlie) and Myrna Loy (as Margit). It is not as well known as their films such as **The Thin Man**, and truthfully, it's nowhere near as entertaining, but it is always fun to see the interplay between these two quick-witted film comedians. Watching Charlie try to figure out how to make Margit's sister fall out of love with him and convince Margit that she is in love with him makes the 87 minutes worthwhile.

FRENCH KISS (1995) is a modern romantic comedy starring Meg Ryan and Kevin Kline. The first time I saw this movie, I didn't really think much of it, but it comes on TV a lot, so I find myself watching it every time. I love watching Kevin Kline's facial expressions and double takes as the roughish Frenchman, who has stolen a diamond necklace, and Meg Ryan is typically adorable as the confused schoolteacher trying to win back her fiancé, who has dumped her for a hot French pastry. Fans of

Kline looking for a laugh can also guarantee a chuckle with **A Fish Called Wanda** (1988) with the brilliant John Cleese, **I Love You to Death** (1990), where Kline is the macho, moron husband of Tracey Ullman, who finds he's just so ornery, he won't stay dead when she tries to kill him, and **Soapdish** (1991), a send-up of TV afternoon soap operas co-starring Sally Field. I've always been a Meg Ryan fan, but wish she had stuck to romantic comedies, and I must confess, I've never thought **When Harry Met Sally** is as great as everyone thinks. But for Ryan fans needing a giggle, I also recommend **Joe Versus the Volcano** (1990), with Tom Hanks. This movie just tanked and is pretty much despised by everyone, but for some reason, I find myself watching it whenever it comes on. Of course there is **Sleepless in Seattle** (1993) and **You've Got Mail** (1998) for those romantic moods, both also co-starring Tom Hanks.

GROUNDHOG DAY (1993) finds snarky and miserable Pittsburgh weatherman Phil (Bill Murray) forced to relive Groundhog Day over and over again until he gets his life right. Each day he falls a little more in love with his producer Rita (Andie MacDowell), while to her it is just another day with the misery that is Phil. Eventually he learns humility and love for his fellow man and manages to make Rita fall in love with him.

LIBELED LADY (1936) features a cast that makes movie fans drool: William Powell, Myrna Loy, Spencer Tracy and Jean Harlow. This slapstick romance features Powell as a rakish reporter that editor Tracy brings in to save the newspaper from a libel suit brought by heiress Loy. Jean Harlow is Tracy's fiancé, who has been waiting forever for him to make an honest woman of her. Of course mayhem ensures, but things have a way of working out for the best. The film was nominated for a Best Picture Oscar.

MY FAVORITE WIFE (1940)—Garson Kanin directed this romantic comedy starring Cary Grant and Irene Dunne. On the eve of his second wedding, widower Grant sees his first wife, Dunne, in the hotel lobby. Which is shocking, since she had been lost at sea seven years ago. Grant, while avoiding his new wife, discovers his first wife had spent those seven years with hunky Randolph Scott and they called each other Adam and Eve. James Garner and Doris Day filmed a remake, **Move Over, Darling**, in 1963. You can't go wrong checking out that title also. Garner and Day have an easy rapport and will charm viewers.

NOTTING HILL (1999) was pretty much box-office gold from the get go—adorably charming Brit Hugh Grant, beautiful and sunny Julia Roberts, a supporting cast of zany characters, and a the story of mega-famous movie star who meets everyday working schlub and falls in love. Of course, seriously who wouldn't fall in love with Hugh Grant or Julia Roberts? The clever script even manages to make brilliant use of her zillion watt smile, which will have moved to your face as the end credits roll.

THE PARENT TRAP (1961)—I can't even pretend to be unbiased about this film. I've adored Haley Mills, Brian Keith and Maureen O'Hara since I was a kid. Mills plays separated-at-birth twins who meet at camp and engage in a slapstick war. When they are forced to room together, they discover they are

twins and their parents have never remarried. The girls switch places, determined to reunite their mom and dad. The scene with Keith's scheming new fiancée being tortured by the sneaky duo is priceless, as is the kitchen scene with Keith and O'Hara. Disney remade the film in 1998 with a fresh-faced innocent Lindsey Lohen as the twins. Dennis Quaid and Miranda Richardson played the parents. This is the film most people will probably remember as one of Richardson's best roles, who, after a tragic skiing accident in 2009, passed away leaving behind husband Liam Neeson and two children.

THE PHILADELPHIA STORY (1940)—Cary Grant, Katharine Hepburn, Jimmy Stewart star; George Cukor directs; and audiences cherish each moment of this brilliant romantic comedy. The snappy dialogue cracks like a whip as the witty wordplay trips off the tongues of the charismatic trio. While Hepburn and Stewart receive most of the acting accolades, including Oscar nominations, which Stewart won, I've always liked Grant best. His C.K. Dexter Haven is low-key but so charming that you hate George Kittredge (John Howard) before you even see him. The 1956 remake, *High Society*, starring Crosby, Frank Sinatra and Grace Kelly doesn't have the acting chops of the 1940 film, but it is filled with great music and Louis Armstrong. The best number is a sharply clever Cole Porter number "Well, Did You Evah?" sung by Crosby and Sinatra.

THE SEVEN YEAR ITCH (1955) stars Marilyn Monroe as the object of lustful fantasies of home-alone husband Tom Ewell. I must confess, this Billy Wilder comedy has never appealed to me. I think it is more a man's film. I guess I just can't find a man fantasizing about cheating on his wife with a beautiful woman entertaining. But Gary said it makes him laugh—which makes me wonder if I should be worried. But then again, since he can't stay awake past 8 p.m., I just don't think he'd have the energy to chase a beautiful neighbor.

SULLIVAN'S TRAVELS (1941)—The tagline for this Preston Sturges comedy was, "A Happy-Go Lucky Hitch-Hiker on the Highway to happiness! He wanted to see the world... but wound up in Lover's Lane!" Joel McCrea and Veronica Lake star as unlikely lovers. The plot involves a director who wants to make a film for the beaten working class salt-of-the-earth people, so he lives in poverty as a hobo to understand his subject matter. Veronica Lake does not play the femme fatale, instead, she plays a terminally cute and sexy love interest. By the movie's end, Sullivan has gotten far more than he bargained for and learned what it means to hit the skids and rise up even more triumphantly afterward. Preston Sturges is at the top of his game here, as both writer and director. Veronica Lake has never been more attractive or likable.

WOMAN OF THE YEAR (1942)—Hepburn and Tracy trade barbs and kisses as an intellectual journalist and a sportswriter, who fall in unlikely love. The real-life lovers starred in nine films together, most comedies and all contain the heat of their on and off screen chemistry. **Guess Who's Coming to Dinner** (1967) was their last film together. Hepburn picked up another Academy Award and Tracy was nominated. Tracy died June 10, of that year, 1967.

TEARJERKERS
(They really do make some people feel better!)

AN AFFAIR TO REMEMBER (1957) is probably the queen of the chick flicks. Nickie (Cary Grant) and Terry (Deborah Kerr) meet on a cruise, try to ignore their attraction—they are both involved with other people—but when fate keeps throwing them together, they give in and fall deeply in love. He even introduces her to his beloved grandmother. On the return voyage they agree to meet in six months at the top of the Empire State Building. Terry is so eager to see him again, she is not paying attention to traffic and is hit by a car and paralyzed. She doesn't want Nickie to be with her because of guilt, and never lets him know the reason she didn't show up. But happily fate once again intervenes. You can't go wrong with the original version called **Love Affair** (1939), starring Irene Dunne and Charles Boyer, and **Sleepless in Seattle** (1993), which is not a remake, but *An Affair to Remember* plays an important part

in this Meg Ryan/Tom Hanks romance. One of the strongest assets of this Nora Ephron-directed film is her musical selection of classic romantic songs including "When I Fall in Love," "In the Wee Small Hours of the Morning," "Stardust" and even "Over the Rainbow."

ANNE OF GREEN GABLES (1985), the classic children's novel, written by Canadian author Lucy Maud Montgomery, has been filmed many times, but the best adaptation was filmed for broadcast on the Canadian Broadcast Corp. and gained legions of U.S. fans when picked up by Public Television. The film stars perky redhead Megan Follows as Anne Shirley, and features a stellar supporting cast of Collen Dewhurst and Richard Farnsworth as the brother and sister who take the orphaned Anne into their home and hearts.

CASABLANCA (1942) has so many memorable scenes that it's difficult to pick a favorite. The film has influenced TV, comics, cartoons, and, of course, romance, for decades. The classic story features the beautiful Ingrid Bergman as Ilsa, the woman who gives up her true love, Rick Blaine (Humphrey Bogart), for Victor Laszlo (Paul Henreid), a hero of the Resistance, who also loves her and needs her. As Victor and Ilsa are trying to flee the Nazi's in Casablanca, she once again meets Rick. And even though they will "always have Paris," when that plane takes off leaving Rick standing on the misty runway, our hearts are breaking. But ultimately, we sigh with contentment at this story of courage, dedication and sacrifice for true love.

DARK VICTORY (1939) is sooooooo sad, but sometimes a good cry is just what the doctor ordered to make us feel better. Bette Davis is spot on as the spoiled rich girl, who only finds kindness, humility and true love after she is diagnosed with a brain tumor. She falls in love with her doctor, George Brent, and though she tries to deny their love to save him from grief, he convinces her that a few glorious months of happiness are more important than an unknown future.

ENCHANTED APRIL (1992) is the story of four unhappy but very different women who find a bond when they chip in to rent a villa in Italy. Lottie (Josie Lawrence) is unhappily married to a cold and demanding husband; Rose (Miranda Richardson) is married to a gauche dandy who writes risqué novels and is having an affair; Lady Caroline (Polly Walker) is bored with life and disgusted with men who are only after one thing (she's also unknowingly having an affair with Rose's husband); and the grumpy Mrs. Fisher (Joan Plowright) lives in the past rather than the present. The women find peace and sanctuary in the beautiful villa, and the enchanted month they spend there turns their lives around—Lottie and Rose reconnect with their husbands, Lady Caroline finds love and Mrs. Fisher learns to live in the present. The film was just being released on DVD in May 2009. The novel, written by Elizabeth von Arnim in 1922, had also been filmed in 1935 and starred Ann Harding and Frank Morgan. Von Arnim, also author of *Mr. Skeffington*, had two very unhappy marriages, which gave her

material for her novels. She wrote with a feminist viewpoint in a period that still placed very little value on women, her first novel was anonymously published in 1898. Interestingly, her bio on The Literature Network states she had a three year affair with H.G. Wells.

GOODBYE MR. CHIPS (1939) is just so sad and so lovely. I'm a sucker for underdog and one-true-love stories, and this film is both. Robert Donat stars as the unassuming, mild-mannered Mr. Chips, a lonely teacher at a boy's boarding school.

Belgium poster for *Goodbye Mr. Chips*

as the gruff grandfather who comes to love the little girl that brings happiness and light to his lonely existence in the beautiful Alps. The two lost souls find safety and comfort together, but that calm is shattered when Heidi's mean aunt kidnaps her and sells the child to a rich man, who wants a companion for his wheelchair-bound daughter. Heidi eventually finds herself in danger once again from her aunt, but grandfather has traveled to the big city to save his little granddaughter. You really can't go wrong with any of the versions, children will love the story of the feisty little girl, who finally finds a true home and happiness.

A LITTLE PRINCESS (1995), a popular Frances Hodgson Burnett novel, has been filmed many times, including an excellent 1939 Shirley Temple version (titled **The Little Princess**), but director Alfonso Cuarón's version is one of the best. Girls of all ages will be enchanted by the story of Sara Crewe. Sara's father takes her to a popular girls' boarding school when he must leave to fight in the war. The nasty headmistress goes out of her way to be nice to the daughter of the rich Captain Crewe. But when Crewe is reported dead and all his money gone, all Sara's lovely things are sold and she is forced to work for her keep, sleeping in a cold attic room. The film has beautiful cinematography and set design that only adds to the magic. One of the most important lessons of **A Little Princess** is the power of imagination to take us from pain and hurt of the real world to a magical land of color and beauty. I fear that today children are not encouraged to develop their imaginations and instead rely on TV and movies, rather than their own minds.

On a walking vacation he meets the vivacious Katherine (a radiant Greer Garson) and the two opposites attract and they fall deeply in love. Katherine brings out the best in Chips and her influence helps make him one of the most beloved teachers on campus. Just in case you've never seen this film (oh my goodness, you have to watch it!), I'm not going to spoil the story. The film was based on the James Hilton novel. Hilton, whose most famous work is probably **Lost Horizon**, based Mr. Chips on one of his boyhood teachers. The film may actually be most remembered because during the 1939 Academy Awards the audience was shocked when Donat won the Best Actor Oscar over Clark Gable's Rhett Butler from **Gone With the Wind**, which pretty much won every other award that night.

In 1969 Herbert Ross directed a musical remake starring Peter O'Toole and Petula Clark. O'Toole also received a Best Actor nomination for his portrayal of Mr. Chipping, but that award would go to John Wayne for **True Grit**. Critics always snipe that Wayne's win was a sympathy vote, but I look upon it as justice since he was not even nominated for his terrific performance in **The Quiet Man** (1952), although John Ford picked up an Oscar as Best Director for the film.

HEIDI (1937), the beloved children's story by Swiss authoress Johanna Spyri, has been filmed numerous times, but the Shirley Temple version remains a favorite. Jean Hersholt is marvelous

LOVE STORY (1970) was released when I was in ninth grade and every girl in the school was begging their parents to be allowed to see it. But the film contained bad language and had dirty nude scenes. So of course, most of us never got to see the film in the theater. But someone managed to find a copy of the novel and passed it around—with all the dirty parts underlined. When my two friends and I did finally see the film in the theater (our parents could only stand so much nagging after a year or so), we sobbed our eyes out, and loved every minute of it. Ali MacGraw and Ryan O'Neal starred as young college students that fall in love and marry against the wishes of his rich family. They are blissfully happy until she becomes terminally ill. I'm sure you know the story, and today it would probably be difficult to find anyone to admit they like the movie. It has become a parody of itself. In fact, in **What's Up Doc?** (1972), Ryan O'Neal says the most famous line from the movie, "Love means never having to say you're sorry," to Barbra Streisand. That line, right from the novel, is probably one of the stupidest in the history of Hollywoodland, as Streisand points out. But when Ali MacGraw said it, we swallowed it hook, line and sinker. **Love Story** is one of the few examples of a film that is better than the book. **What's Up Doc** is another great candidate for cheer me up film. It's quirky and silly with dynamite performances by Madeline Kahn, Kenneth Mars and Austin Pendleton, in addition to Streisand and O'Neal.

NOW, VOYAGER (1942) is one of my very favorite films. I'm not even going to mention the story, just go watch it. Bette Davis plays an ugly duckling who becomes a swan, Paul Henreid impresses as the suave lover who is in a loveless marriage and Claude Rains has never portrayed a kinder part, as an understanding doctor who helps Charlotte emerge from her sad existence. Oh, just watch it. Today the film might seem hokey, silly and campy, but just forget today and wallow in the old-fashioned love story. Lighting up a cigarette never seemed sexier.

POLLYANNA is another popular movie subject adapted from a beloved children's novel. Eleanor H. Porter penned the classic novel, which was published in 1913, and for that we're very glad. Mary Pickford starred as Pollyanna in the first film version, a silent film made in 1920. It is the 1960 Disney version that is our favorite. Hayley Mills stars as the impish orphan Pollyanna, whose joy and innocent common sense turn the sad and bitter town of Harrington into a happy haven and melts the cold heart of her Aunt Polly (Jane Wyman), who runs the town with a no nonsense grim determination. I read some modern reviews and it was depressing to find most of them written by snarky men who raged against the syrupy story. But I say what do they know? It might be cool to be mean and cynical, but then I've certainly never been cool. And they're not going to cheer me up when I feel down, but Pollyanna's "look on the bright side of life" story most certainly will.

RANDOM HARVEST is so over-the-top, you just have to love it. Suave Ronald Coleman is an injured WWI vet who has lost his memory and identity and must start life all over again. He flees the mental hospital and meets Paula (Greer Garson), who nurses him back to health. They fall in love, marry and have a child, and he becomes a successful writer. But just as their life is at its most perfect, he has another accident, regains his past memory but loses all memory of what happened after the war, forgetting Paula and his child. I know—what man could forget Greer Garson, but work with me here. He returns to his original rich and privileged life. Years pass and we worry about what's happened to poor Paula. But we're soon to find out when his extremely efficient secretary enters his office and—it's Paula! **Random Harvest** is based on another James Hilton novel and was directed by Mervyn LeRoy. The film received seven Oscar nominations.

RETURN TO ME (2000) is a more modern day romance but still manages to tug the heartstrings. David Duchovny does a 180 turn from *The X-Files* as a happily married man who loses his beloved wife in a tragic accident. A year later he is still trying to recover and move on. He manages to begin a new relationship with waitress Grace (Minnie Driver), whom he

52

meets at a small family restaurant. But things seem to fall apart when they discover she is the recipient of his wife's donated heart. Bonnie Hunt directed the film, and she manages to bring a cheerful hominess to the restaurant scenes between Grace's grandfather (Carroll O'Connor) and his roguish old friends Robert Loggia, William Bronder, and Eddie Jones. The sense of love and support provided by the extended family and the thought that love can survive, in one form or another, beyond death makes this romantic story something special.

THE SECRET GARDEN (1949 and 1993) is another children's novel adapted into two films that I find myself hooked on and return to often. Frances Hodgson Burnett, author of **The Little Princess**, is also the author of **The Secret Garden**, and both stories concern orphans who had been raised in India but are forced to return to the dark and scary world of England. I cannot decide which version is my favorite, so I'm advising people to watch both. The Margaret O'Brien black-and-white 1949 version is pure magic, with the added cinema gimmick that when the children enter the secret garden they have lovingly brought back to life, the film transforms into intense color photography (but only when they are in the garden). It's truly magical, much like the feeling we have when Dorothy opens the door into Munchkinland in **The Wizard of Oz**. This version boasts a cast of classic actors including Herbert Marshall, Dean Stockwell, Gladys Cooper, Reginald Owen, George Zucco and Elsa Lanchester. The 1993 version, directed by female director Agnieszka Holland, has a British cast that is mostly unfamiliar to U.S. audiences, although Maggie Smith appears as the grim Mrs. Medlock.

A STAR IS BORN (1937 and 1954) is the story of big stars, fragile egos, raw new talent, jealousy, devotion, sacrifice and love. We know the story. A big star whose popularity is on the decline because of his partying ways meets a fresh new talent and makes her a star. They fall in love and marry, but as his star declines, her star is on the rise and soon he is a supporting player. Both versions are excellent, but the 1954 version has Judy Garland burning up the screen with her intensity, as she tries to make a Hollywood comeback after almost destroying herself, much like the Norman Main character in the film. Incredibly this would be Garland's first Oscar nomination. Everyone was so convinced she would win, a camera was placed in her hospital room, where she had just given birth to her son. Groucho Marx quipped her loss was, "the biggest robbery since Brinks." Grace Kelly won for *The Country Girl*. Both James Mason and Garland were nominated, as were Janet Gaynor and Frederic March for the same roles in the 1937 version.

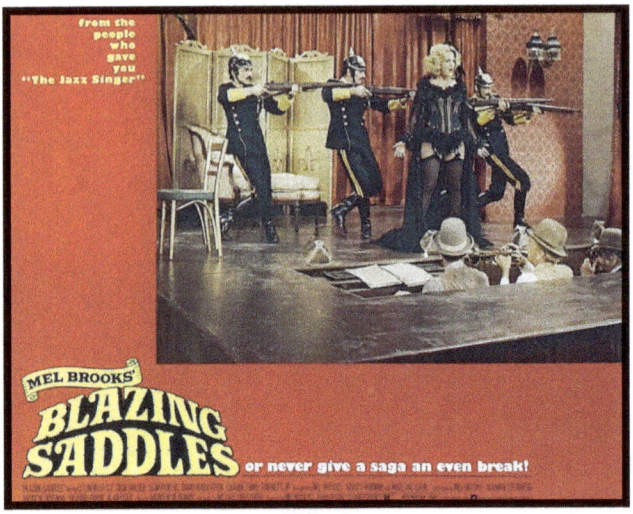

WESTERNS

BLAZING SADDLES (1974) by Mel Brooks might well be the very first film to use farts as a comic set piece. But you know, that's still the scene most fans laugh about and remember first—that and Mongo (Alex Karras) punching the bull. There are so many silly jokes and puns in this story of a black sheriff (Cleavon Little) that takes on corruption and the nasty villain, Hedley Lamarr (Harvey Korman). Audiences can almost see Korman twisting his mustache like a silent movie villain. Madeline Kahn is brilliant as usual as Lili Von Shtupp. Pretty much guaranteed to provide at least one hearty laugh for everyone.

CAT BALLOU (1965), like **Blazing Saddles**, is a spoof of classic Westerns. The film stars the super cool Lee Marvin as twin gunfighters, one evil and one, well, good, but in a drunken way. Jane Fonda manages to be both tough and tender as Katherine "Cat" Ballou, who turns to a life of crime to avenge her father's murder. A sort of hillbilly Greek chorus of Stubby Kaye and Nat King Cole croon clever lyrics throughout, as Cat finds love and justice in the old West. Marvin picked up the Academy Award, the BAFTA and a Golden Globe for his dual role.

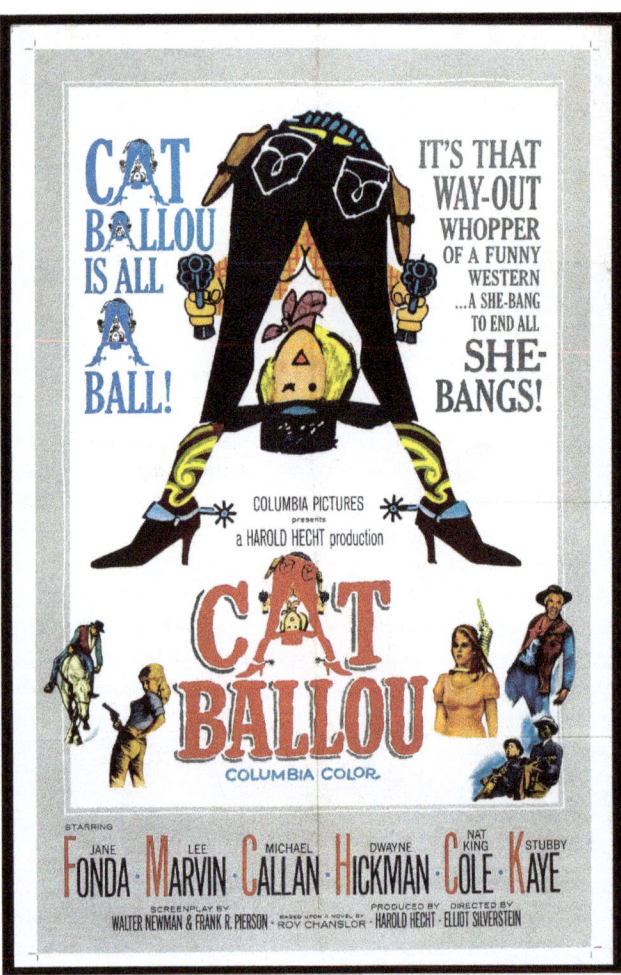

MAVERICK (1994), based upon the popular TV series, had a Hollywood heavyweight cast of Mel Gibson, Jodie Foster and James Garner, plus a cameo list that reads like a who's who of old time Westerns and country music. Garner portrayed Bret Maverick in the TV series, but in this film, Mel Gibson takes on the smooth-talking con man role, playing a character who prefers charm to a sidearm. Garner stars as Marshal Zane Cooper (a tribute to famed Western author Zane Gary and actor Gary Cooper). Jodie Foster is Annabelle Bransford, who manages to outsmart both men. Maverick is lots of fun, has great stunts, is full of intrigue and double crosses and offers a

surprise finale. James Garner's **SUPPORT YOUR LOCAL SHERIFF!** (1969) is also worthy of inclusion in our list of feel good Westerns.

McLINTOCK! (1963)—I have to admit that I'm biased when it comes to this film. My dad, who was my hero, loved John Wayne movies and I can remember being packed into the family station wagon, along with my four younger brothers and sisters, to see this at the drive-in. When we grew up, drive-in movies (the only kind we ever saw) were a special treat to be anxiously awaited and planned with care. The five kids would all be stuffed into our PJs, Kool-aid and popcorn by the gallon would be stowed in the back, along with blankets and pillows and after much ado, we'd be off. As the oldest, I usually managed to make it long enough to see the dancing hotdogs after the first movie and maybe the cartoon. And now back to our movie. What makes **McLintock!** so darn good is the chemistry between the tough-guy with the big heart, John Wayne, and the beautiful but equally feisty Maureen O'Hara, as the battling husband and wife at the center of the film. I had never realized that **McLintock!** is considered a Western version of "The Taming of the Shrew," which puts it right up there with **Kiss Me Kate** as my favorite version of the Shakespeare play. The best scene in the film is the over-the-top fight scene that takes place in a huge mud pit. Eventually the entire cast gets thrown down the slippery slope and dumped into the slimy stuff. Great fun, and if you've never seen it, well, it's out on DVD. Another favorite Wayne film that has lots of action and humor is **HELLFIGHTERS** (1968), starring Wayne and Jim Hutton. Other John Wayne films that are rambunctious fun include **DONOVAN'S REEF,** (1963) with Lee Marvin, and **RIO BRAVO,** with Dean Martin and Ricky Nelson. Two rare Wayne comedies, **WITHOUT RESERVATIONS** (1946) with Claudette Colbert, and **A LADY TAKES A CHANCE** (1943), with Jean Arthur, also should be viewed.

HORROR/SCIENCE FICTION

ABBOTT AND COSTELLO MEET FRANKENSTEIN is considered by most fans to be the best of the horror comedies. Bud Abbott & Lou Costello meet up with Frankenstein's Monster (Glen Strange), Dracula (Bela Lugosi) and the Wolf Man (Lon Chaney, Jr.) when Dracula and a mad doctor (Lenore Aubert) team up to steal Lou's brain and transplant it into the Monster. A&C took quite a few dips into the horror dungeon when they met up with **Dr. Jekyll and Mr. Hyde** (1953), **The Killer, Boris Karloff** (1949), **The Invisible Man** (1951) and finally **Go to Mars** (1953).

THE APE MAN (1943) is one of the classic Bela Lugosi Poverty Row movies that, despite their low-budgets, always manages to entertain. Lugosi's success in these films was his ability to take each part seriously, no matter how campy or silly the role. As cheap sets frame

his every scene and supporting players merely walk through their roles, Lugosi pretends he is playing Shakespeare and elevates the film because of his commitment to his performance. Other Lugosi adventures that will bring a grin to the skull of your classic horror film lover include **CHANDU THE MAGICIAN** (1932), **THE PHANTOM CREEPS** (1939), **THE GORILLA** (1939), **THE DEVIL BAT** (1940), **SPOOKS RUN WILD** (1941), **GHOSTS ON THE LOOSE** (1943) and **BELA LUGOSI MEETS A BROOKLYN GORILLA** (1952), and, of course, the Ed Wood period including **BRIDE OF THE MONSTER** (1955) and **PLAN 9 FROM OUTER SPACE** (1959).

BUBBA HO-TEP (2002) stars Bruce Campbell, who has become the king of horror comedies. Campbell rose to cult fame as one of Sam Raimi's Bat Pack including 1981's **The Evil Dead**, **Evil Dead II** and the *coup de grâce* of the Evil Dead cycle, **Army of Darkness**. Along the road of darkness, Campbell managed to appear in over 70 films and over 31 TV appearances. One of our favorite TV shows that Campbell starred in was **The Adventures of Brisco County, Jr.** (1993-1994), which was a creative mix of humor, Westerns and sci-fi. Currently Campbell lights up the small screen on **Burn Notice** as Sam Axe, a hedonistic former spy with a heart of gold that is in constant war with his sense of self-preservation. But this is about his turn as another King, Elvis in **Bubba Ho-Tep**. Now pay close attention, because this is going to get weird. Elvis, sick of his whole existence, pays an Elvis impersonator to take his place. Elvis changes places and happily spends his days in relative obscurity. Eventually the actual King lands in a nursing home in Texas, where he meets a black man who tells him he is JFK. The two discover a mummy is sucking the souls from the residents and set about destroying the creature. They limp and groan their way through the battle of good vs. evil. It's crazy, silly, warm, charming and heart-breaking, all at the same time.

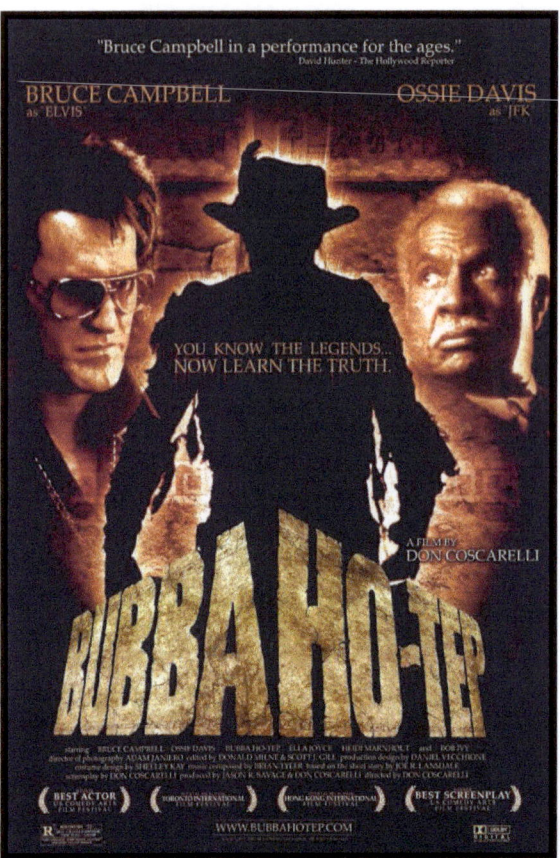

GALAXY QUEST (1999) is probably one of the biggest movie surprises since we found out the identity of Luke's father in **Empire Strikes Back.** The reason I love this movie is the script's approach to sci-fi fans. Rather than treat them as misanthropic geeks, the fanboys and girls actually help save the day. **Galaxy Quest** stars Tim Allen, Alan Rickman, Sigourney Weaver and Tony Shalhob as unemployed cast members of a once popular TV space opera, à la **Star Trek**. The has-been cast has a battle royale with the egotistical "star" of the show, but when he is rude to a fan and then misses a personal appearance, they know something is up. What's up is their spaceship, which has been constructed by a race of brilliant but naïve aliens, who think the cast are real heroes that will save them from evil villains out to destroy them. While poking gentle fun at the mythos of sci-fi movies and shows, the movie manages to also respect the genre and the people who find adventure from the safety of their homes. In addition to Allen, Weaver and Rickman, several familiar TV actors provide excellent support, especially the amazing Tony Shalhob (the neurotic cab driver on *Wings* and the defective detective **Monk**) and Enrico Colantoni (so good in everything he's in including *Veronica Mars*, *Just Shoot Me!* and *Flashpoint*).

GHOST BREAKERS stars Bob Hope as a cowardly radio personality, who is accused of a murder and takes the first boat out of harm's way. Unfortunately, he meets and falls for a lady in distress (Paulette Goddard) and winds up in Cuba at a haunted house filled with ghosts and zombies. Hope is always good for a chuckle and some particular favorites include **The Cat and the Canary** (1939), another eerie old-dark house mystery with Paulette Goddard, John Beal, George Zucco and Gale Sondergaard, any of the Road pictures with Bing Crosby, such as the first in the series **Road the Singapore** (1940). Also greta fun is **My Favorite Brunette** (1947), which has an all-star cast that includes Peter Lorre, Lon Chaney, Reginald Denny and Dorothy Lamour. Hope and Goddard have such a lively chemistry that Universal paired them up again for **Ghost Breakers**. Both Goddard films are silly fun, but I lean a little more toward **Ghost Breakers** because it features Willie Best as Hope's level-headed but equally frightened assistant, and Noble Johnson as a very frightening zombie.

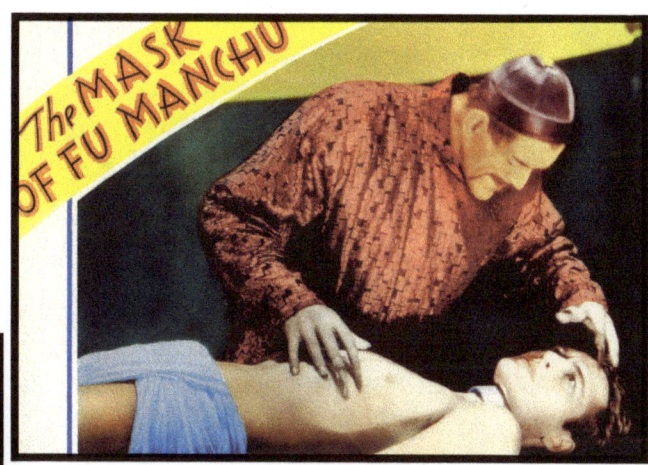

GHOSTBUSTERS (1984), starring **Saturday Night Live** alumni Bill Murray, Dan Aykroyd plus Sigourney Weaver and Harold Ramis, was a runaway hit at the box office. The film had a huge budget for the 1980s, 30 million, but more than made up for the production budget with a worldwide gross of almost 300 million. Aykroyd is the academic genius researching paranormal activity and Murray and Ramis also trudge along as professors at Columbia. The three get tossed and decide to form a company to rid people of their ghosts. Boy are they surprised when first they find some ghosts, and then discover that Aykroyd's silly machine actually works. **Ghostbusters** was the top moneymaking film of 1984. That year Hollywood produced an impressive array of horror, sci-fi and fantasy films including **Gremlins**, **Indiana Jones and the Temple of Doom**, **The Last Starfighter**, **Night of the Comet**, **Romancing the Stone**, **Splash**, **Starman**, **Star Trek III: The Search for Spock**, **Streets of Fire**, **The Terminator**, **2010**, **All of Me** and **Dune**, Any films on that list will entertain viewers and transport you to your happy movie place for a couple of hours. **Night of the Comet, Street of Fire, 2010** and **All of Me** are lesser-known titles, but deserved a wider audience. David Lynch's **Dune** is pretty much despised by everyone, but I think it deserves another look and do my best to defend the movie in the book *Guilty Pleasures of the Horror Film*.

THE MASK OF FU MANCHU (1932) stars Boris Karloff as the mega-evil villain Dr. Fu Manchu and lovely, sweet, witty Myrna Loy has a grand old time playing his equally evil and most decidedly kinky daughter, Fah Lo See. While Fu makes eyes at the hero and his sword, Fah Lo See manages to convince daddy to let her play with him for a while. Our poor hero winds up tied to a table as Fah gloats over him. The movie is so much a product of the time, that it has become a campy classic. But the star power of Karloff and Loy make this early 1930s fantasy adventure a genuine delight.

RAIDERS OF THE LOST ARK (1981) is one of my favorite films of the 1980s. For some reason, it slipped under my radar, and when Gary and I went to see it, I think, it was our second or third date (our first date was to see Ray Harryhausen at the AFI Theater in D.C.), we were just blown away. It was like a rollercoaster ride without the fear and nausea. From the first frame of the film until the last, it was an exciting, funny, charming and scary adventure that we didn't want to end. I think I will always despise *Chariots of Fire*, because it won the Best Picture Oscar rather than **Raiders of the Lost Ark.** Seriously, does anyone still say, wow, *Chariots of Fire* was a great film. No, they say it had that good instrumental song, but cannot remember anything else about it. You know, I'm still annoyed about that. I think that was the beginning of my apathy for the Academy Awards, and sad to say, it's just gotten worse as the years go on.

SHAUN OF THE DEAD (2004) is one of the few modern films you'll find in our list. I'm not sure if it's because I'm a sucker for British TV and humor, or it was the quirkiness of the movie that captured Gary's attention, or just the need to watch something silly with absolutely no redeeming qualities that makes this an excellent choice to escape reality for a while. However, if you absolutely cannot stand any kind of gore, skip this one. Today, it's pretty much impossible to sell a horror movie without sex and gore, but I just closed my eyes during the gross stuff. Our slacker heroes (Simon Pegg and Nick Frost) seek the most secure place they know when they finally realize zombies are a deadly plague overtaking England—their favorite pub. There they plan how to survive with just their wits and a cricket bat. Oh dear. The film is filled with zombie movie in-jokes as well as references to **Spaced**, the Britcom that Pegg and Frost starred in. The funniest thing about the movie is the point

that people today are so self-involved they don't even notice the zombies devouring people in their neighborhood, as they blindly embark on their daily rituals of life. I really think this would happen today, especially if people were texting at the time. What an annoying habit, and how stupid has the population gotten when our state of Maryland had to pass a law against texting while driving! Who is that dumb? Most people can't walk and chew gum, let alone drive and work a keyboard, at the same time. Mankind is doomed, hummm, maybe this isn't much of a cheer up movie, but it's fun and silly and you'll laugh. So just worry about the destiny of humanity some other time. Simon Pegg and crew returned in **HOT FUZZ** (2007), a laugh-filled spoof of cop/buddy pictures. Pegg is on his own in a David Schwimmner (Ross on *Friends*) comedy, **RUN, FATBOY, RUN** (2007).

Belgium poster for *Topper*

SHREK (2001)—I think is probably the funniest animated movie ever made. Yes, Mike Myers, Cameron Diaz and John Lithgow are wonderful, but the reason this movie just makes me happy is quite simply Donkey, voiced to perfection by Eddie Murphy. I love Donkey!!! I love how the animators gave him the sly but equally charming Eddie Murphy grin. I love the clever lines the writers came up with. And finally I just love Eddie Murphy's performance. I truly believe he should have received an Academy Award for his work in **Shrek**. I know Eddie gets trashed by critics—a lot, but even in his worst films, he can still make you smile. If, like me, you are an Eddie fan, also check out **48 HRS.** (1982, his first feature film), **TRADING PLACES** (1993, so much fun when Eddie and Dan Aykroyd one up those evil rich dudes, old pros Ralph Bellemy and Don Ameche—we always watch the film at Christmas), **BEVERLY HILLS COP** (1984), **COMING TO AMERICA** (1988), **DOCTOR DOOLITTLE** (1998, great fun for kids of all ages, and the animals are so adorable), **LIFE** (1991) and **DADDY DAY CARE** (1993, another film the critics hated, but it made me laugh).

TOPPER (1937) isn't the funniest film of the 1930s, but it has Constance Bennett and Cary Grant as Marion and George Kerby, a wealthy, wild, witty and hedonistic couple who are killed in a car crash after an evening of wild partying. Unfortunately, they can't seem to get off the Earth and decide they must do something good to enter the gates of Heaven. So they decide to give their poor old banker a makeover, turning the dull, henpecked Topper (Roland Young) into a suave debonair man about town. Poor old Topper doesn't know what hits him when Marion takes a little too much of an interest in him, causing George to rage with jealousy. You can't go wrong with any film that stars Cary Grant, he's handsome, charming, funny, can do seri-

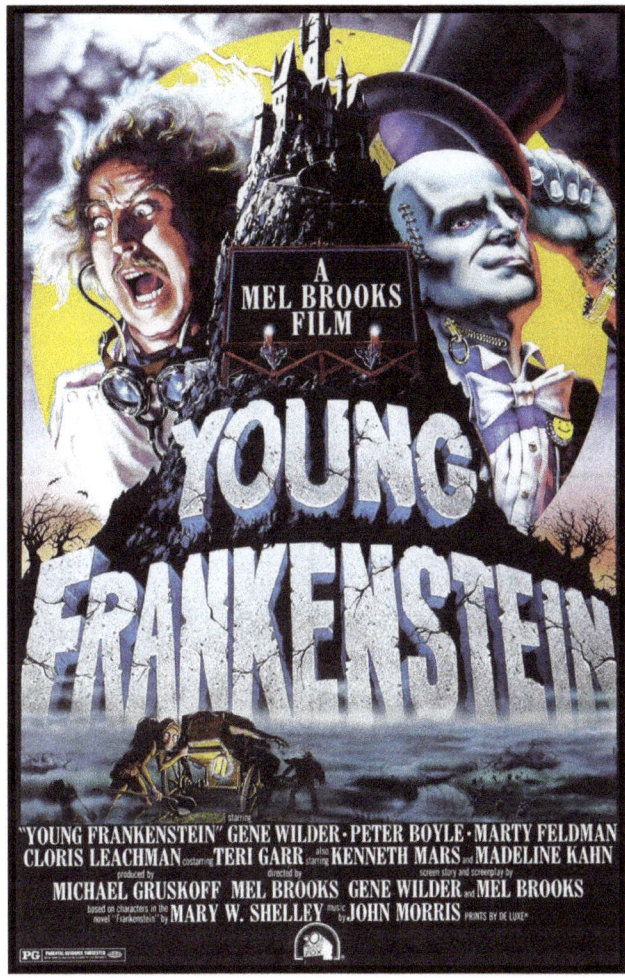

Dracula the spoof treatment with Leslie Nielsen, still reeling in the popularity of his *Naked Gun* movies, as Dracula and a brilliant Peter MacNicol as Renfield in **Dracula: Dead and Loving It**. I must confess, the first time we watched this, we hated it, and most critics couldn't resist using headlines like "Dracula: Dead and Loving it Bites." But each time we see it, we notice clever bits of atmosphere pulled directly from classic vampire movies of the 1930s and 1940s. If you're in the mood for zany movie spoofs, stick with **Young Frankenstein** followed by **AIRPLANE!** (1980), **THE NAKED GUN** (1988), **SCARY MOVIE** (2000), **HOT SHOTS** (1991) and **SPIES LIKE US** (1985), **THE MUMMY** (1999) and **TROPIC THUNDER** (2008).

FANTASY

IT'S A WONDERFUL LIFE (1946) is a bittersweet tonic that arrives once a year, usually during the Christmas season, forcing all of us to re-evaluate the value of our lives. This Capra classic is seldom laugh-out-loud funny, but its for-the-times clever premise forces everyone who watches to imagine what the world would have been like without our presence, as if we were never born. Jimmy Stewart's landmark performance swims from youthful hope and exuberance to adult disappointment and depression, finally skirting with ideas of despondency and suicide. So what's there to feel good about? Ah! The final act reunites family, community and friends who all band together, chip in with the cash and resolve all problems in a satisfying yet rather pat manner. As we are reminded, "a man is never poor who has friends," then everyone raises glasses of cheer and voices to *Hark! The Herald Angels Sings*. As **It's a Wonderful Life** proves, sometimes we have to hit rock bottom to appreciate the joy and magic in all our lives.

ous, romantic and pretty much anything thrown at him. I have several of his comedies on my list but you might also want to catch **HOLIDAY** (1938), **HIS GIRL FRIDAY** (1940), **MY FAVORITE WIFE** (1940), **ARSENIC AND OLD LACE** (1944), **THE BACHELOR AND THE BOBBY-SOXER** (1947), **THE BISHOP'S WIFE** (1947), **MR. BLANDINGS BUILDS HIS DREAM HOUSE** (1948), **I WAS MALE WAR BRIDE** (1949), **TO CATCH A THIEF** (1955) and **THAT TOUCH OF MINK** (1962).

YOUNG FRANKENSTEIN—To us, anyway, is so much funnier than *Blazing Saddles*. Of course, as major classic horror film fans, that's probably to be expected. There are so many funny bits in the film that even now, over 30 years later, they still make me laugh just sitting here thinking about the movie. I still can't hear "Puttin' on the Ritz" without seeing Peter Boyle and Gene Wilder dancing and croaking their demented version. Mel Brooks and Gene Wilder penned the story and screenplay together and lovingly pay tribute to the Universal Frankenstein series, especially 1939's *Son of Frankenstein*. Director Brooks even uses the original Kenneth Strickfaden laboratory equipment that was used in the original *Frankenstein* (1931) and *Bride of Frankenstein* (1935). Any fan of classic horror films can't help loving **Young Frankenstein**, especially since Wilder and Brooks are brother fanboys at heart. In 1995 Brooks gave

THE SEVENTH VOYAGE OF SINBAD (1958) is pure visual imagination, fueled by equal parts heart, spirit and adrenalin, becoming the baby boomer generation's most vivid cinematic fantasy adventure, brought to life by master animator Ray Harryhausen. As kids we were exposed to the fairy tales of Hans Christian Andersen and the Brothers Grimm, but director Nathan Juran's fairytale masterwork combines all those exciting elements from the printed page and brings them to life—heroes bravely facing monsters; damsels in distress; magical evil curses that needed to be undone; frightening castles and lairs of evil; and genies who offer help and salvation. Every child, and every adult harboring the kid within, can feel renewed energy returning time and time again to "the land beyond all hope and fear" in this classic bat-

tle between good and evil, where evil is always defeated. Torin Thatcher becomes the perfect dragon-and-skeleton producing villain to Kerwin Matthew's courageous sword-wielding hero. Along with the original **King Kong**, **The Seventh Voyage of Sinbad** becomes the classic example of stop-motion special effects in the movies.

MUSICAL

Pretty much any musical will put me in a good mood, but here are a few of my faves. I didn't have room for so many favorites like MAME (1974) and CENTER STAGE (2000), KISS ME KATE (1953), etc, etc. etc.

THE BAND WAGON (1953) is my second favorite musical and contains one of the most beautiful dance scenes ever filmed, "Dancing in the Dark," Fred Astaire and Cyd Charisse providing the magic. The setting is classic, Central Park in the moonlight, the costumes simple and the dancing breathtaking. Astaire stars as a washed up Hollywood song and dance man, who tries to make a comeback on Broadway. He's nervous about dancing with a professional ballerina (Charisse), and things go from bad to worse when the simple musical, written by his friends Lester and Lily (based on screenwriters Aldoph Green and Betty Comden), is turned into an arty version of *Faust* by the pretentious director. Of course things go horribly wrong and the cast must band together and turn the disaster into a hit. The musical numbers are all winners, but the first number "Shine on Your Shoes" is a Technicolor orgy of motion. One song, written especially for **The Band Wagon**, would become a Hollywood anthem, "That's Entertainment," and that certainly describes **The Band Wagon**.

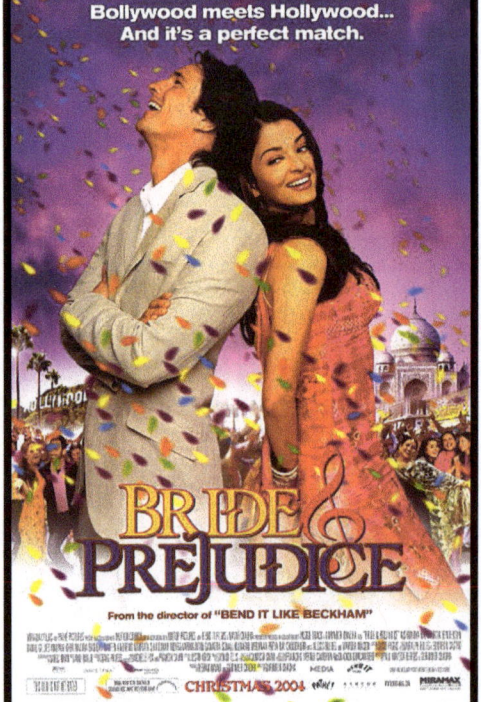

BRIDE AND PREJUDICE (2004) will force you to become a fan of Bollywood movies. The joyful songs, dances and brilliant colors remind me of the classic days of MGM movie musicals, something Hollywood wouldn't touch today with a 10-foot pole. Director Gurinder Chandha gained worldwide acclaim for **Bend it Like Beckham** (2002), and followed that film with **Bride and Prejudice**, which she and co-writer Paul Mayeda Berges adapted from Jane Austen's **Pride and Prejudice**. Aishwarya Rai, who played Latlia (the Elizabeth Bennet-inspired role), was crowned Miss World in 1994, and from there went on to a huge career in the Indian film industry. **Bride and Prejudice** was her first English language film. The Bingly-inspired role was played by Naveen Andrews, who is known to millions of fans as Sayid on cult-TV hit *Lost*. If you have never seen a Bollywood film, make this your first one. Another Bollywood-style film you'll enjoy is **The Guru** (2002) with Heather Graham. While not a true Bollywood film, the dance numbers are still fun and there is enough silliness to entertain.

BYE BYE BIRDIE (1963) stars Janet Leigh, Dick Van Dyke, Paul Lynde, Bobby Rydell and Maureen Stapleton, who are all left in the dust by Ann-Margaret, in her third film. Loosely based on Elvis Presley's leaving for the Army, Ann-Margaret plays the girl nextdoor that is chosen to kiss the idol goodbye on national TV. While the movie doesn't reach the heights of great musicals, there are enough sparkling numbers to keep us happy, especially the opening number, "The Telephone Hour," "One Last Kiss," A Lot of Livin' To Do" and "Put on a Happy Face." A remake is supposedly in the works, now in the hands of Adam Shankman, the choreographer-director of many of today's dance and musical films, including **Hairspray** and **Step-Up**.

A FUNNY THING HAPPENED ON THE WAY TO THE FORUM (1966)—Just reading the cast list will make you happy—Zero Mostel, Phil Silvers, Buster Keaton and a very young, pre-*Phantom* Michael Crawford. In ancient Rome, a slave (Mostel) hatches a complicated plan to gain his freedom that involves acquiring a virgin, who is being sold by the local house of ill-repute, for his smitten young master (Crawford). Meanwhile, a fierce soldier is arriving for the virgin and will destroy anyone who gets in his way. The twisted plot mounts as Mostel sends Crawford on a quest for horse sweat, while playing puppetmaster. Even Gary, who is a tough audience, has to laugh at the bawdy musical numbers, especially "Everybody Ought to Have a Maid." The Stephen Sondheim musical also features the well-known "Comedy Tonight."

GENTLEMAN PREFER BLONDES (1953) is one of my favorite Marilyn Monroe performances. Monroe and Jane Russell steam up the screen as two showgirls from Little Rock, on a transatlantic cruise to Paris. Lorelei Lee (Monroe) plays the dumb blonde bit for all it's worth, but manages to outwit all the men who cross her path, and Monroe nails that character. I think Monroe always had a sad look in her eyes—I suppose it's as difficult being treated as an empty-headed sex-fantasy as it is being treated as stupid, because you're overweight or do not fit society's idea of beauty. But we're talking about movies that lift us out of our doldrums, so on with the show...

Lorelei is in love with rich milquetoast Gus (Tommy Noonan), but his father does not approve and hires a PI to tail the girls. Lorelei can't help herself when old Beekey shows her his wife's diamond tiara and she sets out to charm the diamonds out of him, and Dorothy (Russell) amuses herself with buff Olympic athletes traveling on the ship. Russell is a teenage wet dream when she does a swinging "Ain't There Anyone Here for Love" (written by Hoagy Charmichael and Harold Adamson), with a chorus line of the more than willing Olympians (the Olympians/dancers included Jane Russell's brother Alvy Moore, from *Green Acres,* and Robert Fuller, star of *Emergency*). When a private detective reports Lorelei has been canoodling with a rich old fart, Sir Francis Beekman (Charles Coburn), Gus cancels all Lorelei's credit and the girls are forced to figure out how to survive, which leads to another great number "When Love Goes Wrong," sung by Russell and Monroe. But of course the most famous number is "Diamonds Are a Girl's Best Friend," from the Broadway show, written by Jule Styne and Leo Robin. Monroe, in a tight pink satin gown, sparkles more than the diamonds she struts. The number has been imitated by Madonna, T Bone Burnette and used in *Moulin Rouge*. Another Monroe recommendation is **HOW TO MARRY A MILLIONAIRE** (1953), this time with three stunning blondes—Monroe, Betty Grable and Lauren Bacall—as models who rent a luxury apartment they can't afford to attract millionaire husbands. The film features

a great cast that includes William Powell, beautiful clothes and a happy ending, as all three get their men and discover that money isn't everything.

THE ROCKY HORROR PICTURE SHOW (1975) certainly isn't your typical musical! But it is laugh out loud funny and the bawdy songs will have you jumping up to do the "Timewarp" with the cast. Tim Curry is brilliant as the hedonistic Dr. Frankenfurter, who in just seven days can make himself a

man—Rocky, which shocks the innocent travelers who have stumbled into Frankenfurter's madcap mansion. While the randy, horror-film-inspired **Rocky Horror** may shock some musical fans, for the rest of the audience it's a tune-filled sexy romp with a bustier-clad mad scientist, who, unlike most of the worlds' female population, can actually pull that look off and look hot while doing it! The film was adapted from the London stage production, and inspired a sequel, **Shock Treatment** (2000), starring Jessica Harper. Harper also starred in another cult musical, Brian De Palma's **Phantom of the Paradise** (1974), starring Paul Williams, who also penned the songs, and which featured a delightfully over-the-top performance by Gerrit Graham, who played Beef.

SILK STOCKINGS (1957) is a musical remake of Ernest Lubtich's **Ninotchka**, the 1939 original starring Melvyn Douglas and Greta Garbo. Fred Astaire is an American movie producer in Paris, who is trying to get a Russian composer to provide the music for a new picture. Three commissars are sent to check up on the composer, but fall victim to the gaiety and decadence of Paris. Jules Munchin, and horror film star Peter Lorre play the commissars. The sight of the height-impaired, rotund Lorre faking his dancing around the pros is one of the funniest things about the movie.

SINGIN' IN THE RAIN (1952) is one of the most perfect films ever made. This loving homage to Hollywood was written by the amazing husband and wife writing team of Betty Comden and Adolph Green, who turned the problems studios faced going from silent films to sound into a comic musical masterpiece. If you can watch the title number as Gene Kelly, happily in love, sings and dances down the street in the rain without smiling, well just put the book down, you're hopeless. One sparkling scene leads to another and this is one of the few musicals where every number is a winner. Donald O'Connor is just brilliant in "Make 'Em Laugh," and Kelly and O'Connor tear up the dance floor with "Fit as a Fiddle" and especially the hilarious "Moses Supposes." Debbie Reynolds joins the duo for the cheerful "Good Morning," and is a charmer in pink in the chorus of "All I Do is Dream of You." Jean Hagen is deliciously nasty as Lina Lamont, the diva with a voice that could stop a train and Cyd Charisse wows as the specialty dancer in the "Broadway Rhythm" finale. I'm sure many people think musicals are silly and dull, but give it a chance. I promise it will make you happy.

STAND UP AND CHEER (1934) is a Shirley Temple movie that I think is as vital today as it was in the 1930s. Warner Baxter is appointed Secretary of Amusement to help America keep its sense of humor during the dark days of the Depression. But evil big business wants him to fail, the Depression is making them tons of money and they'd be happy if it never ended.

Shirley Temple as Charmaine in 1932's *Baby Burlesk War Babies*, obviously made before the Hays Code!

What did I tell you, history always repeats itself. James Dunn and Shirley Temple appear as a father and daughter duo that performs "Baby Take A Bow." That one number saved the film and made Shirley Temple a mega-star, who pretty much saved Fox Studios. Prior to this film, Temple had made a series of Baby Burlesk one-reel shorts. I find the Baby Burlesk shorts really odd when seen with today's sensibilities. They take adorable tiny tots aged 3, 4, and 5 and used them as the actors in adult stories. *War Babies* (1932) is a spoof of *What Price Glory?* The film takes place in a French bar and the three-year-old Temple plays a "dancer" who is paid in lollypops. You can see the Baby Burlesk's on You Tube.

THAT THING YOU DO! (1996), written and directed by Tom Hanks is the tuneful story of the Wonders, a small PA band that, in the early 1960s, joins Play-Tone records' bus tour of State Fairs. Their song, "That Thing You Do," begins to climb the charts and soon the boys are famous. But alas, things begin to fall apart when they hit the big time in Hollywood. They really do become the one-hit Wonders. The song is catchy and you'll find yourself humming it throughout the day. *Bosom Buddies* Tom Hanks and Peter Scolari both appear in the film. The two leads remind me of younger versions of the duo. Tom Everett Scott, a virtual clone of a young Tom Hanks, is Guy Patterson, the cheerful, jazz loving drummer who gives the song a faster beat that catches on with the kids. Steve Zahn as the skirt-chasing Lenny, reminds me of Peter Scolari. The love interest, Liv Tyler, is excellent as always, and Johnathon Schaech is suitably annoying as the pretentious Jimmy.

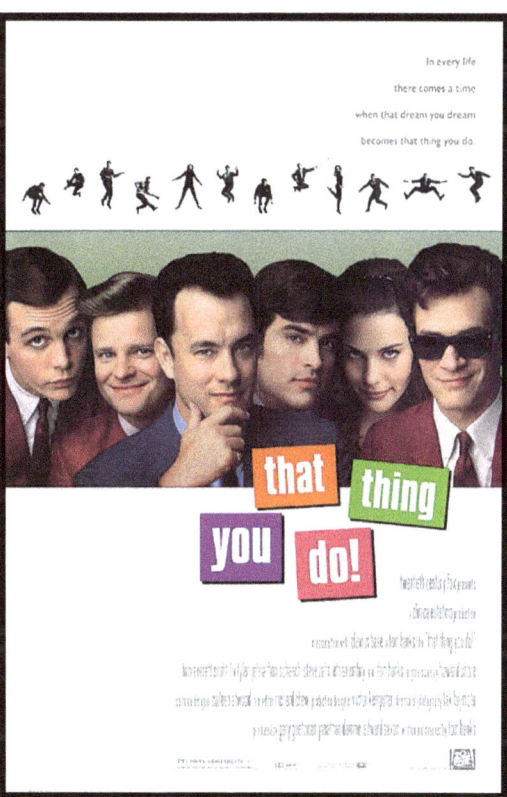

VIVA LAS VEGAS (1964), well let's just cut to the chase, the chemistry between Elvis and Ann-Margaret is Hot, Hot, Hot! With a tagline like "It's that "go-go" guy and that "bye-bye" gal in the fun capital of the world!" how can you not have a good time? Elvis is a racecar driver who needs money for a new engine, so he gets a job at a Vegas hotel. The hotel is having an employee talent contest and Lucky (Elvis) is a sure winner—until Rusty Martin (Ann-Margaret) slinks onto stage in a white fur coat and starts to sing. The story is more movie-of-the-week quality, but really, who's watching this for the plot. Elvis, Ann-Margaret, the sparkling title musical number and the funky clothes are the real reason to watch. Director George Sidney has a huge list of musicals on his resume and had just finished *Bye Bye Birdie* with Ann-Margaret the year

Yung and, best of all, Keye Luke) than he would ever be by the villains. Capturing the bad guys is easy compared to controlling the audacity and sometimes stupidity of his children. But once in a while, even with such hare-brained ideas, Chan's son manages to save the day. But mostly, each offspring makes things worse. When Monogram took over the series, perhaps its most creative contribution was the addition of classic funnyman Mantan Moreland to the mix, playing comical sidekick Birmingham Brown. The comic repartee between wizened father Chan and foolishly naive sons was further enhanced by the shenanigans of the detective's comic foil, Mantan Moreland. Of course Chan's son of the moment would team with the masterful Moreland for even funnier comedy results, but the mystery plots remained as intriguing as ever. Finally, one of the joys of the Chan series is seeing major stars pop up from time to time, giving inspired performances. Boris Karloff, Bela Lugosi, Lionel Atwill, George Zucco, Ray Milland, Robert Young, J. Carrol Naish, Cesar Romero, Victor Jory, etc. all appeared in the series. Even though the Charlie Chan series was a classic B programmer, it struck the right chord between comedy and mystery, keeping audiences guessing whodunit until the very end.

earlier. The two films make a great double feature since both feature Ann-Margaret getting to meet the worlds most famous rock star. Make some popcorn, prop your feet up and start the evening with a cartoon of *The Flintstones* "Ann-Margrock Presents." Most Elvis films are cheerful fun, especially **BLUE HAWAII** (1961), **FOLLOW THAT DREAM** (1962) and **IT HAPPENED AT THE WORLD'S FAIR** (1963).

MYSTERY

CHARLIE CHAN movie series (released via 20th Century Fox and Monogram)—Be it Warner Oland or Sidney Toler as Charlie Chan (we can forget Roland Winters for the moment), whether we are looking at the more lavish Fox productions or the low-rent Monogram productions, the bottom line is that all the Charlie Chan movies make for superb entertainment. First of all, the character of Chan, always smiling too broadly and humbling himself before authority figures, is wilier than he appears. With the evidence and clues out of reach for local police authorities, it is the self-depreciating Chan that eventually solves the case. Charlie Chan is more frustrated and baffled by the actions of his numerous sons (all played to comic perfection by actors such as Benson Fong, Victor Sen

FARGO (1997) is a quirky comedy, but it is also horrifically brutal and forces audiences to never look at wood chippers in quite the same way again. The writing-directing team of Joel and Ethan Coen are at the pinnacle of their game with **Fargo**, a movie that serves as comfort food in a world of mayhem, deception and good plans gone badly. First and foremost we have a pivotal performance from William H. Macy, who plays Lundegaard, the sales manager of his father-in-law's car dealership. Unfortunately, Lundegaard is skimming money from the company and is in debt and about to be caught by father-in-law, Gustafson (Harve Presnell). Lundegaard presents Gustafson with his scheme to make a fortune from a parking lot deal, but he needs Gustafson's front money to make it happen, something he soon convinces himself will never occur. Fearing the worst, Lundegaard hires two semi-professional hit men (the jabbering and inspired Steve Buscemi and his silent Swede partner, played by Peter Stormare, who is all business and little personality) to kidnap his wife for ransom, offering the criminals $40,000. Of course things go wrong, to full comedic potential, and the avenging angel becomes pregnant police chief Gunderson (Frances McDormand), whose exaggerated Minnesota accent (equally mimicked by the full cast of characters) becomes a delightful running gag. Gunderson, not accustomed to such violent crimes, becomes headstrong in her dedication to bring justice to her winterized community. Never a warm and cozy movie experience, **Fargo** instead presents characters that populate this odd universe and who happen to be cozy and comforting. Even the perky hookers who service the criminals are innocently cute. Steve Buscemi is never less than interesting, and his incessant talking, trying to hold a conversation with an almost mute partner, becomes hilarious. Add these well-honed characterizations to a riveting plot with clever dialogue, and **Fargo** becomes a movie that invites repeat viewings. Just watching the small-town pregnant Gunderson work her charms and ultimately capture the bad guys (that is, the ones who survive) is a delight, as is the ending, a satisfying scene with husband and wife intimately discussing the birth of their child, his hand rubbing her big belly, as they speak of non-job related topics too long delayed by the demands of the job.
Note from Sue: As a fan mystery novels, I think the Coen brothers were slyly commenting on cozy mysteries read by mostly women and their fascination with grisly murder plots, as long as they were contained in a book whose crime is solved by an amateur detective, a handsome cop or even a dog or cat.

MURDER BY DEATH (1976) and **THE CHEAP DETECTIVE** (1978) were directed by Robert Moore and written by Neil Simon, and both featured Peter Falk and a cast of Hollywood royalty. **Murder by Death** is a must see for mystery fans, as five famous detectives are brought to a mysterious old dark house to solve a mystery. The detectives are comical caricatures of famous literary detectives and their assistants. The film stars Falk, Eileen Brennan, Truman Capote, James Coco, Alec Guinness, Elsa Lanchester, David Niven, Peter Sellers and Maggie Smith. **The Cheap Detective** is a comic homage to *The Maltese Falcon* and *Casablanca*, with Falk as

the Bogart character. His female admirers include Ann-Margret, Eileen Brennan, Stockard Channing, Louise Fletcher and Madeline Kahn. Sid Caesar, James Coco, Dom DeLuise and John Houseman are also along for the fun.

NORTH BY NORTHWEST (1959), considered by many as director Alfred Hitchcock's masterpiece, becomes the ultimate popcorn thriller for the ages. Take an average businessman, in this case the always likable Cary Grant, and place his life

in jeopardy for reasons of which, at first, he remains totally unaware. Everyone appears to be after him, and people simply want him dead. Grant's cross-country trek leads him to the iconic chiseled stone faces on Mount Rushmore, from where he dangles, holding on for dear life. Even Midwestern cornfields, where a seemingly innocent crop-dusting plane flies overhead, become locations of death. Assassins can be the pleasantly smiling man standing right next to you. The feel good aspects of the movie come from the adrenalin produced by the film's expert scripting (by Ernest Lehman) and direction. The classic Bernard Herrmann musical score only adds to the film's iconic status. Grant plays the Everyman who fights to learn the truth, that is, if he can remain alive long enough to get to the bottom of the conspiracy. Also, his protecting and rescuing of Eva Marie Saint, a classical blonde beauty, only adds to the fun. When Grant flees for his life, so do we all. When Grant wins at the end, every man wins. How can we not feel good after the intense suspense dissipates and the common man triumphs!

THE THIN MAN (1934) demonstrates the warmer and fuzzier side of pulp-noir writer Dashiell Hammett, author of *The Maltese Falcon* and creator of fiction's archetype noir detective, Samuel Spade. To be honest, the screenplay by Albert Hackett and Frances Goodrich takes the hardboiled pulp aspects out of the equation and plays up the onscreen chemistry between Nick Charles (William Powell) and his wife Nora (Myrna Loy), whose comedic yet sizzling relationship dominates the clever whodunit plots. Coming in the wake of the American Depression, still crippling the economy in 1934, audiences wanted to see glam and ritz and former detective Nick Charles marries money in the lovely form of Nora, and the duo live to drink and party. Nick still has enough of the detective bloodhound in him to become irritated when the police seem to blow off leads and search in the wrong direction. Slowly but surely he involves himself in the case, always wondering how his professional commitment will interfere with his cocktails and romantic interludes with Nora. William Powell produces his iconic portrayal as the always slightly buzzed yet fully in control detective/husband who can outsmart the criminal element, even

if running on semi-sobriety. But this elegant couple, demonstrating that wealth, work and love can mix, allow plenty of time for fun and hedonistic pleasures, while still maintaining adult responsibility and getting the job done correctly. **The Thin Man** paints a comforting portrait of the romanticized American character for a post-Depression world.

MILITARY

DR. STRANGELOVE OR: HOW I LEARNED TO STOP WORRYING AND LOVE THE BOMB (1964) becomes perhaps the only sardonic comedy focusing upon the nuclear destruction of the planet—the film ends on the explosive imagery of a mushroom cloud as the quaint English folk ditty, "We'll Meet Again," plays over the soundtrack. After the Cold War heated up to the boiling point with the Cuban Missile Crisis in 1962, how could the intensity of world politics and "the bomb" not be the object of satire and humor, as the world was looking for any excuse to laugh at such absurdity? Peter Sellers portrays multiple parts including the bland president of the U.S.A. (in direct contrast to the charismatic John Kennedy, who occupied the White House at the time), but his spastic, wheelchair-bound Dr. Strangelove (supposedly influenced by Henry Kissinger), ranting and attempting to keep his out-of-control body under control, becomes his finest moment. Paranoid General Jack D.

Ripper's (Sterling Hayden) sexual inadequacies (constantly speaking of his contaminated "precious bodily fluids") and quietly intense paranoid lunacies (based upon his theory of the Commie infiltration of the American water supply) become the impetus for world annihilation. General "Buck" Turgidson's (George C. Scott), hawkish yearning for all-out nuclear war, believes that such a war can be won, so he is equally crazy as Ripper. But everyone relates to simple, good-hearted Major "King" Kong (Slim Pickens), who rides the atomic bomb out of his jet, bucking bronco style, doing all he can for his country, even sacrificing his own life, but having one hell of a time doing it. Anything that could make America laugh at imminent world destruction in 1964 must certainly be the ultimate feel good film.

OPERATION PETTICOAT (1959) stars Cary Grant and Tony Curtis in this WWII comedy. Grant is the commander of a run-down submarine held together by luck and rubber bands. Curtis is his shifty executive officer whose larceny helps keep the sub afloat. Through a series of events the sub winds up painted pink, carrying a group of sexy nurses and manages to hold its own in the war effort.

MISTER ROBERTS (1955) is the type of military-at-sea comedy that initiated an entire sub-genre that continued through the mid-1960s (i.e. **The Wackiest Ship in the Army, Operation Petticoat, Ensign Pulver, Don't Give Up the Ship**, etc.). However, no matter how humorous, **Mister Roberts** is also very much a drama, especially its gut-punch finale. Directors John Ford (who left the production when he became ill) and Mervyn LeRoy create a concoction of comedy and superb character interaction (between Henry Fonda, William Powell and Jack Lemmon) that still delights to this day. Lt. Doug Roberts (Fonda) is the type of military leader that underlings would gladly die for. He is a leader in the most laid-back and humanitarian way. He leads by example. His cohort and wise elder (and major hedonist) is Doc, played by an aging (but gracefully so) William Powell. Ensign Pulver, a youthful Jack Lemmon, provides the scheming high-jinks and confrontation with authority that create the loudest chuckles. But the villain is the stick-in-the-mud ship's captain, Morton, played by James Cagney as a play-it-by-the-book naval officer, whose love and protection of his palm tree (kept alive aboard a naval cargo ship) provides a lion's share of the laughs. The problem is, no matter how crucial Roberts is to this ship and crew, he longs for combat duty before WWII is over, and by the film's end, he gets his wish. Up until this tearful finale, **Mister Roberts** is a comedy classic with a few serious overtones. The film touches the heart as well as tickles the funny-bone.

STRIPES (1981) stars Bill Murray and Harold Ramis as two sad sacks, who decide to change their pathetic lives by joining the Army. After butting heads with the DI, Murray is forced to whip his misfit platoon into shape. They manage to pull it off and wind up trying to rescue their friends from behind the iron curtain. The cast includes P.J. Soles and Sean Young as MPs the boys fall in love with, and John Candy and Judge Reinhold as members of the platoon. Mindless laughs and fun, much like Goldie Hawn's **PRIVATE BENJAMIN** (1980).

ROMANCES

MOONSTRUCK (1987) is the type of movie I can watch over and over and over. Cher is a delight as Loretta Castorini, a widow who agrees to marry a harmless Italian man, Johnny Cammareri (Danny Aiello), whom she likes but does not love. Johnny rushes off to Italy to be with his dying mother, but asks Loretta to find his brother Ronny (Nicholas Cage) and invite him to the wedding. There is bad blood between the brothers and Johnny wants to make it right. Loretta immediately falls for the bad-boy baker Ronny, who seduces her with arguments, surliness and grand opera. His monologue on love, that it does not make things better, it only manages to tear things apart, is perhaps Cage's best on screen moment. The scene where Loretta gets ready and attends the Metropolitan Opera is just fabulous—heartbreaking, beautiful, touching, all those adjectives, but you get the idea, I like it—a lot. **Moonstruck** looks at the love of couples of all ages, and even the love of her weird old grandfather and his many mangy mutts. Another powerful moment occurs when the family is eating at the kitchen table. Olympia Dukakis

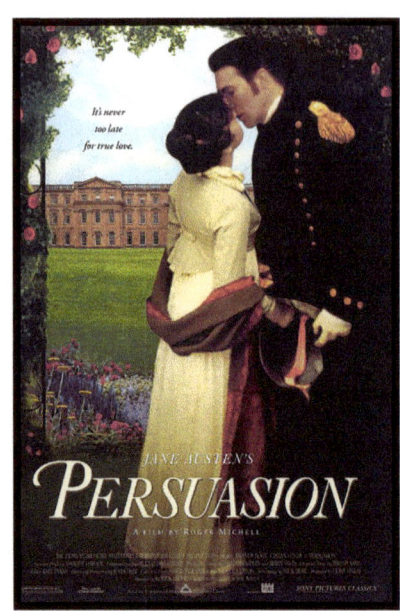

confronts her husband, who is having an affair, and she demands he ends the relationship (after he cites a fear of death as being the reason he strayed). Sitting stoically at the table, he slams his hand down and agrees, his love for his wife, even in their past-prime years, is still very important. This movie just makes me happy. The film was nominated for numerous Oscars, and Cher and Olympia Dukakis both took the statue home, as well as screenwriter John Patrick Shanley.

JANE AUSTEN MOVIES—I'll pretty much watch any Jane Austen adaptation. I won't love them all, and some I quite dislike, but the ones that are good make me feel so warm and cozy and content, that I usually fall asleep watching them. But if you have never seen a Jane Austen film (and shame on you), your best options are **PRIDE AND PREJUDICE** (1995, BBC), yes, the Colin Firth one, where he exits a pond in his clingy white shirt and is obsessed over by Bridget Jones. I don't know why this mini-series fascinates me, perhaps because people had to be so careful never to give offense, or the idea of true love and destiny and good beating out evil. Jennifer Ehle is the ideal Elizabeth Bennet, smart, brave and beautiful. Julia Sawalha portrays the extremely silly Lydia. Sawalha is worlds away in this production from her main claim to fame, as the put upon daughter Saffy in the laugh-out-loud Britcom **Absolutely Fabulous**. Another Austen favorite of mine is **PERSUASION** (1995), which stars Amanda Root as the downtrodden Anne Elliot, daughter of a vain and stupid man. Anne is persuaded to give up the man she loves because he is not in the same social class as her family. Austen skewers the follies of the upper-crust as she manages to get the two lovers back together after many years apart. **SENSE AND SENSIBILITY** (1995) was directed by Ang Lee and was nominated for several Academy Awards, winning one for star Emma Thompson, but not for acting, but for adapting the screenplay. The film also won a slew of BAFTA Awards. Thompson and Kate Winslet play sisters who are forced to move from their beloved home due to reduced circumstances, after the death of their father, whose estate must go to their half-brother. Hugh Grant, Alan Rickman and Greg Wise are the men in their lives. **EMMA** (1996) stars Gwyneth Platrow as the self-centered but good-hearted Emma, who was Austen's favorite character. **CLUELESS** (1995), starring a sparkling Alicia Silverstone, is Amy Heckerling's modern version of **Emma**. The film brought Austen to a younger audience and picked up numerous MTV Movie Awards and a Kid's Choice Award for Silverstone. You won't go wrong with any of these, and you might even get the man in your life to watch them (but don't start with the mini-series, that will scare them away).

THE QUIET MAN is a sigh-inducing romance with a capital R. Macho he-man John Wayne and beautiful spitfire Mau-

reen O'Hara battle with words and fists as Irish lovers, Sean Thornton and Mary Kate Danaher, who can't come to terms because she wants him to stand up to her bully brother and bring to their home the cash and belongings her mother left her. But she doesn't know that Sean accidentally killed a man in the boxing ring and lives in terror of hurting someone else. John Ford pulls no punches in this rowdy Irish comedy, where everyone good-naturedly battles everyone else, the Catholics vs. Protestants, the men vs. the women, the Irish vs. the Brits, the priest vs. the minister, brothers vs. sisters…but Ford believed that you thrash out your troubles with words or fists and forgive all when the dust has settled. My mother always called John Wayne (and Elvis) an ooooww man. When I was much, much younger, I asked her what that was and she said that when she saw them she went ooooww. I didn't know what she meant at the time, but even back then I knew Wayne reminded me of my dad and I would always admire him.

SPORTS

CADDYSHACK (1980) isn't what you'd call a good movie, but it's got great comic parts and those parts are worth the wait. Rodney Dangerfield is weirdly engaging, but my favorite part is the gophers and their battle of wits with Bill Murray. Of course the cute cuddly gophers win.

FIELD OF DREAMS (1989) becomes the male version of the female chick flick, allowing even the most hardcore guy to connect with his emotions and face his failings and his regrets in the most redemptive sense. Laid back farmer Ray Kinsella (Kevin Cosner) hears a booming disembodied voice declare, "If you build it, he will come." Of course that means he has to mow down his own cornfield, risk financial ruin, and build a baseball diamond. Before long the eight ghostly figures of the disgraced Chicago White Sox World Series team of 1919 appear and start to play some ball. Soon Kinsella is off on a quest searching for both reclusive writer Terry Mann (James Earl Jones), a man who longed to play baseball even more than write, and former ace baseball player Moonlight Graham (Burt Lancaster, in one of his finest late career performances), now an aging doctor who gave up his desire to play baseball in order to become a small town physician. In one sentimental sequence, Moonlight regains his youth and gets to live out his fantasy of playing baseball, but when Kinsella's daughter is choking to death, Moonlight has to make a decision, retain his youth and play ball, or exit the field of dreams and save the girl's life, becoming old once again (without any chance of returning to that field of dreams). Of course, just as he made that decision earlier in life, Moonlight forfeits his youth and dreams to save a life. The film's ultimate tearjerker ending occurs when Kinsella, alone on the baseball diamond, has a chance to reconnect with his young father, who is full of life and energy and the desire to just play a little catch. In the current period of time, Kinsella's father is dead, and all Ray knew of his dad was that the man was beaten down by life, drained of any joy and excitement. But here, Kinsella gets to bond with his father long before that tragic fall from grace, and both men, alone, play a little catch and get to know one another as each would want to be remembered by the other. Kinsella did build it, and he did come. And a warm Midwestern wave of what might have been permeates both the baseball field and our straining hearts. And as a double feature

Belgium poster for *The Quiet Man*

69

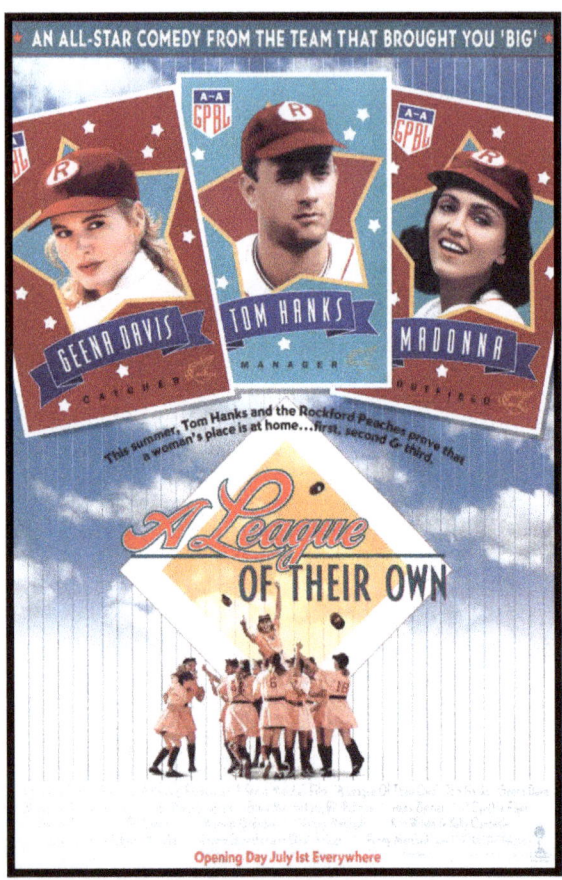

how about **A LEAGUE OF THEIR OWN** (1992), a Penny Marshall-directed valentine to the oft-ignored players in the first woman's professional baseball league, created when most able-bodied men were off fighting WWII.

MAJOR LEAGUE (1989)—*The Washington Post* trashed **Major League** saying it was trying to be **Bull Durham** and failing. My point is, I never found **Bull Durham** (1988) that funny, and it's one of my least favorite baseball movies, and I love baseball movies. Mind you, I don't like to watch the games on TV; I just like the movies. **Major League** is the underdog tale of the losing Cleveland Indians and how their coach, Tom Berenger, turns a bunch of weird misfits into a winning team. The weirdoes include Charlie Sheen, Corbin Bernsen, Dennis Haysbert and Wesley Snipes. Bob Uecker is sidesplitting as the Indians' weary announcer.

ROCKY (1976) might well be the most classic underdog film ever made. The story of the film's pre-production parallels the actual story told in the screenplay. Struggling actor Sylvester Stallone felt if he wrote himself the ultimate part, he would be cast in the movie and rise quickly to the top. The producers, of course, wanted to purchase the screenplay, but they wanted top-drawer Hollywood talent to play the title role, not unknown Stallone. Stallone held out, and while the film's budget was sliced in half, Stallone proved that he was the best actor to play Rocky Balboa, the Italian Stallion, and ultimate underdog, both on screen and off. The film entertains so well for many reasons. First of all, the screenplay, sentimental and formulaic as it might be, works. The character interactions (Talia Shire as Rocky's paralyzingly shy love interest Adrian; Adrian's annoying brother, the down and out Paulie, played by Burt Young; grizzled old fart trainer Mickey, played by an enthusiastic Burgess Meredith; arrogant champion boxer Apollo Creed, played by Carl Weathers) seem unglamorous and realistic, yet each performance touches our hearts. Here is a Philadelphia working class world populated by people battered down by life, but people who refuse to give up or give in. When the heavyweight champion decides to give a Philly "bum" a chance at the title, instead of taking the money and falling to the canvas, Rocky sees this as his only chance to make his mark on life, and entrusting his fate to battered trainer Mickey, they both put everything on the line. The classic musical score by Bill Conti, his music becoming the basic for the visual rhythms, accentuates the marriage of sight and sound. As the featured title fight progresses, masterfully edited, it is the sense of both visual and musical rhythm that builds to the climax, Rocky winning a spiritual victory, as his battered face cries out for beloved Adrian, as she runs to the ring and both quietly declare his/her love for one another. The musical score brings this visual to a satisfying conclusion, as all of us underdogs leave the theater feeling we also have a chance to rise above. If you can resist the sight of Rocky running up those stairs as the music soars, maybe you should think about happy pills.

TELEVISION

ADVENTURES OF OZZIE AND HARRIET (1952-1966), along with **FATHER KNOWS BEST** and **LEAVE IT TO BEAVER**, became the archetype for the 1950s American family, TV-style. Even though we never knew what Ozzie's job was, he rushed home from the office, gallantly attired in a coat and tie, and read the newspaper awaiting the full course meal cooked by dutiful wife Harriet. Their children, David and Ricky, were the ideal 1950s teenagers, ruggedly handsome, polite, intelligent and popular at school (as well as being good students academically). True, Ricky veered off into the exploding rock 'n' roll world, but even when singing with his rather clean-cut rockabilly band, fueled by ace guitarist James Burton, Ricky always sang safe, innocent tunes (such as *Lonely Town*). He had the looks but lacked the menace and sneer of Elvis, Eddie Cochran, Gene Vincent, Johnny Burnette and other musical rebels of the time. In the world of the Nelsons, neighbors were just about your only friends and everyone had an open door policy, allowing neighbors to enter and exit at will. But once again, Ozzie and Harriet offered a world of frivolity, white-picket fences, well-manicured lawns, prosperity and warmth shared by one and all. It was almost as though the world envisioned in the 1956 film *The Invasion of the Body Snatchers* had come to vivid life.

THE AMOS 'N ANDY SHOW (1951-1953) is television's most unfairly maligned situation comedy series. Coming to television from radio, where the series' white creators voiced the voice characterizations of black characters, the show allowed an entire company of black performers to work professionally and make money. But frightened and politically correct networks and TV stations were nervous that such slow-drawled black stereotypes were insulting to the African American race and the show was canceled. The show was not shown in syndication or offered, legally, on home video. Today, we realize that most network situation comedies made white people out to be stereotypes—the men stuipd louts and the women shrews or bimbos. But as enacted by a troupe of gifted performers, **Amos 'n Andy** still entertains to this day. Alvin Childress played the show's fairly normal cab driver, the narrator and moral conscience for the conniving Andy (Spencer Williams) and the classical oily Kingfish Stevens (Tim Moore). In a sense we can see a lot of Jackie Gleason and his relationship to Ed Norton from **The Honeymooners** in the series, with Andy being both gullible but also a schemer, much in the same sense that Ed Norton was. The Lodge that Ralph and Ed attend is similar to the The Mystic Knights of the Sea Lodge that Kingfish and Andy attend. And the shrewish wife to Kingfish, Sapphire (Ernestine Wade), always the one who takes charge, is very similar to Ralph's wife Alice. Perhaps one of the funniest episodes is when the Kingfish and Andy buy a roadside diner, not knowing that the major traffic route has been diverted, so cars now bypass the diner. In hilarious fashion, when Kingfish sees a car off in the distance, he repeatedly tells Andy to "turn on the grill," but no one ever stops. For the Kingfish, never the working man but a full-time conniver, sometimes the funniest situations revolve around the paybacks that life delivers, often in the most humorous ways.

THE ANDY GRIFFITH SHOW (1960-1968) was simply infectious, from its catchy whistled title song, to its inspired cast of characters. Mayberry was most likely fictional to the American south even during the 1960s, but the berg's innocence and dream of a lazy, unstressed America was mighty appealing, back in the day. Remember, even Otis, the town drunk, had a key to the sheriff's jail cell and would lock himself up when on a drunk. Add to the mix simplistic yet goofy Gomer Pyle, loopy Floyd the Barber, grandmotherly Aunt Bee, and best of all, high-strung deputy, Barney Fife, portrayed by underrated television comedian Don Knotts. Of course star Andy Griffith, as the slow-talking and smiling Sheriff Andy Taylor, demonstrates the power of personality and wisdom over weaponry (best displayed by Barney Fife's comical mishandling of his pistol, with the bullet stored in his pocket, safely out of harm's way). Young Ron Howard as Andy's son Opie allows the Sheriff's wisdom to extend to matters of the family, and the heart. Bottom line, we all yearned to grow up in Mayberry, in a family like the Taylor's.

71

THE COSBY SHOW (1984-1992) and **ROSANNE** (1988-1997) were wildly popular television, but it was their very realness that set them apart from other TV sitcoms. Forget the fact that **The Cosby Show** crossed color barriers and became the number one show in the country, it was those loving threats that Cliff and Clair uttered to their rambunctious brood that struck home. How many times had we heard those exact same words from our parents. While the Huxtable family battled with the problems of parenthood and family life, money was not one of the problems in their upscale world. **Rosanne** broke new ground by featuring a blue-collar family dealing with job loss, dead-end jobs, frustrating bosses and insane relatives. In other words, the life most Americans lead. But the brilliance of Rosanne Barr was her ability to make us laugh at our troubles and see that love and humor can always make everything better. The final season of Rosanne was reviled by critics, but I think it was brilliant. Our family lost our father at a young age, only 42, leaving my mother with six kids, between the ages of 6 through 17. Those daydreams that made up the final season really hit home with my family. Maybe you had to live through a rough year like that to understand it. Even today, both the Huxtable and Conner clans are still relevant and are always good for a laugh.

THE CAROL BURNETT SHOW (1967-1978) is probably one of the greatest variety shows ever. It's difficult to decide what was funniest on the show, the soap opera sketches "As the Stomach Turned," or the movie parodies, especially *Mildred Pierce*, *Sunset Boulevard* and *Gone With the Wind*. But I had the most fun watching Tim Conway try to crack up Harvey Korman in front of the live audience. I don't think we need say anything other than this show featured brilliant comedy that will never age.

CHEERS (1982-1993) became one of television's longest surviving series, simply because of its terrific ensemble cast, whose life problems could be discussed or forgotten simply when entering the Boston community bar Cheers, "where everyone knows your name!" Actual life was lived outside the confines of the bar, but reactions, plans and regrets were the substance of most of the episodes. Plots were mostly confined to character interaction. That included likable, though heavily flawed, people including bar owner, Sam (Ted Danson), a former professional baseball player with a drinking problem (so of course he buys a bar!). His love interest, a former graduate student, is Diane (Shelley Long), a character who eventually splits with Sam and leaves the series, allowing Rebecca (Kirstie Alley) to become his new frictional love interest. The lovable yet simple Coach (Nicholas Colasanto) allows the more sarcastic Sam to often put his foot in his mouth. Head waitress Carla (Rhea Pearlman) creates some of the show's best comic barbs, yet she sometimes becomes the mother figure to a troubled Sam. Let's not forget accountant Norm (George Wendt), who seeks refuge at Cheers to get a break from his wife, and mailman Cliff (John Ratzberger), who lives with his mother and becomes the annoying member of the entourage. There's new dumb bunny farm boy Woody (Woody Harrelson), who replaced Coach. But perhaps the most classic character was Dr. Frasier Crane (Kelsey Grammer), whose narcissism and conflict with wife Lilith

provides the show's most comedic moments (of course his character got his own series eventually). **Cheers** succeeded because everyone in the bar was "broken" and either reminded us of ourselves or of people we know. In spite of such flaws, viewers got to know and eventually truly care about these people, and just like in real life, we come to see beyond people's flaws and find the soul that lies buried beneath.

THE DICK VAN DYKE SHOW (1961-1966) taught us what it was like to be hip, young and married in the dawning 1960s. Rob Petri (Dick Van Dyke) and sexy wife Laura (Mary Tyler Moore) raised the perfect son, Ritchie, a child who rarely caused his parents any real problems, and when he did, they were easily (and comically) solved.

While 1950s comedy kept the action generally focused at home, here, the focus occurred on the job site, at the office, with Van Dyke playing one of three writers of TV's fictional *The Alan Brady Show*. Carl Reiner portrayed the erasable Brady (the show's running gag concerned his vanity and hair piece), and Rose Marie and Morey Amsterdam played Rob's two writing cohorts, equally whacky. Van Dyke's long, lanky physique, bolstered by his propensity for pratfalls and slapstick, created the persona of the almost in-control 1960s breadwinner, a role model that kept his world intact both at the office and at home. Mary Tyler Moore started out as an **I Love Lucy** clone, but she soon morphed into the "Thoroughly Modern" Mary persona, who while ditzy, was still intelligent and resourceful. And no one could cry more comically than Mary Tyler Moore. Fans of **The Dick Van Dyke Show** should also check out the film **My Favorite Year** (1982), which stars Peter O'Toole, Mark Linn-Baker, Jessica Harper and Joseph Bologna, in this fictional homage to Sid Caesar's **Your Show of Shows** (which is another show that provides more than enough belly laughs to cheer you up).

FATHER KNOWS BEST (1954-1960), along with **The Adventures of Ozzie and Harriet**, became the template for how the modern American family would be depicted on television. Robert Young, who by 1954 was more the grandfather image, becomes the wise father who can solve any family problem, hardly working up a sweat (and that would be disastrous, when sitting home in a full suit and tie!). Imagine the perfect American family: stately father Jim Anderson (Robert Young), always beautiful looking wife Margaret (Jane Wyatt), eldest daughter Kathy or Princess (Elinor Donahue), son Bud (Billy Gray) and youngest daughter Kathy or Kitten (Lauren Chapin). Bud, who wore slicked-back hair, was never a rebel, with or without a cause. Innocent troubless at school or with the family car were his biggest problems. Princess was always treated too gingerly, and her crying spells were the result of not being asked to the high school dance or experiencing problems with friends. Kathy was

the family brat and always got her way, although her problems, likewise, were molehills projected by her as mountains. Today, looking back, **Father Knows Best** was a fantasy even during its time; however, it was a program where youngsters of the baby boomer generation learned morals, social skills and how to survive and work together as a family. Where a bad hair day might be the basis of a half-hour episode, hardcore reality was never the focus in the world of the Andersons. However, the show visualized an ideal that was both warm and comforting at the time and has become even more so decades removed.

FRASIER (1993-2004) — When **Cheers** ended production 1993, **Frasier** became television's most famous off-shoot production by sending pivotal character, psychiatrist Dr. Frasier Crane (Kelsey Grammer), from Boston to Seattle, after his divorce. So basically Kelsey Grammer played the character (either as supporting or lead) from 1982 until 2004, making the arrogant and boorish hot-aired radio shrink one of television's defining characters. Relocating to Seattle, Dr. Crane moves into the ultimate bachelor pad, until his handicapped ex-cop father Martin (the marvelous John Mahoney), moves in. Within a short time Martin and Eddie, his loveable mutt, totally invade Farsier's turf. Must the worst thing of all, to Frasier anyway, is

Martin's broken down (but comfy) green lounge chair (which

73

is totally out of place in Frasier's world). Crane, overly pretentious and quirky in his tastes, shares an infinity with his equally comical and weird brother, Dr. Nils Crane (the show's ace-in-the-hole David Hyde Pierce). Alone, Frasier Crane is totally obnoxious, but interacting with brother Nils, we can see both adults as terribly flawed, perhaps even sympathetic, and wonder how such a normal working stiff as Martin could have produced two sons so far removed from his policeman reality. The love interest (for both Frasier but mostly Nils) comes from lovely Jane Leeves as Daphne, Martin's home care physical therapist, recently arriving from England. The interaction between all four members of the household (and of course we have the supporting cast of loonies at the radio station, most notably the much too sexually active Roz, played by Peri Gilpin) fuels the scripts. **Frasier** is perhaps one of the funniest TV series ever produced, but its odd concoction of characters and twisted plots makes the show an anomaly, but it's funny as hell and we grow to love all these daffy people, warts and all.

FRIENDS (1994-2004) was another home run for NBC's must see Thursday night. The show, about six friends living in New York, relied on the quirks and charisma of its talented cast and their instant chemistry. The show rarely had a dull season and managed to exit at the top of their game. The cast of friends really did become friends for millions of viewers. The show, now in repeats all over the place, still makes you laugh, especially the untraditional Thanksgiving shows.

THE GEORGE BURNS AND GRACIE ALLEN SHOW (1950-1958) took the movie comedy team of Burns and Allen and transplanted them into suburban America, trying to recapture their intelligent verbal repartee for the masses, in a half-hour format no less. The heart of the team's chemistry relied upon wife Gracie's seemingly zany and confused dialogue, which in reality turned out to make more sense than at first suspected. Husband George, with deadpan smile and cigar in mouth, is the calm reactor who makes a few low-key verbal responses to Gracie's verbosity. To transpose this stand-up style to the small tube, the situation comedy added neighbors to fuel the fire. Comedian and announcer Harry von Zell played energetic neighbor Harry von Zell, but it was the Fred-and-Ethel based conflict between neighbors Blanche (Bea Benaderet) and husband Harry (played by both Fred Clark and Hal March at various times) that fueled the festivities. Blanche, in her 1950s conniving manner, always brought volatile husband Harry to a full boil, because of her antics. Gracie, her friend and often partner in crime, would blabber to husband George about the neighbor's problems, thus allowing George to make editorial comments. George would always play the calm observer, much like the viewing audience, and his quips would provide both humor and wisdom. Frequently the show would end with Burns and Allen doing some of their classic repartee stand-up comedy routines, and often this ending section became the highlight of the episode.

THE HONEYMOONERS (1955-1956), besides **I Love Lucy**, is the other iconic comedy of the 1950s. While **I Love Lucy** debuted in 1951, **The Honeymooners**, which appeared in 1955, always looked decidedly lower rent (it was produced by the DuMont Network) and old-timey (no three camera setups from cinematographer Karl Freund) when compared to **I Love Lucy**, but nonetheless, the wonderful scripts and the character interaction between Ralph (Jackie Gleason), Alice (Audrey Meadows) and "pal-of-mine" Ed Norton (Art Carney) produced classic comedy that remains just as hilarious over 50 years later. The premise, based upon the toxic friendship between bossy bus driver Ralph and his affable best friend, sewer worker Ed Norton, focuses upon Ralph's attempts to prove he is dominant and smarter, but although not too bright, Ed's loyalty, friendship and love always melts Ralph's stubborn heart. And speak about toxic relationships, the marriage between Ralph and Alice works so well because Alice can dish it out just as well as Ralph does, and she seldom falls for his pranks. In other words,

she is his equal (but yes, she is much smarter than he is). Even when threatening he will "fly her to the moon," Ralph truly loves Alice and gets into most of his tight jams when trying to make her happy. For 39 classic episodes, **The Honeymooners** is tough to beat for tender heartwarming comedy.

I LOVE LUCY (1951-1957) is perhaps the most innovative, influential and funniest of TV's classic situation comedies, ever. Based upon a simple premise of a not-so-young daffy woman (Lucille Ball was a red-haired beauty who played in comedies, musicals and film noir during the 1940s, check out **Ziegfeld Follies** [1946] for the number that has Lucy wearing a skin tight pink gown, as a sizzling lion tamer who cracks her whip over the heads of a sexy chorus line and black-clad kittens), with aspirations toward show biz, marries a Cuban bandleader-singer who tries to convince himself he has his family situations firmly under control. Add to the mix two much older neighbors, Fred and Ethel, as the best friends in the apartment nextdoor (to perhaps make Lucy and Desi appear young and hip), the comic shenanigans revolve around Lucy and Ethel teaming up against Desi and Fred. Plus we have a gifted comedy writing team who could create classic laugh riots involving Lucy getting drunk while filming a commercial many times over, losing control while working the conveyer belt at a chocolate candy manufacturing factory and embarrassing herself when meeting any and every star in Hollywood. The characters were iconic, the scripts crisp and focused and the comedic talents of Lucille Ball undeniable.

LEAVE IT TO BEAVER (1957-1963) came after **Father Knows Best, Burns and Allen** and **The Adventures of Ozzie and Harriet,** but this definitive portrait of the suburban white-picket-fence American family of the late 1950s-early 1960s is iconic and still popular today. Hugh Beaumont (as father Ward Cleaver) and Barbara Billingsley (as wife June) continued the tradition of relaxing around the house in suit and tie for Ward or crisply fresh daytime dress and pearls for June. Of course, June tended to the house and kids and Ward returned from a hard day at the office, never even bothering to loosen his tie (sometimes he switched out of the formal sports jacket for an equally formal cardigan sweater, still with tie). Unlike the earlier shows that focused on the adults, this show's success was based upon getting into the mind of a child, in this case the terminally cute Theodore or "Beaver" (Jerry Mathers), always getting himself into trouble. Sometimes older brother Wally (Tony Dow) could save his butt, but mostly Beaver corrupts Wally and has to tumble and fall and be picked up by the wise, always smiling, father Ward. The boys' friends become another focus of the show: rotund Larry Mondello, Lumpy Rutherford (and his officious father, played by Richard Deacon) and the classic sneaky weasel Eddie Haskell (Ken Osmond). Somehow the morality of Beaver always shines through, and his own guilty conscience punishes him long before the scouring face of Ward intervenes. But along the way, we wish we had parents like Ward and June and a brother like Wally, not to mention goofy friends, a hot teacher such as Miss Landers and even that priceless community relic, Gus the fireman. **Leave It To Beaver** is as comforting as a can of Campbell's tomato soup and a grilled cheese sandwich. It creates a world that any of us would love to inhabit.

Warner Bros.' **LOONEY TUNES** were always considered cartoons for adults, and as a child going to the movies during the 1950s and 1960s, almost every feature was introduced by a Warner Bros. **Looney Tunes** (or they could be viewed at home, as they were broadcast on television weekly). Perhaps your favorite character is Bugs Bunny and Elmer Fudd, or perhaps Tweety and Sylvester, The Road Runner and Wile E. Coyote or even Daffy Duck. It does not matter. With those brilliant Technicolor hues, those insane musical cues, whatever character was featured in the current cartoon was not as important as knowing the team behind the execution held high creative standards. We had masterful Mel Blanc providing the vast majority of all voices. We had writers such as Mike Maltese and Warren Foster. We had directors such as Chuck Jones and Robert Clampett. In these seven-minute animated masterpieces, we had a consistent factory focused on producing the funniest and cleverest cartoons ever made. Whether the subject was spoofing classic Hollywood or showing how a frisky hare could outsmart everyone around him, the Warner Bros. animated unit

knew how to tickle our funny bone. But not all the humor depended upon chases, flying boulders from above or physical confrontations. Just as much of the cartoon humor derived from parody and satire, sometimes political (their caricatures of Japanese soldiers during WWII) and sometimes social (their censored version of Coal Black and De Sebben Dwarfs, which forced the animation unit to research black jazz nightclubs for visual and musical inspiration). Even though children might laugh at the antics, especially the physical ones, Warner Bros. cartoons were geared toward intelligent adults, adults who knew the world in which these cartoons were produced and adults who knew something about culture. A child might giggle at What's Opera, Doc? But an adult who understands something of the opera on which the cartoon is based will laugh the loudest. And that's the secret of the Warner Bros. animation unit. They captured our curiosity as children, but they challenged us even further as we grew into adults. And all this art created in seven-minute chunks!

Love of cartoons is something the entire family can enjoy—they are truly one of the few art forms equally popular with kids of all ages. With the Cartoon Network, Disney Channel and Nickelodeon, a quick fix of cheer is available 24 hours a day. **SPONGEBOB SQUAREPANTS, THE PENGUINS OF MADAGASCAR** and **THE FAIRLY ODD PARENTS** can hold their own with Bugs and Daffy and the gang. Nickelodeon's TV Land broadcasts many of the classic shows on this list as well as original comedies made for kids, but I find these shows have some of the cleverest writing on TV. Check out i**CARLY, EVEN STEVENS** (with a young Shia LeBeouf), **NED'S DECLASSIFIED SCHOOL SURVIVAL GUIDE** and **DUCK DODGERS**.

THE MARY TYLER MOORE SHOW (1970-1977), besides being hilarious and comforting, was a landmark series in that a young, single woman becomes empowered as she moves to a strange new city, Minneapolis, and takes a job as associate newsroom producer at a small television station. What we love about Mary Richards (the character the lovely and perky Mary Tyler Moore plays) is her vulnerability. She is not afraid to make decisions, and her competence always shows through, yet at the same time she makes mistakes, is often tentative and afraid and she has to depend upon her support network (friends Rhoda, Phyllis, Murray and even boss Lou Grant) to find her way. But as the classic theme song bellows, "You're gonna make it after all," a song deemed so cool that punk band Husker-Du covered it in all its ferocity. Once again the situational comedy derives from the on-the-job interactions. We have low-key head writer Murray (Gavin MacLeod), intelligent and friendly and a person that Mary can turn to frequently because he is non-judgmental. At the other extreme is Ted Baxter (Ted Knight), the vain TV anchorman who can barely read his script and whose arrogance

and air of superiority is brought down to earth by his comical flaws. But it is the wizened newsman Lou Grant (Ed Asner), whose gruff exterior and crustiness makes Lou a frightening boss to Mary, but in reality he is the doting father-figure or at least professional mentor, who both understands Mary's strengths and potential to grow. But at the same time he seldom lets on how much he cares about his employee. And as Mary struggles, we all pull for her and know, in spite of the comedic challenges afoot, that Mary will make it after all.

MY LITTLE MARGIE (1952-1955) was a perennial favorite of mine as a child, and the show's premise explains why. Many times early television took either B actors or fading A stars from the movies and cast them into television series. Here is B star Gale Storm (having the 20-something Margie role) cast along-

side 1930's matinee favorite Charles Farrell (who plays 50-something father Vern). The plot's either focused upon Vern's concern with his young and innocent daughter's day-to-day problems and love life, or with Margie's concern that some hussy might snare her debonair and quite defenseless single father, whose romantic drive makes him blind to the craftiness of scheming women. It should it be mentioned that Vern and Margie live in a luxury high-rise apartment, and that they seem fairly affluent, making Vern prime pickings for the right woman. However, the affable Margie, seemingly worldly and always in charge, sometimes is also blind to the pitfalls of the world. So here we have a show where father and daughter are best friends, both watching out for the best interests of the other, with comic potential tapped to the fullest.

SEINFELD (1990-1998) demonstrates that stand-up comedians, at least the most gifted ones, can make the leap from comedy stage to Hollywood flawlessly. Show creator Larry David stated he wanted to produce a situation comedy about nothing, and **Seinfeld** is the result. Each show began with a brief stand-up comedy routine that somehow tied into the episode. The world of Seinfeld is a whacky one that depends upon the supporting cast of eccentric characters. We have the pudgy

and balding George (Jason Alexander), whose immorality and coldness would make many people hate him if we could not see beyond his underlying flaws and thus sympathize with him. We have the totally crazy Kramer (Michael Richards), the skinny, tall and wild-haired comedian whose physical trips and pratfalls created perhaps the loudest and longest laughter of the series. Elaine (Julia Louis-Dreyfus) became the only girl of the ensemble, but her classic inability to dance, when she thinks she is Miss Rhythm Nation, makes her another lovable whack case. Simply put, these characters belong together (Jerry is by far the most normal and sympathetic of the lot) because who else could stand them or put up with their shenanigans? Such an unlikable crew of characters somehow gets under our skin, and we at least laugh with them, if not actually like them. But how can we not find the "soup Nazi" episode funny ("No soup for you!") or the entire episode spent with the cast waiting around to be seated, even though they have a reservation at a Chinese restaurant. Or, better yet, the entire episode spent in the underground parking garage trying to find a car. Stupid people, often unpleasant people, who are put into strange circumstances, can sometimes become hilariously funny. **Seinfeld** proves the point.

THE SMOTHERS BROTHERS COMEDY HOUR (1967-1969) was an anomaly, breaching the safe insulated world of the early 1960s folk music scene and the explosive politically volatile world of the Psychedelic drug-induced Hippie era. On the safe side we had Tom and Dick strumming away and singing safe variations of the authentic Harry Brown-archived American folk music scene, which earlier acoustic groups such as The Kingston Trio and Peter, Paul, and Mary made palpable

for mainstream college audiences. But then Tom and Dick opened their mouths to speak, and the political rhetoric flowed. The brothers complained of CBS censorship and studio infringement of their First Amendment rights. The show featured tamer artists such as Mason Williams, John Hartford, Glenn Campbell and others. But newly emerging rock artists such as Jefferson Airplane, The Doors and other threatening (to parents) rock acts appeared. So this home-brewed and

safe Americana existed side-by-side with the explosive birth of a newer, more politically active and violent generation. Depending upon your age and political leanings, the show was definitely entertaining. Also check out **THE SONNY AND CHER COMEDY HOUR** (1971-1974), which was filled with quirky comedy sketches, witty one-liners, dazzling Bob Mackie costumes and made a star out of the multi-talented Cher. And, of course, **ROWAN & MARTIN'S LAUGH-IN**, which may only be funny to those of us alive in the 1960s, but with the cast of prime comedians and cutting social commentary, it's a precursor to **THE DAILY SHOW WITH JON STEWART** (1996-),

which features biting news stories, that although true, are so ridiculous it's almost impossible not to laugh at the foibles of mankind. **The Daily Show** is nothing short of brilliant and well deserving of the praise and accolades received.

TAXI (1978-1983), another quirky character-driven comedy, explores the world of New York cab drivers and the big dreams all of us harbor. Alex (Judd Hirsch) is the most normal of the cabbie crew and his friendship with cute and perky Elaine (Marilu Henner) forms the basis of the show. Both Tony Danza and Jeff Conaway portrayed young cabbies, frisky and full of life and libido, who at times are nurtured and advised by veteran father-figure Alex. The comedy comes from boss and dispatcher Louis De Palma (Danny DeVito), a short little man who barks out commands from the safety of his protected cage. Weird characters on the crew include the burned-out Reverend Jim (Christopher Lloyd) and East European odd-ball Latka, played by the even stranger Andy Kaufman, in his breakout TV series. The series, always containing warmth and humanity behind the situational gags, wins us over by the sheer strength and commitment of the characters to struggle through life, trying to reach bigger dreams. This was truly a golden age for sitcoms. Other favorites include **NIGHT COURT, THE BOB NEWHART SHOW, BARNEY MILLER,** and several more current faves include **SCRUBS, THE SIMPSONS, EVERYBODY LOVES RAYMOND and HOME IMPROVEMENT.**

YOUR SHOW OF SHOWS (1950-1954) with Sid Ceasar, Imogene Coca and Carl Reiner is another variety show that never fails to entertain, although it is a little difficult to locate, but the program is well worth the effort. The show was broadcast live, making the flubs and ad-libs some of the best laughs. The skits were snappy and silly, sometimes risqué, but entertainment that never played down to the audience, if only that were still true today. But the real talent was behind the scenes—the writers, without whom TV would

have been a much duller place—Mel Brooks, Larry Gelbart (**M*A*S*H**) and Neil Simon. One of the funniest shows I have ever, and I mean ever, seen was a documentary called **Sid Caesar's Writers—A Reunion of Writers from Your Show of Shows and Caesar's Hour** (1996). This was filmed at a Writer's Guild of America evening, which taped the show.

BRITCOMS have a huge fan base in the U.S., and I have to say, I'm hooked. I can watch them over and over and see something new each time. The thing I love about British TV is that they cast actors rather than faces. It's so refreshing to watch great actors doing comedy, and to me, one of the best things is that I can tell the actors apart—they are more like real people than Barbie dolls. If you've never seen any British comedies, check out PBS, also BBCAmerica occasionaly runs them. Of course most of them are on DVD. So check out **FAWLTY TOWERS** (will actually make your side hurt from laughing), **THE VICAR OF DIBLY, ABSOLUTELY FABULOUS, FATHER TED, MY HERO, KEEPING UP APPEARANCES, AS TIME GOES BY, BLACK ADDER, COUPLING, ARE YOU BEING SERVED?, CHEF, JEEVES AND WOOSTER** (a hilarious pre-*House* Hugh Laurie), **MR. BEAN** and of course **MONTY PYTHON.**

AFI 100 TOP LAUGHS

This is the American Film Institute's list of America's 100 Funniest Movies, selected by AFI's blue-ribbon panel of more than 1,500 leaders of the American movie community. And while we don't agree with all their choices or the numerical arrangement of them, they are still good medicine for bad times.

1. SOME LIKE IT HOT, 1959
2. TOOTSIE, 1982
3. DR. STRANGELOVE OR: HOW I LEARNED TO STOP WORRYING AND LOVE THE BOMB, 1964
4. ANNIE HALL, 1977
5. DUCK SOUP, 1933
6. BLAZING SADDLES, 1974
7. M*A*S*H, 1970
8. IT HAPPENED ONE NIGHT, 1934
9. THE GRADUATE, 1967
10. AIRPLANE!, 1980
11. THE PRODUCERS, 1968
12. A NIGHT AT THE OPERA, 1935
13. YOUNG FRANKENSTEIN, 1974
14. BRINGING UP BABY, 1938
15. THE PHILADELPHIA STORY, 1940
16. SINGIN' IN THE RAIN, 1952
17. THE ODD COUPLE, 1968
18. THE GENERAL, 1927
19. HIS GIRL FRIDAY, 1940
20. THE APARTMENT, 1960
21. A FISH CALLED WANDA, 1988
22. ADAM'S RIB, 1949
23. WHEN HARRY MET SALLY, 1989
24. BORN YESTERDAY, 1950
25. THE GOLD RUSH, 1925
26. BEING THERE, 1979
27. THERE'S SOMETHING ABOUT MARY, 1998
28. GHOSTBUSTERS, 1984
29. THIS IS SPINAL TAP, 1984
30. ARSENIC AND OLD LACE, 1944
31. RAISING ARIZONA, 1987
32. THE THIN MAN, 1934
33. MODERN TIMES, 1936
34. GROUNDHOG DAY, 1993
35. HARVEY, 1950
36. NATIONAL LAMPOON'S ANIMAL HOUSE, 1978
37. THE GREAT DICTATOR, 1940
38. CITY LIGHTS, 1931
39. SULLIVAN'S TRAVELS, 1941
40. IT'S A MAD MAD MAD MAD WORLD, 1963
41. MOONSTRUCK, 1987
42. BIG, 1988
43. AMERICAN GRAFFITI, 1973
44. MY MAN GODFREY, 1936
45. HAROLD AND MAUDE, 1972
46. MANHATTAN, 1979
47. SHAMPOO, 1975
48. A SHOT IN THE DARK, 1964
49. TO BE OR NOT TO BE, 1942
50. CAT BALLOU, 1965
51. THE SEVEN YEAR ITCH, 1955
52. NINOTCHKA, 1939
53. ARTHUR, 1981
54. THE MIRACLE OF MORGAN'S CREEK, 1944
55. THE LADY EVE, 1941
56. ABBOTT AND COSTELLO MEET FRANKENSTEIN, 1948
57. DINER, 1982
58. IT'S A GIFT, 1934
59. A DAY AT THE RACES, 1937
60. TOPPER, 1937
61. WHAT'S UP, DOC?, 1972
62. SHERLOCK, JR., 1924
63. BEVERLY HILLS COP, 1984
64. BROADCAST NEWS, 1987
65. HORSE FEATHERS, 1932
66. TAKE THE MONEY AND RUN, 1969
67. MRS. DOUBTFIRE, 1993
68. THE AWFUL TRUTH, 1937
69. BANANAS, 1971
70. MR. DEEDS GOES TO TOWN, 1936
71. CADDYSHACK, 1980
72. MR. BLANDINGS BUILDS HIS DREAM HOUSE, 1948
73. MONKEY BUSINESS, 1931
74. 9 TO 5, 1980
75. SHE DONE HIM WRONG, 1933
76. VICTOR/VICTORIA, 1982
77. THE PALM BEACH STORY, 1942
78. ROAD TO MOROCCO, 1942
79. THE FRESHMAN, 1925
80. SLEEPER, 1973
81. THE NAVIGATOR, 1924
82. PRIVATE BENJAMIN, 1980
83. FATHER OF THE BRIDE, 1950
84. LOST IN AMERICA, 1985
85. DINNER AT EIGHT, 1933
86. CITY SLICKERS, 1991
87. FAST TIMES AT RIDGEMONT HIGH, 1982
88. BEETLEJUICE, 1988
89. THE JERK, 1979
90. WOMAN OF THE YEAR, 1942
91. THE HEARTBREAK KID, 1972
92. BALL OF FIRE, 1941
93. FARGO, 1996
94. AUNTIE MAME, 1958
95. SILVER STREAK, 1976
96. SONS OF THE DESERT, 1933
97. BULL DURHAM, 1988
98. THE COURT JESTER, 1956
99. THE NUTTY PROFESSOR, 1963
100. GOOD MORNING, VIETNAM, 1987

© 2002 American Film Institute

For some people, like my husband Gary, a dark, depressing noir will brighten them right up. For the misogynists in the bunch, and we do know a few, a nice gruesome slasher film will do the trick (I won't even get started on how repellant I find those films!) For most people, a rib-tickling comedy will chase the wolves from the door—at least for a few hours. For me, it's a love story...

IT'S A LOVE STORY: OUR FAVORITE ROMANTIC SCENES

As I was watching *Pride and Prejudice* for the nth time, I began to think about my favorite romantic scenes in films. And, being a naturally curious person, I wondered what other people found romantic about the movies. We asked readers of our website and magazines, *Midnight Marquee* and *Mad About Movies,* to send us their five favorite love scenes. And, since it was my idea, I thought I'd throw in my two cents.

I love romantic movies. I love to sit on the couch under an afghan and sigh with contentment when, in *Pride and Prejudice*, Elizabeth and Mr. Darcy glance at each other across the room and realize they adore each other. Or I happily sob away when, in the finale of the Bette Davis weeper *Dark Victory*, reformed socialite Judith sends her physician husband away to an important medical conference, even though she knows she only has left a few brief hours. I couldn't limit myself to five and I'm sure I'll think of many, many other favorite titles later, but here are a few of my favorite sigh-inspiring romantic film moments in no certain order:

The aforementioned *Pride and Prejudice* (1995, BBC). Jennifer Ehle as Elizabeth Bennett and Colin Firth as Mr. Darcy inspire so many silly grins of utter delight, it's difficult to pick just one. One of the most touching occurs when Mr. Darcy demands that Elizabeth tell him if her feelings for him have changed, and she admits she now loves him. You can feel they long to throw their arms around each other in a passionate embrace, but society's mores allow them to only politely acknowledge their mutual affection.

The cruise where Charlotte (Bette Davis) and the unhappily married Jerry (Paul Henreid) fall in love in *Now, Voyager* (1942). Well, really, the entire film from that point onward—Jerry lighting two cigarettes (I know, smoking is bad, yadda, yadda) and handing one to Charlotte, aka Camille. Sigh...

Loretta (Cher) preparing for her first opera, *La Boheme*, and a date with her fiance's brother Ronny (Nicolas Cage) in *Moonstruck* (1987). We are with her every step of the way as she transforms herself from a frumpy widowed bookkeeper, via a new hairstyle and fabulous scarlet dress, and feel our hearts flutter as tears roll down her face at the end of the tragic opera and Ronny reaches for her hand. Second place goes to Loretta's moonstruck Aunt Rita (Julie Bovasso) and Uncle Raymond (Louis Guss), who still feel the electricity of true love.

When Elinor (Emma Thompson) learns her one true love, Edward Ferrars (Hugh Grant), is not married and still loves her in *Sense and Sensibility* (1995). She is so overwhelmed that she clutches her chest and begins to sob uncontrollably. Her mother and sisters quickly remove themselves from the room, as Edward declares his love. Runner-up scene is the wedding of Marianne (Kate Winslet) and Colonel Brandon (Alan Rickman).

Annie (Meg Ryan) listens to the radio on Christmas Eve as Jonah Baldwin (Ross Malinger) tries to find a wife for his widower father Sam (Tom Hanks), in *Sleepless in Seattle* (1993). Another favorite sequence is when Annie sits at a table peeling an apple in one long string, something Sam helped Jonah remember about his late mother.

The spaghetti supper in *Lady and the Tramp* (1955).

Fred Astaire and Cyd Charisse "Dancing in the Dark" in *The Band Wagon* still thrills.

Gene Kelly after seeing Debbie Reynolds' home and realizing he's in love and expressing his elation by dancing and *Singin' in the Rain*; this scene never, ever fails to make me smile.

Gene Kelly is *Singin' in the Rain*

Judy (Vera-Ellen) convincing Phil (Danny Kaye) they need to get engaged to encourage Betty (Rosemary Clooney) to hook up with Bob (Bing Crosby) in *White Christmas*.

John Wayne and Maureen O'Hara together in anything, but especially *The Quiet Man*.

The magical love between homely Laura (Dorothy McGuire) and scarred Oliver (Robert Young) in *The Enchanted Cottage* (1945)—their enchanted cottage (really the magic of their deep love for each other) has made them beautiful.

Cursed lovers Navarre (Rutger Hauer) and Isabeau (Michelle Pfeiffer) almost touch at sunrise in *Ladyhawke* (1985).

The romance between Katherine (Greer Garson) and Mr. Chipping (Robert Donat) in *Goodbye Mr. Chips*.

The finale of *The Women* (1939), when Mary (Norma Shearer) goes back to her wayward husband after getting the best of slut Chrystal Allen (Joan Crawford).

Tracy (Katharine Hepburn) decides to take control of her messy life and explains to her wedding guests that the marriage to old George is off, and then C.K. Dexter Haven (the yummylicious Cary Grant) whispers her lines to her, and she automatically repeats to the guests that they will witness the wedding they originally missed, in *The Philadelphia Story* (1940).

I've had my say, so now on with the show...
—Susan Svehla

♥   ♥   ♥   ♥   ♥

by Anthony Ambrogio (editor *You're Next*):

In compiling my list of the top-five romantic scenes from the cinema, I realize that so many of them are melancholy. I don't know what that says about movie romance (or, more precisely, my idea of it—maybe I've confused romantic with "moving"), but, for better or worse, here are my choices (in chronological order).

Charlie Chaplin and Virginia Cherrill in *City Lights* (1931). The Little Tramp, more threadbare than ever after a stay in the penitentiary, encounters the formerly blind young woman who's regained her sight through his machinations (passing himself off as a rich man, "stealing" the money she needed for her operation). Now the successful owner of a florist shop, she presses a coin into the hobo's reluctant hand and realizes, by his touch, that he is her secret benefactor. Their series of close-ups and the inter-titles' simple dialogue ("You can see?" "Yes, now I can see") convey a sense of heartache and hope unparalleled in cinema before or since.

Bob Hope and Shirley Ross in *The Big Broadcast of 1938* (1938). Exes Buzz and Cleo Fielding use song ("Thanks for the Memories" by Leo Robin and Ralph Rainger) to relive their former relationship (constantly returning to the refrain, "Thank you, so much") until the bittersweet reminiscences become too much for her and she rushes out, breaking off with a choked, "Thank you, so much." The infectious Oscar-winning tune, Hope's signature for over 60 years, has acquired so many other connotations since, but in context, the clever lyrics and interplay of the cast create a moving moment even for people who only associate it with the beginning and end of a TV special.

James Cagney and Olivia de Havilland in *Strawberry Blonde* (1941). In the not-so-Gay-'90s, Biff Grimes, released from prison for a crime he didn't really commit, meets his faithful wife, Amy, waiting for him on a bench in the park. Their quiet greeting to each other speaks volumes about his newly found, incarceration-instilled humility and their deep love.

Humphrey Bogart and a piece of paper in *Casablanca* (1943). Rick Blaine, at the Gare de Lyon, receives Ilsa Lund's (Ingrid Bergman's) "Dear Rick" letter, saying she won't be joining him. As he stares at the words in disbelief, the rain, his metaphorical tears, causes them to vanish before his eyes, just as Ilsa has. Heartbreaking visual poetry from Michael Curtiz. My loving spouse, Anca Vlasopolos, suggested this one to me—along with about a dozen others, in the space of three minutes. It took me three days to come up with mine (which shows who's the more romantic of we two). Her most romantic scene is between Cary Grant and Ingrid Bergman in Hitchcock's *Notorious* (1946), when Devlin finally declares his love for Alicia by pulling her from her deathbed, guiding her down the stairs and out of the house of her hapless Nazi husband, Alex Sebastian (Claude Rains).

Ernest Borgnine and Betsy Blair in *Marty* (1955). At the Stardust Ballroom ("It's loaded with tomatoes"), after watching a fragile, plain young woman unceremoniously dumped by a jerk ("I only get one Sattidy night off every three weeks, and I wanna wind up with somethin'"), Marty Pilletti follows her to the terrace, where she has fled, taps her on the shoulder, and asks, "Excuse me, Miss, would you care to dance?" Touched, she folds into him, silently sobbing, and he, nonplussed, tentatively embraces her without touching, fingers fluttering in a "There, there" gesture. This could be the beginning of a beautiful relationship.

Can't help but mention Patrick Swayze and Demi Moore in *Ghost* (1990)—the moment when Oda Mae Brown (Whoopi Goldberg) channels Sam (Swayze) and "becomes" him so he can dance with/embrace Molly (Moore) one last time. Music (the Righteous Brothers' "Unchained Melody") and editing (the

Patrick Swayze and Demi Moore in *Ghost*

"transgressive moment" of white female hands holding black female hands, and then the smooth transition from Goldberg to Swayze, obviating any risible "girl-girl" fondling) combine with performance to create a well-earned romantic *frisson* in the audience.

♥ ♥ ♥ ♥ ♥

by John Clymer:

The love scene in *The Big Easy* (1987)

Chaplin courting the blind girl in *City Lights*

Most scenes between Bogart and Bergman in *Casablanca*

Most scenes between Bogart and Bacall in *The Big Sleep* (1946)

The "portrait" scene in *Titanic* (1997)

♥ ♥ ♥ ♥ ♥

by Stan Campbell:

First, the tried and true:

To Have and Have Not (1944): Bacall to Bogart, "You know how to whistle, don't you Steve? You just put your lips together and blow."

Casablanca: Bogart to Bergman, "We'll always have Paris. Here's looking at you, kid."

And, perhaps less obviously:

Shane (1953): Jean Arthur to the disgraced Shane (Alan Ladd), standing outcast in the rain, "I think we know (pause) Shane."

The Lion in Winter (1968): Katherine Hepburn (Queen Eleanor) to Peter O'Toole (Henry II), "I should have been a great fool not to love you."

Some Like it Hot: The love-mad millionaire Joey Brown to the in-drag Jack Lemmon, who has just revealed that he is a man and cannot marry Brown, "Nobody's perfect!"

There are also scenes that, while not romantic in the usual sense, are classically *romantic*. Consider:

The door closing on Ethan (John Wayne) at the conclusion of *The Searchers*.

William Holden, Ernest Borgnine, Warren Oates and Ben Johnson marching to their deaths in *The Wild Bunch* (1969).

At the conclusion of *The Hunchback of Notre Dame* (1939), Charles Laughton, as Quasimodo, watching Esmeralda, far below his perch on the Notre Dame Cathedral, as she leaves with the callow young poet, turns to a stone gargoyle and says, "I wish that I were made of stone like you." (That might be a slight paraphrase.)

♥ ♥ ♥

by B. Kurek:

Any scene from the late 1940s British movie *Brief Encounter* (1945).

Editor's note: Directed by David Lean and based on Noel Coward's "Still Life," Brief Encounter, *starring Celia Johnson and Trevor Howard, tells of two married strangers who meet in a train station and fall in love over a period of time. Guilt and despair eventually separate the star-crossed lovers.*

♥ ♥ ♥

by Mark Clark (author *Smirk, Sneer and Scream*):

Rick Blaine (Humphrey Bogart) says goodbye to Ilsa Lund (Ingrid Bergman) at the airport at the end of *Casa-*

blanca—Perhaps the most romantic scene ever filmed and certainly the most iconic moment of heartbreak in movie history. "Here's looking at you, kid."

Gathered around a telephone receiver, while Sam Wainwright babbles about plastics, George Bailey (James Stewart) pastes a kiss on Mary Hatch (Donna Reed) in *It's a Wonderful Life* (1946). Not only very romantic, but this scene crackles with pent-up sexual tension. (Who knew we could expect that from Stewart and Reed?) Of course, as a result George misses his chance to become a plastics magnate.

Lovestruck Don Lockwood (Gene Kelly) goes "singin' and dancin' in the rain" in *Singin' in the Rain* (1952). As perfect a representation as we're ever likely to see of the pure bliss love can inspire.

The Little Tramp (Charles Chaplin) casts a last, longing look at the flower girl (Virginia Cherrill), whose blindness he helped cure, in *City Lights* (1931). The look on Cherrill's face registers the sudden realization of the devotion and sacrifice the tramp has made on her behalf (she thought he was rich). And Chaplin's Mona Lisa smile informs us that he knew all along that if his efforts succeeded, she would leave his life forever. One of the most moving sequences ever lensed.

C.K. Dexter Haven (Cary Grant) asks Tracy Lord (Katherine Hepburn) to marry him (again) in *The Philadelphia Story* (1940). The movie presents love as an inexorable force, destined to pull these two together despite themselves. For further study of this phenomenon, see Grant in *The Awful Truth* (1937).

♥   ♥   ♥   ♥

by Robin Smith:

In *Gone With the Wind* (1939), when Rhett (Clark Gable) grabs Scarlett (Vivien Leigh) at the bottom of the stairs, tells her that this is one night she is not turning him out, and sweeps her off her feet, right up those stairs and into their bedroom. This sequence leaves so much to one's imagination. That's why it's a classic!

Watching Cary Grant cry as he realizes that Deborah Kerr, the woman he loves, is also the woman in the wheelchair that bought his painting. I can never get through this scene in *An Affair To Remember* (1957) without crying like a newborn.

Any scene with William Holden and Jennifer Jones in *Love is a Many-Splendored Thing* (1955).

When Boris Karloff as the Frankenstein Monster first lays eyes on his so-called Bride (Elsa Lanchester) in *Bride of Frankenstein*.

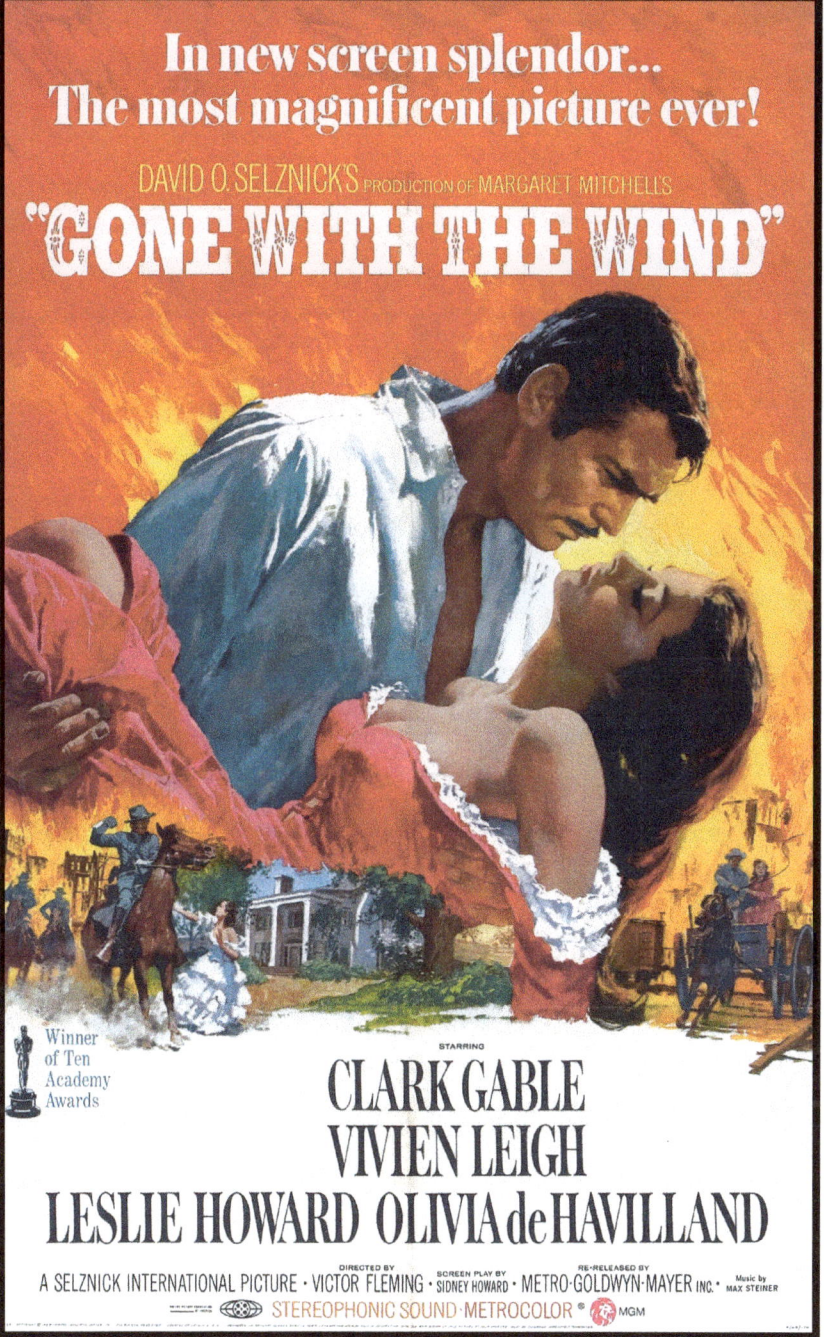

In *Days of Wine And Roses* (1962), when Joe Clay and his wife Kirsten (Jack Lemmon and Lee Remick) were actually sober as they literally rolled around in the hay outside her father's green house. Just goes to show, you don't need booze to have a good time!

I am probably the only person who will have these scenes listed in their top five, but I am who I am, and these will always be some of my favorite movies.

♥   ♥   ♥   ♥   ♥

by Bob Bloom:

Elizabeth Taylor and Montgomery Clift on the balcony in extreme close-up in *A Place in the Sun* (1951).

Kevin Costner explains his credo about sex, women and dating to Susan Sarandon in *Bull Durham* (1988).

King Kong gently pets Fay Wray before he falls to his death from the Empire State Building. No fooling, it is very touching and you feel sorry for the big ape—no pun intended.

Jimmy Stewart sweeping Katharine Hepburn off her feet in the swimming pool sequence of *The Philadelphia Story*.

Teresa Wright hugging Gary Cooper, portraying a dying Lou Gehrig, as they talk about their future plans in *Pride of the Yankees* (1942).

♥ ♥ ♥ ♥ ♥

by Betty Cavanaugh:

Scarlett and Rhett up the stairway in *Gone with the Wind*
Ginger and Fred dancing in any of their movies
The *Casablanca* good-bye
Lauren Bacall–"You know how to whistle, don't you?" from *To Have and Have Not*.
Katherine Hepburn verbally sparring with anyone

♥ ♥ ♥ ♥ ♥

by Jesse:

Now, Voyager (cigarette scene at end)
An Affair to Remember (final scene)
Romeo and Juliet (1936), Shearer and Howard's Balcony Scene; both are too "old" to play Romeo and Juliet, but they carry it off)
Vertigo (when Novak comes out in the same dress/hairstyle)
Robin Hood (Flynn and de Havilland's balcony scene)

♥ ♥ ♥ ♥ ♥

by Neil Vokes (co-author/artist *The Black Forest*):

ONLY five, Sue...? -yeesh-

West Side Story (1961)—The balcony scene: it always reminds me of that pure, passionate, blind young love you felt the first time.

Spartacus (1960)—Kirk and Jean by the lake, where she's been swimming—she tells him that she's pregnant—the unadulterated love they have for each other, mixed with North's score, gets me every time.

Ladyhawke—Many great scenes, but the moment where Rutger and Michelle lie next to each other and the sun is rising—he's changing from wolf to man and she, woman to hawk, for an instant, they see each other as themselves, and nearly touch—oh God.

Spider-Man (2002)—When Toby bares his soul to Kirsten in his aunt's hospital room—heck, even I fell in love with him.

Nightmare Before Christmas (1993)—When Jack and Sally walk together, at the climax, singing to each other Elfman's beautiful music.

Whew—that was tough.

♥ ♥ ♥ ♥ ♥

by Steve Haberman: (writer *Life Stinks*, 1991):

Kim Novak emerging from the bedroom and sitting by the fire after James Stewart rescues her from drowning, in *Vertigo* (1958).

John Wayne finding Maureen O'Hara in his house after she cleaned it for him, in *The Quiet Man*.

The "just whistle" scene between Humphrey Bogart and Lauren Bacall in *To Have and Have Not*.

Grace Kelly's entrance and the slow motion kiss in *Rear Window* (1954).

Henry Fonda escorting "Clementine" to the unfinished church, in *My Darling Clementine* (1946).

♥ ♥ ♥ ♥ ♥

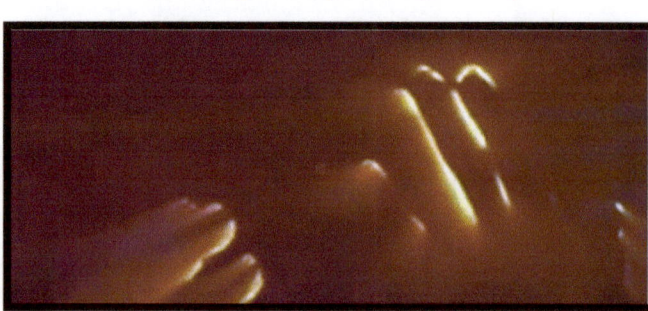

Before they change, cursed lovers Navarre and Isabeau almost touch as the sun rises in *Ladyhawke*.

by Erich Kuersten:

Greta Garbo and John Barrymore's one night together, in *Grand Hotel* (1932).

Christian Slater and Patricia Arquette on the rooftop, in *True Romance* (1993).

Bogart and Bacall shuffling between rooms with the bottle, in *To Have and Have Not*.

Leaving Las Vegas (1995), Nick Cage and Elizabeth Shue on the couch.

Winona Ryder and Gary Oldman sipping absinthe, in *Bram Stoker's Dracula* (1992).

by John Comito:
My favorite romantic scene in an old movie must be from *Top Hat* (1935), with Fred and Ginger, in the scene where Fred sings "Isn't It a Lovely Day to be Caught in the Rain."

by Gary D. Dorst:

The dance sequence between Amanda Bearse and the vampire, in *Fright Night* (1985).

Kevin McCarthy and Dana Wynter huddled together in the abandoned mine, before she turns, in *Invasion of the Body Snatchers* (1956).

Bruce Cabot's corny attempt to show his love for Fay Wray on the boat before she is kidnapped by the natives, in *King Kong*.

Barry Andrews' love scenes in the bedroom with Veronica Carlson, in *Dracula Has Risen from the Grave* (1968).

Ingrid Bergman with Spencer Tracy in her bedroom, when he treats her for her various fake injuries, in *Dr. Jekyll and Mr. Hyde* (1941).

Editor's Note: Can you tell that Gary watches mostly horror films?

by Sam Borowski:

That famous last scene between Humphrey Bogart and Ingrid Bergman in *Casablanca*. She loves him, and wants to be with him, but he wants her to live a better life without him and to help her husband fight the Nazis. Each one is more worried about the other's feelings and needs, and they are completely in love. This one does it for me.

A pretty close second is the scene between Jimmy Stewart and Donna Reed in *It's a Wonderful Life*, when the two of them are on the phone together sharing the receiver and listening to Sam Wainwright talk. No matter how hard Jimmy Stewart tries to ignore it, he cannot stop himself from kissing—and ultimately falling in love with—Donna Reed. The big kiss scene was very passionate for an older movie, at least in my humble opinion.

Jerry Maguire's (1996) final scene in the living room where he has to do his romantic best as the "Lord of the Living Room" to convince Renee Zellweger he really does love her and can put her needs first. He has to do it in front

Gary Oldman and Winona Ryder in *Dracula*

of all of the lonely women in Bonnie Hunt's women's group, and I think it's both touching and humorous and a very underrated scene, in a very underrated movie.

The scene right before the famous staircase scene that ends *Notorious* (1946). When Cary Grant comes to save Ingrid Bergman from Claude Rains, her Nazi "husband," who is poisoning her and she is near death. Despite the fact that she is half comatose, Bergman is still very happy to see Grant come to her side. And in that very brief moment, he has to convince her he *does* love her, so he can help get her strength back to try to walk her down the stairs and out of the house. He, of course, does love her, despite his jealousy that she is "married" to Rains, really just a spy assignment, and one that Grant could have easily convinced her *not* to do. But his pent-up passion and her happiness to see him, despite her drugged-up state, all come out in this scene.

Here is one that I guarantee no one else will bring up, but I love it anyway, and consider it very underrated: The scene where Max Cherry and title character *Jackie Brown* (1997) are having coffee in her kitchen, and a mid-40s Jackie, in trouble with the law, asks Max how he feels about getting old. He reveals how he had some kind of hair transplant to make him feel better about himself. Their honesty, along with the mel-

low romantic vibes in the background, is very poignant. I love this scene. It's no wonder that this one scene helped Robert Forster get nominated for an Oscar and resurrected his career. The only surprise is that Pam Grier was *not* nominated. Still a great scene, though.

♥ ♥ ♥ ♥ ♥

by J. Lansberg:

Buster Keaton and Marceline Day in *The Cameraman* (1928). The scene is in the beginning of the film, when Buster is working as a street photographer. Lindberg's tickertape parade goes by and the crowd presses Buster and Marceline Day together.

Humphrey Bogart and Lauren Bacall in *To Have and Have Not*. The scene where Bacall says "You know how to whistle, don't you Steve?"

Ricou Browning and Julie Adams in *Creature from the Black Lagoon* (1954). The scene where Adams is swimming in the lagoon and the creature is swimming under her, looking up.

Does inter-species romance in horror films count? What about King Kong and Fay Wray? There are a lot of good romantic scenes in horror films, although they are sort of doomed romances. (Lon Chaney and Mary Philbin, etc.)

What about Peter Lorre and Frances Drake in *Mad Love* (1935)? The part where the mad doctor has the wax statue of Drake in his apartment, and he realizes that it is really Drake.

Stan Laurel and Dorothy Christy in *Sons of the Desert*. The scene where Stan agrees to tell the truth to his wife about the convention he attended with Ollie, and Stan and the wife make up. She starts, playfully, messing up Stan's hair, much in the same way he usually does himself.

♥ ♥ ♥ ♥ ♥

by the eternal softie, Arthur Lundquist:

Okay, coming up with this list was a lot of fun, but I've got a feeling that these are not the most romantic scenes of all time, as much as the first ones I could think of. The more I think, the more I come up with.

In what has got to be the single most romantic movie I have ever seen, *The African Queen* (1951), middle-aged Kate Hepburn goes to middle-aged Humphrey Bogart the morning after their first night of love, and asks him with infinite vulnerability, "Dear, what is your first name?"

Who says you can't have romance *and* nudity! The most romantic moment in the most romantic movie of the 1980s, *Racing with the Moon* (1984): Elizabeth McGovern gives herself to Sean Penn as they swim in a secluded lake. Ah, a moment for eternity!

In *Love Me Tonight* (1932), a tailor (Maurice Chevalier) sings a song of love, "Isn't It Romantic." A customer hears his song and begins to sing it. He goes outside singing, and wherever he goes, people hear the song and begin singing it, until all Paris sings of love. The song makes its way across the French countryside, until at last it is heard and taken up by a French noblewoman (Jeanette MacDonald), whom the tailor will soon meet and fall in love with.

You will never know the true poetry of romance until you have seen Gene Kelly sit beside Leslie Caron on the banks of the Seine, late at night, and begin to sing "Our Love is Here to Stay," in *An American in Paris* (1951). "In time/the Rockies may crumble/Gibraltar may tumble/They're only made of clay. But/Our love is here to stay." Sigh.

In *The Abyss* (1989), trapped in a quickly inundating mini-sub, Mary Elizabeth Mastrantonio allows herself to die in the freezing water,

1970s reissue Italian poster for *An American in Paris* features Gene Kelly and Leslie Caron dancing on the banks of the Seine.

Ed Harris and Mary Elizabeth Mastrantonio in the heartbreaking drowning scene in *The Abyss*.

trusting her body to Ed Harris, who then moves heaven and earth to save her.

No, no! My romantic soul balks at the injustice of keeping myself to only FIVE titles! What is life without the pain of loss, the love that transcends death, the understandings that bind, the trust and respect that transcends worlds, expressed in the following titles:

WARNING: THEY ARE ROMANTIC SPOILERS, ALL!

At the end of *Matewan* (1987), the eternally wandering Chris Cooper dies, and so he will forever stay near the woman he truly loves, Mary McDonnell.

At the end of *La Strada* (1954), Anthony Quinn collapses on a beach, giving vent to a flood of tears for the loss of Giulietta Masina, whose love he had never valued until this moment. (Sob!)

At the end of *Double Indemnity* (1944), fatally bleeding Fred MacMurray tells insurance investigator Edward G. Robinson that he never found the killer in an insurance scam, because the murderer was as close as his office desk. "Closer than that," says Robinson. "I love you too," says MacMurray. Greater love hath no man.

At the end of *The Day the Earth Stood Still* (1951), before ascending into the heavens, alien Michael Rennie reaches out to Patricia Neal, with a universal gesture that bridges hearts and worlds.

Ah, love, love. Or as Countess DeLave (Mary Boland) says in *The Women* (1939)—*l'amour, l'amour*!

♥ ♥ ♥ ♥ ♥

by James J.J. Janis (contributor to *Midnight Marquee*):

Romantic scenes are tough for me, since it is not a genre I memorize. So, with your indulgence...

The Age of Innocence (1993)—The whole movie.

The Charge of the Light Brigade (1936)—The noble sacrifice of Errol Flynn, so his brother and his true love can find happiness together.

The sock in the jaw at the end of *Johnny Eager* (1942).

Jack Holt letting an incriminating letter fly out the window, so his friend and Fay Wray can be happy together, in *Dirigible* (1931).

Quasimodo and the gargoyle at the end of *The Hunchback of Notre Dame*: "Why was I not made of stone like thee?"

Runners up:

The noble sacrifices of so many men, so that their wives and children may survive, in *A Night to Remember* (1958).

The scene with Spartacus on the cross, when Jean Simmons tells him, "This is your son, Spartacus," in *Spartacus*.

The conclusion of the 1935 *A Tale of Two Cities*.

♥ ♥ ♥ ♥ ♥

by K. Kurek:

The Bride Came C.O.D (1940): The scene in the mineshaft where Bette Davis thinks she and Jimmy Cagney are trapped together, and she begins to warm to him (until she figures out the truth).

Also, any segment of *Portrait of Jennie* (1948), with Joseph Cotten and Jennifer Jones, or the final scene of the original movie, *The Ghost and Mrs. Muir*.

♥ ♥ ♥ ♥ ♥

by Buc:

Here's my quick vote for most romantic scenes...

The sweater scene in *The Americanization of Emily* (1964)—very sexy without much of any flesh showing—two people giving way to the inevitable conclusion of their love and passion (two totally different things).

87

Nickie (Cary Grant) introduces his grandmother (Cathleen Nesbitt) to Terry (Deborah Kerr) in *An Affair to Remember*.

Of course *Casablanca*—at the airport—two people in love who want something they can't have—the only acceptable deviation from love's true course—duty and honor must put romance on hold. Strangely we see this duel in *Star Wars* and it is one of the strongest underlying themes, even reflected in the music where the call-to-duty theme dominates.

An Affair To Remember—amazingly the greatest love moment is when Grant's character takes Kerr's character to meet his grandmother—a gesture that says "my grandmother is most precious to me, and for me to allow you to get close to both of us, you are precious also."

The Night of the Iguana (1964)—Kerr once again, describing a fetisher asking her for something personal. She gives that item to him, which is an amazing gesture of love for humanity (albeit a different kind of love and romance) and none of it happens on the screen—it's all narrative.

Betsy's Wedding—a great script from Alan Alda and great ensemble performances—while Alda's policewoman daughter is dancing with Anthony P., they discuss his love letters. All the women in this house just melt during this scene (I don't get it), but it seems that the give-and-take in this scene, as they interrelate and react to words not verbalized, takes mental romance to a new ecstasy.

♥   ♥   ♥   ♥   ♥

by Don G. Smith:

Well, you have really come up with a difficult assignment this time. Nevertheless, here are what I consider the most romantic scenes in the cinema (and I know I am forgetting some good ones!).

Leonard Whiting and Olivia Hussey in the balcony scene from Zeffirelli's *Romeo and Juliet* (1968). Unfortunately, most people have only seen parodies of this classic scene, and many who have seen a straight version do not fully grasp its beauty. The dizzying power and seriousness of young love has never been conveyed more beautifully. This version works better than most because, throughout screen history, older actors have had to play the lovers, because young actors lacked the talent, experience and range to carry it off. Hussey and Whiting succeed, making this balcony scene the pinnacle of screen romance.

Victor Moore and Beulah Bondi in the "Let Me Call You Sweetheart" scene from *Make Way for Tomorrow* (1937). Romance comes at both ends of the age spectrum. In this story, Moore and Bondi play an elderly couple whose financial difficulties and self-centered children require that they be separated at the end of their long life together. On their last afternoon together, knowing that after a few hours they will probably never see each other again, they go to a hotel ballroom and want to dance one last time. As they finally make it out onto the dance floor during a slow song, the band concludes and breaks into a swing number. Slowly, the disappointed couple begins to shuffle off the floor as the young swingers take over. But the band leader happens to notice the old couple, stops the orchestra, and begins "Let Me Call You Sweetheart." As Moore and Bondi hold each other on the dance floor, they speak of what their life together has meant. There is no happy ending to this film, but the ballroom scene is one of the most romantically poignant and tearful moments of cinema I have experienced.

Wuthering Heights French 1970 Re-issue poster

The promise on the moors scene from *Wuthering Heights* (1939). Laurence Olivier and Merle Oberon are Heathcliff and Cathy, in what must be one of the most romantic moments in screen history. They are young, and Cathy vows to Heathcliff that the moor will always be their castle and she will always be his queen. Having a classic score play in the background helps too. The final scene of the lovers' ghosts walking the moors makes the earlier scene even more memorable.

The final kiss montage from *Cinema Paradiso* (1988). You have to see this scene in the context of the entire film to realize its romantic impact. The movie concerns a boy growing up in Italy. His father, who runs a movie theater, must cut out all kissing scenes because of government regulations. Later, the boy finds the cut scenes edited together and runs them. This final scene is a fantastic testament to the power of film to produce the magic of romance.

Spencer Tracy's final monologue in *Guess Who's Coming to Dinner* (1967). To-

Lauren (Diane Lane) and Daniel (Thelonious Bernard) finally get their gondola ride in *A Little Romance*.

day this film can be considered mawkish and politically correct. Nevertheless, Tracy's final monologue, in which he gives his wholehearted blessing to his white daughter's love for a black man, is a lasting testament to the power of love to overcome all obstacles. The fact that he is also delivering a heartfelt message to co-star K. Hepburn adds to the film's overall power. In fact, Hepburn, knowing that this is Tracy's final great moment on screen, sheds real tears as she listens.

I would give honorable mention to the scene from *A Little Romance* (1979), in which runaways Diane Lane and Thelonius Bernard finally get to ride under the Bridge of Sighs in Venice in a gondola, and to the final scene from the very underrated *A Walk with Love and Death* (1969), in which Anjelica Huston (in her first film) and Asaf Dayan, playing doomed lovers in 14th-century France, await certain death in each other's arms, knowing that in the end not even death can overcome the power of love.

Well, these are my picks. I look forward to seeing what others come up with since I would predict little agreement in an area this personal.

♥ ♥ ♥ ♥

by Steve Thornton:

Here are my choices. Just to be creative, I decided to take all my selections from silent cinema. I think it turned out quite well, although I doubt that many others have seen these films. Enjoy!

The Big Parade (1925) — The conclusion of this powerful wartime drama finds wounded John Gilbert hobbling across hill and valley to be reunited with French peasant girl, Melisande (Renee Adoree). She sees him in the distance, recognizes him instantly and rushes to be by his side. This becomes a moving reminder of the obstacles that two lovers will overcome to be together.

The Gold Rush (1925) — In the wilderness of Alaska, the Lone Prospector (Charlie Chaplin) has invited lovely Georgia Hale and friends to a New Year's Eve banquet at his cabin. But the girl has blown off the invitation, thinking it was all in jest. The hours tick by and Charlie, after dreaming of the festive celebration, awakens to find himself all alone. The film demonstrates unrequited love at its most bittersweet.

The Student Prince in Old Heidelberg (1927) — Crown prince Karl Heinrich (Roman Novarro) must agree to an arranged marriage for the sake of his kingdom. But first, he pays a final call on Kathi (Norma Shearer), the commoner who has stolen his heart. They spend one last idyllic moment together, sharing smiles and tearful embraces, and then they part, knowing they will never see each other again.

Sunrise (1927) — Guilt and mistrust have splintered the relationship between rural couple George O'Brien and Janet Gaynor, after a temptress goads the man into contemplating murder against his long-time spouse. The unhappy pair then journeys to a distant city, where the urban distractions bring them no joy until they pause to witness a marriage in progress. As they listen to the words of commitment and fidelity, the spark of their love begins to rekindle and forgiveness finds its way into their hearts.

Lonesome (1928) — Jim (Glenn Tryon) and Mary (Barbara Kent) meet and spend a carefree day at Coney Island, until an accident splits up the pair, who then get lost in the crowd. Not knowing how he will ever see her again, Jim walks the long path back to his lonely apartment. Then, to his joy and astonishment, he discovers that the girl of his dreams has been living in the same building all along. Like life itself, love can have its surprises.

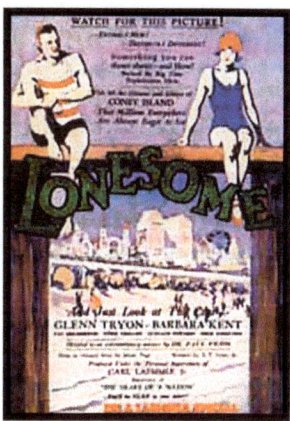

♥ ♥ ♥ ♥ ♥

by Jeff Thompson (contributor *Midnight Marquee*):

Almost any scene in *Somewhere in Time* (1980), "It is you?"; Elise and Richard's day together; the lovers' reunion in the afterlife, etc., but especially the moment when the photograph (of Elise), which makes Richard fall in love with Elise in 1980, is taken as Elise is gazing at Richard in 1912.

The exquisite flying scene between Lois and Superman in *Superman* (1978).

The final scene of *Titanic*—Rose, young again, reunites with Jack, in the afterlife.

The final scene of *Now, Voyager*—"Oh, Jerry, don't let's ask for the moon; we have the stars."

The final scene of *Casablanca*.

♥   ♥   ♥   ♥   ♥

by Ray Mooney:

Being a die-hard sci-fi man, I thought I could not conjure up thought of any such "girlie" films. But then I thought of a special film that is indeed romantic in the truest sense of the word. It is one of my favorites and one not seen much anymore. It is called *Make Way For Tomorrow* (1937) and used to be shown on AMC. It starred Beulah Bondi and Victor Moore as an elderly couple married over 50 years, who have lost their

home. Their ungrateful children who, for various reasons that unfold throughout the film, do not want their parents to live with them, decide that the mother should go to an old ladies' home and the father to live with one child, living far away, who will take him. Without rambling on too long, the romantic part of this film occurs when the couple have one last fling together in NYC and revisit the hotel where they spent their honeymoon. It is both touching sentimentally and romantically. They are wined and dined by the management, and there is a great scene where the bandleader Carlton Gorman (played by Gene Morgan) spots the couple on the dance floor trying to keep up to a modern fox-trot. He stops the band and strikes up "Let Me Call You Sweetheart," to which the couple waltz to the approval of all on the floor. The thank you from Victor Moore to Morgan and his nod in return is a great scene. But the ending is the part that causes "not a dry eye in the house." The couple are saying their last farewell at a train station, where Moore is about to board the passenger car that will take him away forever.

In a simple speech, they tell each other that the last 50 years were wonderful, that there could never have been anyone else, and that they will always love each other. This is ended with a last kiss. And all of this to the strains of "Let Me Call You Sweetheart." The final scene of Bondi trying to smile as she waves good-bye to the departing train, and the smile turning to tears as she turns away, pulls the trap door on the tears.

I guess what I am trying to say about this movie, and especially these scenes, is that age has no claim on romance. This elderly couple expressed love that was still as fresh as it was when they first met 50 years before.

But as far as a list of more romantic films goes, the closest I can come is when Jeff Morrow (Mitch McAfee) kissed Mara Corday in *The Giant Claw* (1957).

Argentinean one-sheet of *From Here to Eternity*

♥   ♥   ♥   ♥   ♥

by Peggy Gervasio:

From Here to Eternity (1953)—Deborah Kerr and Burt Lancaster embrace on the beach as the tide washes over them.

Love is a Many-Splendored Thing (1955)—William Holden and Jennifer Jones reflect on their love for each other, while standing on the hill that overlooks her hospital.

An Affair to Remember (1957)—The look on Cary Grant's face when he realizes that Deborah Kerr was the crippled woman depicted in his oil painting. He is upset until she says, "If you can paint, I can walk."

A Farewell to Arms (1957)—Jennifer Jones embraces Rock Hudson when he returns from the war, then decides to have a passionate session with him inside the hospital. You see her close the door to the room, then we jump to the next scene, which opens with the next morning.

Waterloo Bridge (1940)—Robert Taylor takes Vivien Leigh to his home. Later dancing to "Goodnight Sweetheart," she realizes that after that night she must never see him again.

♥ ♥ ♥ ♥ ♥

by Paul M. Jensen:

One reason why I found this a most difficult exercise, I eventually realized, is because romance usually implies a relationship in the process of evolving, so it is hard to identify a single scene that embodies that evolution. At the same time, I do not tend to seek out what might be called "Romantic Films," so I feared I would have little to draw on. But romance is a basic element of human nature and I soon found examples in more films than I expected—and sometimes in films that surprised me. Eventually, I even had to discard examples, including scenes from *Trouble in Paradise* (1932), *I'm No Angel* (1933), *The Scarlet Empress* (1934), *To Catch a Thief* (1955), *Vertigo* (1958), *Doctor Zhivago* (1965), *Petulia* (1968) and *Time After Time* (1979). The more I examined my choices, the more I realized that romance is usually an intoxicating concoction of uncertainty mixed with knowledge, of the unknown mixed with freshly minted intimacy, of comfort touched with an edge of tension--a simultaneous sensation of anticipation and satisfaction. It usually involves desire on the verge of being fulfilled, or just starting to be fulfilled, or just being recognized. Yet the emotional range can also involve frustration or anticipated loss; in a few cases, it might even feature stability and familiarity.

The following, then, are my current Five Favorite Romantic Scenes (in no particular order):

Queen Christina (1933)—Christina (Greta Garbo) "memorizes" the room in which she has discovered love.

True Heart Susie (1919)—William (Robert Harron), caught in a loveless marriage, gazes one night out his window as Susie (Lillian Gish) thinks of him and does the same, with each not realizing what the other is doing.

Swing Time (1936)—The characters played by Fred Astaire and Ginger Rogers are drawn together in a dance number that moves gracefully from tentative contact to enthusiastic commitment.

Cabaret (1972)—The "Maybe This Time" sequence captures the freshness of a newly intimate relationship, as Sally (Liza Minnelli) privately hopes for the best, while fearing another disappointment.

The Thin Man—Romance that endures over time and familiarity is captured in the banter of Nick (William Powell) and Nora (Myrna Loy), during their first scene together.

♥ ♥ ♥ ♥ ♥

MOVIES WE MUST HAVE IF WE WERE LOST ON A DESERT ISLAND!

*Just sit right back and you'll hear the tale,
the tale of a fateful trip,
that started from a tropic port aboard a tiny ship.
The mate was an obsessed film fan,
the skipper loved films more,
five passengers set sail that day for a three hour tour, a three hour tour.
The weather started getting rough,
the tiny ship was lost,
if not for the courage
of the fearless crew
the Bounty would be lost.
The ship set down on the shore
of this uncharted desert isle,
with Bryan Senn, Greg Mank too,
Gary and his wife,
MidMar's other stars,
the Professor and a DVD, LOST on MidMar's isle!*

Here's the scenario we gave our crack writing staff. Your wife or family has taken a crowbar and pried your couch potato butt off the living room sofa, pulled your latest *MidMar* from your clutching hands and is making you go on a cruise. Oh no! No movies for a week! But then you heave a sigh of relief, you sneaked a peek at the cruise brochure and found out they have, YES—a DVD player in each stateroom! You wait 'til nobody is home, quickly open your luggage, and shove in your three most favorite movies in the world (2 had to be horror/fantasy/SF), movies you know you can watch over and over and over. You board the ship, happily knowing you can hide from the horrors of *The View* and *The Hills*, while relaxing in your cabin with a flick. But wait, what is that noise? We're in a storm! We're shipwrecked on a desert island! And you're the only one with entertainment! As you peddle your bicycle made of palm leaves, creating electricity for your television and DVD player, you grin, happily secure in your good taste, obvious intelligence, and stellar movie choices.

• • • • •

Bryan Senn

Only *three* movies?!! Forever?!! How can one possibly choose from so many wonderful cinematic jewels? But...if such a dastardly event occurred and I was indeed trapped on the proverbial desert island with my DVD player and only three movies, I'd have to select *The Old Dark House* (1932), *King Kong* and *Young Frankenstein*.

The Old Dark House: James Whale's quirky, macabre masterpiece. As a brilliant character study, it only grows more fascinating—and more humorous—with each viewing. It is one of those rare gems that delivers something new every time you see it, whether it be through the witty dialogue, the eccentric performances and mannerisms of its impeccable cast, or Whale's subtle directorial sleight-of-hand. And having only three films to watch over the course of untold years (God—and jungle fever—willing), such a quality would be a definite plus.

King Kong: The ultimate adventure movie. Whenever I watch Kong battle those lifelike denizens of time-gone-by or search valiantly for that tiny symbol of his unrequited love, I never fail to be gloriously entertained. Besides, *Kong* is not simply the tale of a giant gorilla, but (sappy as it may sound) a symbol of the innate nobility—and tragedy—of the human spirit and condition. So whenever I start dejectedly kicking sand around, I'll just pop in the *King* for a *Kong*-sized lift of spirits. (Plus, I might get a few hut-building pointers from the Skull Island natives.)

For my third and final choice: *Young Frankenstein*. Being stranded on a desert island may not be so bad for a time, but I'm sure at one point or another I'd come within spitting distance of losing my sense of humor. And, bar none, Mel Brooks' loving parody is (to me) the funniest film ever made. Beyond that, it cleverly walks that thin line between honoring and poking fun at three of my favorite films (*Frankenstein*,

Bride of Frankenstein, and *Son of Frankenstein*)—without a single misstep. Consequently, watching *Young Frankenstein* is like viewing four films in one, for it immediately conjures up in my mind's eye images from those three beloved classics. So, if I start thinking what a lousy hand the deck of fate had dealt me by turning me into a modern day Bob Denver, I'll just chant along with Gene Wilder as he shouts, "Des-tin-nee, Des-tin-nee, no escaping, that's for me!"—and have another piece of coconut cream pie.

• • • • •

John Stell

Ignoring the unlikelihood that, even if I could have my choice of three films to pass the time on a deserted isle, the Professor would be along to make electricity, my triple feature would be selected on the criteria of fast paced, fun entertainment. Great films such as *Rosemary's Baby* (1968) may be better, artistically speaking, than my personal choices, but I certainly couldn't watch that film over and over again without wanting to eventually feed myself to the sharks—*Jaws 5* anyone? Now then, the envelope please.

As a fan of horror's first Golden Age, I would have to choose one of the Universal classics. *Bride of Frankenstein* wins in a heartbeat for two reasons: it offers not one but three great performances, and it was directed by James Whale, the premier director of the 1930s. *Bride* lets us see Karloff at his finest, bringing many different levels to the monster. In the blind man sequence, Karloff runs the emotional gamut: He is nervous and timid at first meeting the hermit, ecstatic at finding a friend, saddened when his happiness turns out to be all too brief and "monstrous" when the "concerned" strangers cause the safe haven to be burned to the ground.

But we not only get Karloff, we also see Ernest Thesiger as the deliciously evil Dr. Pretorius and Colin Clive as the most admirable of mad scientists. While Clive's doctor still means well, the eccentric Thesiger nonetheless blackmails him. The result, of course, is the ultimate creation scene, with Whale's camera brightly lighting the anxious scientists as they await the upcoming "wedding." Whale's sense of black humor aside, *Bride* strikes an emotional chord (a teary-eyed Karloff at film's end) unmatched by many horrors of the same period. It is a film close to my heart for nostalgic reasons admittedly, but it is also the high point in the series of Whale's, and Universal's, classics.

Since, in fact, horror stars frequently make a horror film ultimately memorable, my next selection would be *The Comedy of Terrors* (1963), which gives us genre greats Vincent Price, Boris Karloff, Peter Lorre, and Basil Rathbone. Again, these actors represent such a vast amount of horror history that watching this one film inevitably brings to mind the participants' previous work. Karloff and Rathbone are hilarious with their slightly bent characters, Lorre is lovable as the unwitting assistant to murder and Price is, well, priceless as the villainous funeral parlor director, who creates his own clientele.

The film is consistently entertaining because one of the four key players is always on the screen having fun, whether it's

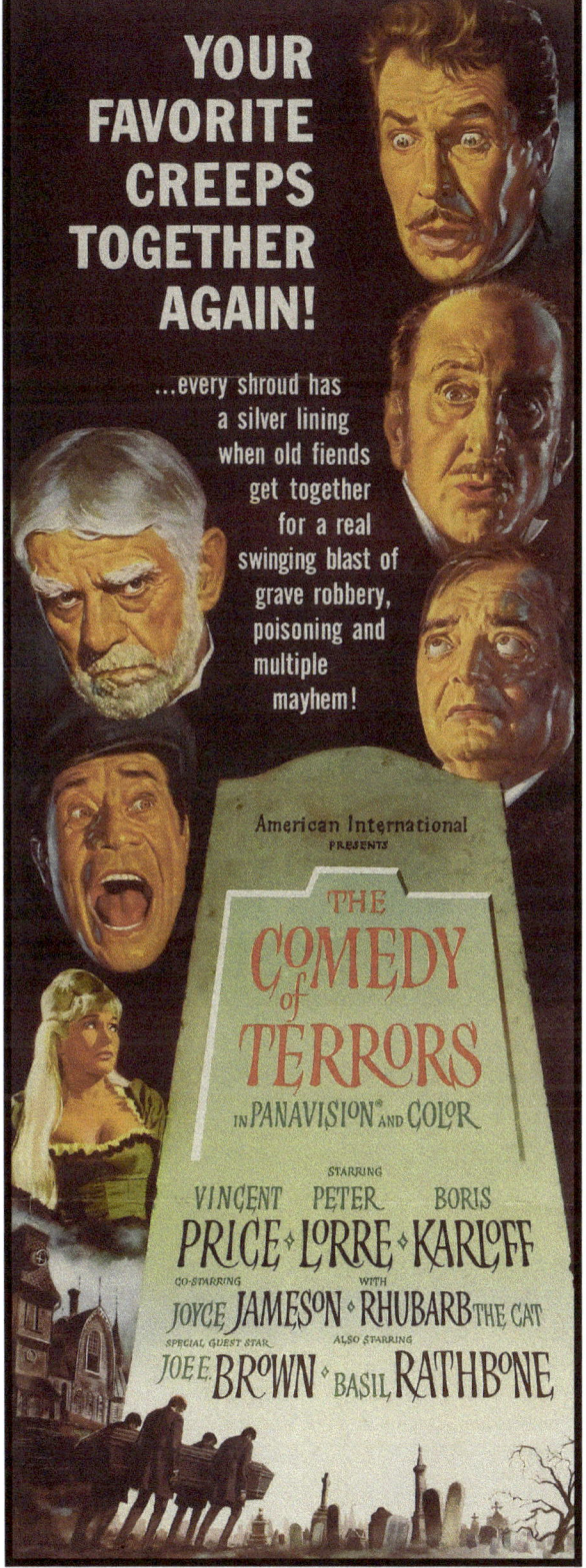

Price hurling insults like there's no tomorrow, or Lorre trying to get up his courage to take action or Karloff whining about his "medicine," or Rathbone asking, yet once again, "What place is this?" The film is unpretentious, wicked black humor, just the sort of thing a castaway horror fan would need.

Lastly, I would require a more recent film title which, although not strictly a horror film, has a horrific atmosphere. The film, *The Usual Suspects* (1994), is one of those "omniscient puppet master killer" movies, wherein a mysterious, unscrupulous villain manipulates those around him, knowing exactly how they will react. But the film works because it provides a constantly twisting plot, more of that black humor I love so much, and an ending which, if not necessarily surprising in the "who" department, does delight in the "how" area with respect to the method the killer utilizes to carry out his deception. The film also harkens back to thrillers of yesteryear, with mystery men donning the quintessential trench coat, hat and dark gloves. Oscar-winning screenwriter Christopher McQuarrie gives the villain a mystical quality, making all those who know the name of Keyser Soze fear him. It's a film that can be watched over and over again, and each time something new arises.

The above three films are certainly not everyone's idea of a good time, on an island or otherwise. But I can think of worse ways to pass the time on a deserted isle, like listening to that Kathie Lee person singing the Carnival Cruise theme over and over again. Some horrors are better left unheard!

• • • • •

Lynn Naron
With the choice of only three movies for a lifetime on a deserted island, I'm struck by the unfairness of the concept. Only three. Three hard, tough choices, but like all adversity in life, choices guaranteed to make a better, stronger person of you—*Earth vs. The Flying Saucers* (1956), *Island of Lost Souls* (1932) and *King Kong*. There, I feel more manly already.

And behind door number one is *Earth vs. The Flying Saucers*. No doubt there are better Harryhausen films, but this is the first of Ray's work I remember. Oh boy and do I remember it well. Every time I watch this little B jewel I'm transported back to Hobbs (the town as pretty as its name), New Mexico. I'm eight years old and mom has finally given in to the eternal pestering of her goofy youngest child. I could go to the movies *alone*! Seated in the dark with my Ma Brown's dill pickle (yes, pickle!), those damn flying discs just scared the living daylights outa me for what seemed like an eternity. I'm trapped in the theater because part of my reasoning to mom was how independent and grown up enough I am to go alone to the theater. No big brother to cling to and just a ratty old seat in a rundown movie house to hide behind; why did I talk mom into this? Jeez, now there's some guy with his brain exposed and saucer men with stiff arms blasting away with deadly rays! Somehow, just somehow, I survived the world's destruction and, after the end credits, I had to walk back home (some 15 or 20 minutes) with the sun setting. By now my imagination is running wild and the possibility of one of those dastardly saucers coming out of nowhere gave wings to my feet as I ran back to the safety of my hearth in record time. But was I deterred by all the mayhem and menace? Heck no! Like the naive hero in *The Howling Man*, my poor mother had unwittingly unleashed the worst of all creatures into the world...a monster loving, film-addicted eight-year-old.

Island of Lost Souls was the very first "must track down and see film" I was able to view before the days of instant VCR gratification. Those of us who struggled to find lost gems before the video explosion well remember the pulse-pounding, heart-racing experience of finally satisfying that aching brain-itch. For me it was Westercon XXX in Vancouver, British Columbia, sometime in the early 1970s, when a tattered, contrasty 16mm print of *ILS* was shown for an enthusiastic bunch of film freaks. Charles Laughton as the absolute best mad scientist (sorry Mr. Clive), a gorgeous heroine, an exotic/erotic femme fatale, a hero who wasn't a complete idiot or as bland as a Yani concert and of course, the Sayer of the Law, Bela Lugosi. Mix these rare ingredients with a sick and twisted screenplay, and you have a perfect recipe for the stuff of nightmares.

Finally my last choice is the eighth wonder of the cinematic world, *King Kong*. The perfect adventure/fantasy film and one I never tire of watching. Ted Turner deserves the undying praise of us all for restoring this incredible classic to as pristine condition as we will probably ever get to see. Midland-Odessa, Texas's *The Million Dollar Movie* would show this marvel during the summer in the late '50s and early '60s. I'd park myself in front of the living room air-conditioner, pissed because the transmission was never super clear and we'd get image ghosting. But, there was Kong, towering 50 feet tall, even if it was on a small TV screen, and soon I would be transported to Skull Island with Denham and Driscoll and finally getting my share of the riches when the big ape would be put on display back in New York. I would cringe and lower my eyes when the planes began their deadly strafing of my hero. Even today Willis O'Brien's artistry in bringing Kong to life and then to death tugs at my heartstrings and brings a tear to my eye.

So slip a disc in the DVD, little buddy, and I know your three selections are going to be just as great as mine.

• • • • •

Don G. Smith

If I were sent off to an island and could take with me only three genre films, my first choice would be *Macbeth* (1971, directed by Roman Polanski). I would choose it for its poetry and for its themes, one of which is the question of human beings as social animals. Sure, the film is filled with witch's prophesies and bloody murder committed in the dead of night, but besides the entertainment inherent in this horror, I would want to consider and reconsider my nature as a social animal and as a human being. No other author has ever matched Shakespeare in his ability to generate, through imagination, the reader's consideration of our multi-faceted human nature. Combine that with the dark artistry of Roman Polanski, and you have a genre film that rewards repeated viewings.

The second film I would take is *Fahrenheit 451* (1967, directed by Francois Truffaut). I am what I have read, and our great books are the repository of the wisdom of Western civilization, which has shaped me. Montague's struggle to be human in the face of a de-humanizing environment resonates with me, and I would want that film on hand to remind me of what is important in living a human life. Of course, Ray Bradbury, the author of *Fahrenheit 451*, is reportedly working on a new film adaptation of his book, and if it becomes a reality, I reserve the right to substitute that version for Truffaut's if I find it superior.

My third choice would be *The Seventh Seal* (1957, directed by Ingmar Bergman). The knight in that film is Everyman, seeking answers to the mysteries of life, while playing a chess game with the personification of death. Set in the Middle Ages

against a backdrop of human carnage, disease and witch burnings, *The Seventh Seal* raises questions of God and the Devil, of good and evil, of meaning and meaninglessness. If I were alone on an island, these issues would remain of paramount importance to me.

• • • • •

Dennis Fischer

In choosing films for a desert island, there are a number of factors to be considered. Presumably, this is a *Gilligan's Island* kind of island where a DVD can work. (If Russell Johnson's Professor could make all those nifty gadgets, surely he could have gotten the castaways off the island. Obviously, he enjoyed being the most eligible bachelor on an island with two attractive women and had the others completely buffaloed.)

Now there are five film classics that I have never gotten tired of, no matter how many times I've seen them (*Citizen Kane* [1941], *King Kong*, *Casablanca*, *Adventures of Robin Hood* and *Thief of Bagdad* [1940]), but if they were the only films I could watch, would that still be true? Perhaps I would want a comedy to distract me from my troubles, yet it doesn't take too many viewings before I'd memorize every line of dialogue in that visually delightful comic fantasy *Monty Python and the Holy Grail* (1975) and it no longer strikes me as being anywhere near as funny as when I chuckled and guffawed my way through it the first time. So as much as I love them, comedies would be out.

Then, perhaps, I should consider films that might help me survive on a desert island. Certainly, *Lord of the Flies* (1960), chronicling the adventures of some English schoolboys who survive a plane crash, warns of the dangers of libertarianism, and demonstrates the chaos that results if there are no rules. *The Most Dangerous Game* (1932) excites and delights as Joel McCrea uses his wits to survive, but probably isn't as much practical use as Luis Buñuel's *Robinson Crusoe* (1952) would be with its great performance by Dan O'Herlihy (*Invasion U.S.A.*, *RoboCop*) as Defoe's shipwrecked sailor, while *Shipwrecked* (1990), an enjoyable pirate yarn, boasts better booby-traps. Even such famous island fare as *Swiss Family Robinson*, *Swept Away...by an unusual destiny in the blue sea of August*, and Nicholas Roeg's *Castaway*, though they offer some thoughtful ideas about the expectations of the sexes, would not bear up under endless re-viewing.

Hence, the films I would select would have to be musicals, because however slight the plot, good music is something one never gets tired of hearing. Some potential genre vehicles I had to reject out of hand because some aspect of them just doesn't hold up (e.g. as marvelous as Mozart is, Bergman's version of *The Magic Flute* (1975) sings the score in the director's native Swedish instead of the original German; Powell and Pressberger's *Tales of Hoffman* (1951) is a visual delight, but Offenbach's score is not an aural experience I could endlessly repeat; *Jesus Christ Superstar* (1973) is a religious fantasy with a tuneful Andrew Lloyd Webber score, but Norman Jewison's visuals look like sub-par Ken Russell.)

So what does that leave? My first choice is Ken Russell's *Tommy* (1975), an audacious film based on The Who's Rock Opera. The first film to be done in Dolby stereo, *Tommy* sweeps the viewer away in a barrage of whacked-out visuals which actually clarify composer Pete Townshend's tale of a young boy who becomes psychosomatically deaf, dumb and blind after witnessing his mother (Ann-Margret) and her lover (Oliver Reed in an incredibly expressive performance, despite being unable to sing a note) kill his father. Tommy becomes a national pinball hero who succeeds because he plays with no distractions. Russell interprets the tale as a religious fable, with Tommy being tempted or abused by the material world as he seeks to be reunited with his father (who is equated with God), gets proclaimed the new messiah and then being rejected by the crowd because Nirvana does not prove to be effortless. It truly is an amazing journey to enlightenment with a powerful pop score and Daltrey's definitive versions of "I'm Free" and "Sensation."

Next would be Brian De Palma's *Phantom of the Paradise* (1974), with a surprisingly rocking score from Paul Williams, a wicked sense of humor and satire and a truly terrific performance by the underrated and underutilized William Finley as temperamental, ripped-off, rock composer Winslow Leach. The film is dazzling, demented, fast and funny, paying tribute not only to *Phantom of the Opera*, but also German expressionism, Hitchcock, *The Picture of Dorian Gray*, Phil Spector and *The Manchurian Candidate,* among other influences. De Palma whips the melange together into an original offering that knocked my socks off when I first saw it; it still does. Filled with great bits by juicy Jessica Harper, campy Gerrit Graham, unsung comedy stalwarts Archie Hahn, Harold Oblong and Jeffrey Comaner, judicious use of George Memmoli, and Paul Williams as a truly swinish Swan.

Lastly I would pick the queen of the midnight movies, *The Rocky Horror Picture Show*, not because it's a brilliant homage to Hammer-style Frankenstein films (it isn't), or because of its risqué philosophy of "Don't Dream It, Be It," which invited cultists to jump up on stage and participate, but dammit, Richard O'Brien's rock score is so lively and so likable, singing as it does about things with which I could easily identify (such as the pleasures of watching sci-fi double features or making out in the back row), that I've never tired of it. Tim Curry's flamboyant performance as the seductive but sinister transsexual scientist from outer space still seems to me a remarkable achievement (here the supremely self-indulgent scientist is truly the monster, yet he too remains sympathetic), celebrating hedonism while condemning it, blurring the lines of gender preferences and making them seem unimportant, and partying to the hilt. He certainly isn't a good role model, but then again, neither is Scarlet O'Hara. Trapped on an island might be less lonely if there was a sense that being totally self-centered is okay, and that, on celluloid, the party can last forever, or at least until one can "time-warp" out of that situation. Let there be lips!

William Finlay in The Phantom of the Paradise

• • • • • •

Nathalie Yafet

My first question is: Why would I have a DVD and a television set if I were stranded on a desert island? That aside, I could not be without *The Black Cat* (1934), *The Black Room* (1935), and *It's a Gift*.

The Black Cat has to be one of the most watchable horror movies ever made. It has style, bravura characterizations, gorgeously sinister music, inner angst and only one weak scene. I was 14 when I first saw this film and I don't think I moved a muscle the entire time. It was 16 years later before I would see it again. My husband Steven and I had just purchased a VCR, and we bought a tape with *The Black Cat* and *The Raven*. That same day, I ran it three times. Steven usually dislikes seeing the same movie more than once, but even he can be coaxed into seeing it—just one more time. All the elements—acting, music, costumes, lighting, screenplay—work together like a well-written symphony. Karloff and Lugosi, in particular, are both at the height of their powers. Lugosi's Werdegast is the heartrending violin and Karloff's Poelzig the sinister bassoon. My favorite scene is Poelzig's eerily beautiful "game of death" soliloquy accompanied by the slow movement of Beethoven's *Seventh Symphony*, with Karloff's Svengali-like voice convincing us that this extraordinarily evil man is also a helpless victim of the war. But if I did have this film with me on my desert island, I would definitely have to slice out the unbearable "comic relief."

My favorite, *The Black Room*, is another film that never bores me. Where else could I get three Karloff performances for the price of one! Robert Allen is tedious, but I do my best to ignore him. I dote on the swaggering, remorseless, unkempt Gregor and the courteous, princely, dog-loving Anton. Their reactions in the "Love is Like Music" scene are perfection—Anton truly appreciating both the woman and her art, and Gregor leering at Thea, clapping boorishly and not giving a hoot about the song. It's a joy to see Karloff's Anton swing into action, with his one good arm, sword in hand, and his perverse brother inciting with his, "Kill him, Thor!" There's a slick little moment later, when Gregor is impersonating Anton and the cheering villagers wave at him in his coach en route to the church; Anton/Gregor's natural sneer flickers over his face for an instant before he covers quickly with a smile. *The Black Room* is a Grimm's fairy tale where the princess does not necessarily get her prince, and good perishes along with evil.

A desert island would be depressing without at least one comedy. My choice is W.C. Fields' tour de force, *It's a Gift*. Fields is Harold Bissonette, pronounced Bis-o-nay, the owner of a local grocery store. He suffers hilariously through one ridiculous situation after another. His family abuses him, he lives in fear of the blind man, Mr. Muckle, who shatters his glass door and breaks light bulbs, is bested by Baby LeRoy, and yet triumphs over every obstacle, becoming fabulously wealthy at the picture's end. The best scene has our hero Bissonette trying desperately to sleep on the back porch after his wife harangues him all night long. He crashes through a porch

glider and is disturbed by—a milkman clinking his bottles up and down all three flights of stairs, a relentless insurance salesman, Baby LeRoy dropping grapes, an icepick, a squeaky clothesline, a vegetable salesman, and finally—a fly. Fields' peerless timing and priceless reactions—together with the whole cacophonous ensemble—make me laugh so hard that my eyes water and my stomach hurts!

• • • • •

Joe Guilfoyle

There have been many tales woven from the premise, "If you were stranded on a desert island..." At parties, after appropriate libation, I can recall serious discussions aimed at selecting everything from the top three "Hammer" ladies with whom to share your island retreat to the best trio of salted snacks to munch on until your ultimate rescue. However, the burden of selecting only three films for the island's movie library would seem the ultimate "ponder puzzle."

After due consideration, my first choice is *The Magnificent Seven* (1960). The film, which was directed by John Sturges, was loosely based on the Japanese picture *Seven Samurai*. The remake might better be called charisma on horseback. For stylized hokum, it has no equal. It offers a first class blend of acting talent, music and quotable dialogue. When it was released in 1961, only Yul Brynner was an international star, but his footsteps would soon be followed in short order by Steve McQueen, Charles Bronson, James Coburn and, to a lesser extent, Robert Vaughn and Eli Wallach. The script by William Roberts (and uncredited Walter Newman) is the equivalent of a testosterone highball with the principals delivering lines like, "We deal in lead, friend," with all appropriate gusto. According to Neele Adams, Steve McQueen's first wife, the set was anything but a happy experience for Yul Brynner, who was constantly dealing with the young "upstarts," all of whom would do anything to steal a scene from the veteran star. In her book, *My Husband, My Friend*, Adams said McQueen and his young co-stars spent their off screen hours inventing bits of business (e.g. McQueen shaking the shotgun shells next to his ear before loading the weapon) to draw the audience's attention from Brynner to them. *The Magnificent Seven* also benefits from the most recognizable score in the history of modern film. Granted, today's audience may not know the source of Elmer Bernstein's rousing music, but it is unforgettable and the perfect background for young action-oriented stars in the first major film of their careers.

The second film for the island library would be *Horror of Dracula* (1958). Arguably Hammer's finest hour (actually one hour and twenty-two minutes), *Horror of Dracula* was the first significant pairing of cinema icons Christopher Lee and Peter Cushing after *Curse of Frankenstein*. It also established Hammer as a company devoted to the production of horror films, a genre it would easily dominate for the next two decades. Based on the novel by Bram Stoker, the film was released in the UK simply as *Dracula*. Directed by the venerable Terence Fisher, *Horror of Dracula* is sinister fun, which easily surpasses all previous adaptations of the novel, including Lugosi's landmark ver-

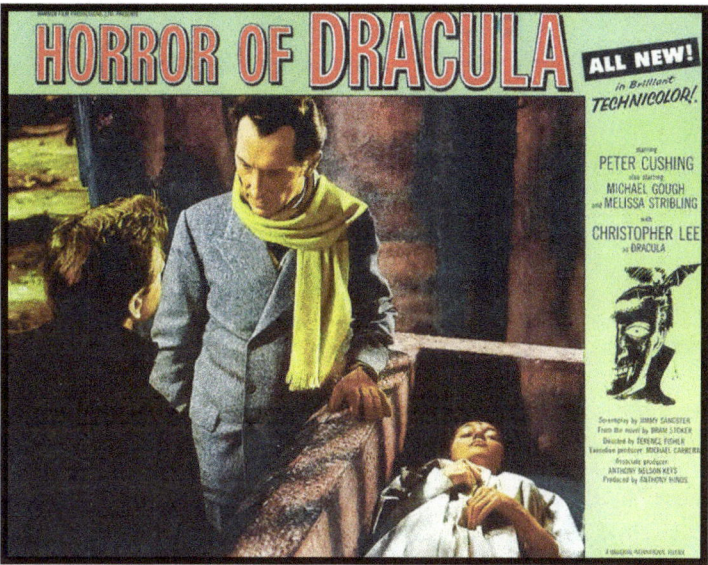

sion. Even film fanatics, whose loyalty and devotion rests with the horror films produced by Universal in the 1930s and 1940s, grudgingly admit *Horror of Dracula* is something special. For Hammer fans it was our first exposure to the studio's famous "style" characterized by first class production values (which we now know were accomplished on very modest budgets) and chillingly perfect scores, in this case, by the brilliant composer James Bernard. Unquestionably, however, the real measure of this classic lies in the performances of Lee and Cushing. Both men may have lost some artistic freedom through their close association with the horror genre, but it did provide them a stature reserved for the celebrated few. Christopher Lee and Peter Cushing would be the defining figures in the horror film for a generation, and *Horror of Dracula* was their finest collaboration.

The third required film for any extended period of isolation is the wondrous *The Seventh Voyage of Sinbad* (1958). After learning his trade from legendary effects wizard Willis O'Brien, Ray Harryhausen began creating his unforgettable magic with

films like *Earth vs. The Flying Saucers* and *Twenty Million Miles to Earth*, but it was his creations for the *The Seventh Voyage of Sinbad*, his first color film, which bewitched a generation. *Voyage* is a near perfect fantasy adventure which is as captivating today as when it was released in 1958. Surrounded by an excellent Bernard Herrmann score, Sinbad (Kerwin Mathews) confronts the arch villainy of Sokurah, the Magician (Torin Thatcher), and, in the process, outwits the mystical beasts of Ray Harryhausen's fertile imagination. In 1995 Mr. Harryhausen was awarded a special Oscar for his contribution to special effects in film. It seems certain the Academy could not forget the Cyclops and sword-wielding skeleton from *The Seventh Voyage of Sinbad* (among his other achievements in "Super Dynamation") in reaching their decision on this overdue honor.

The desert island scenario forced me to leave behind a number of wonderful films, some of which could be argued are "better" movies than the ones I've selected, but for me, this is an exercise more of the heart than the mind. Sitting in the dark of the theater, precious few films during my life have been able to take me away and open my imagination to the heroes, the villains and primordial creatures of different places and different times. When you find such flicks, you should never be without them.

• • • • •

David H. Smith

Castaway on some deserted island, one can only hope there are enough modern conveniences to make salvaging three videos a viable endeavor. Hopefully there'll be a comfy chair, a big screen TV and a DVD, and a generator to juice the blamed thing. And, since this is *Midnight Marquee* after all, some of the creature comforts should deal with creatures.

First of all, I would have to have at least one movie that bore a relation to my circumstances. The finest of all, without a doubt, from its soaring theme music to its volcanic finale, has to be *Mysterious Island* (1961). The intelligentsia might claim I should look to the Jules Verne source before watching a movie adaptation, but how on earth can the French author's tale of Civil War soldiers marooned on a deserted island populated only by the occasional capybara or dugong compare to the stirring sights of Ray Harryhausen's marvelous stop-motion crabs, bees and octopi?

I muddled though the basis novel as best I could as a youth and perhaps I should give it another chance, but I doubt anything in its pages could equal the adventure wrought on screen by director Cy Endfield. After a group of Union army soldiers escape from a Confederate prison and wash ashore on the title

bit of real estate after descending from a transcontinental and Pacific balloon ride, the stops are pulled for a pic of stirring adventure that is impossible to dislike. The saturnine presence of Captain Nemo explains the mysteries, and the wonder of it all comes to a head in a race against time to salvage a sunken pirate ship even as the island sinks beneath the waves. The filmmakers were even inventive enough to figure out a way to get a couple of women cast ashore as well, fulfilling the genre requisite quotas for romance as well as terrified shrieks. Again and again, over and over, *Mysterious Island* is a terrific film.

If that all seems a bit trite, then surely my second selection for repeated viewings rates a bit higher on the originality scale. *Highlander* (1986) takes what could have been a laughable notion and imbues it with enough lusty adventure, whimsy, tragedy and romance to satisfy even the most curmudgeonly film fan. With director Russell Mulcahy's fast-paced editing and the rapid-fire scenario, the saga of men cursed (as opposed to blessed) with immortality, fighting among themselves through the centuries to attain a mysterious "prize," is a film epic that, in other hands, would have easily and understandably fallen apart. But not here, and repeated viewings do little to dilute its grandiosity.

Immortality has been the focus of many a motion picture—vampire films all deal with it, of course, as do adaptations of H. Rider Haggard and James Hilton novels. But here in *Highlander*, the theme is treated not so much as a wonderful existence but as often an effort to endure. The weight of the passing years, the inherent loneliness, the boredom that inevitably comes and the loss of identity are all handled sensitively and with a kind of sweeping grandeur. The hero waxes tragic on occasion, but he is justified in his bitterness, and one can feel the burden of four centuries wearing him down. On many levels, including new ones I find on every viewing, *Highlander* is a wondrous and thought-provoking film.

Getting those synapses in gear is half the fun with my third choice. The other half is simply turning off your brain and delighting in *Head* (1968), the only feature film effort of The Monkees. Rather than repeating their stock television personae for the big screen, the four members of the band (as script co-writers) opted to deride their own manufactured image, mocking Hollywood stereotypes at the same time and delighting in showing themselves as distinct and not necessarily compatible parts of a synthetic sum.

The movie is a Möbius strip of vignettes, looping back at the finale to its beginning. The band members had grown considerably as actors, songwriters and musical performers (in spite of, or perhaps more likely *to spite*, their detractors) in their two years together, and they probably knew *Head* represented their grand valediction. It is a plot-less film that can be end-

Australian poster for *Head*

the signal fire, Friday, and shoot the flare pistol, Gilligan—we've got to get home!

• • • • •

Lou Gaul

A desert island. A lifetime there. Only three movies.

How cruel can Gary and Susan Svehla be?

Here it goes.

I'd pack *Shane* (1953), *The Exorcist* and *Abbott and Costello Meet Frankenstein*. Stop snickering.

For those narrow-minded purists who consider *Shane* strictly a Western, not a horror film, think again. Dressed in more black than Dracula, wearing a killer's smirk that would chill Steven Seagal and wound tighter than Demi Moore's stomach muscles, Jack Palance represents death as the gunfighter Wilson. He's out to obliterate a frontier family by physically destroying the father, psychologically maiming the mother and totally traumatizing their eight-year-old son. Even Hannibal Lecter would tip his hat to Wilson, whose death-like presence is suggested when director George Stevens photographs the character entering the bar with antlers—the symbol of death—clearly mounted above and beside the saloon's swinging doors. He places the gunslinger in the middle of the frame.

With his bright blonde hair and shiny buckskin garb gleaming in the sunlight, Alan Ladd's Shane, like Peter Cushing's Van Helsing, obviously represents the good in the world. During the climactic saloon gunfight, Shane's bullets to the heart send Wilson reeling backward into barrels, which all symbolically bury him, much like a vampire put to rest. But Shane is also injured, riding away wounded and hanging slightly from the side of his horse, suggesting that good may also be dying in a world becoming progressively more ruthless, cold and ugly. Even Clive Barker doesn't have thoughts this dark.

Taking along *The Exorcist* is a no-brainer. It's so psychologically chilling, horrifically devastating and physically numbing that people remember where they were the first time they saw it, just the way they remember where they were when JFK

lessly scrutinized by pundits for hidden meanings and deeper insight, or it can be simply dismissed as a self-indulgent home movie of swollen egos and palatine teen heartthrobs having a pot party. Either way, it's a hummable, fun excursion with images of 1960s' psychedelia that hasn't aged badly at all.

With those three being marooned on a desert island might be just a bit more tolerable. But wait! What's in that issue of *Variety* that washed up on shore? All four Monkees have reunited for a new record and tour? A "director's cut" of *Highlander* with additional footage has just been released? Light was shot. (I was in South Jersey's Westmont Theater on opening day with my wife, who refused to even glance up at the screen, stared at the floor for more than two hours and was petrified just by the sounds William Friedkin created. She's still angry at me for taking her to see it and doesn't believe I had no idea how frightening it would be. For the 24 years of our married life, pea soup has never been part of our dinner menu.)

Lean, mean, and obviously intended as an assault on the audience, *The Exorcist* didn't play by any rules. My Catholic upbringing made it almost seem like a documentary, one that said evil can be anywhere and everywhere, including within an innocent little girl. Even the nuns, with the possible exception of the two-fisted Sister Saint George in eighth grade, never scared me that much.

Why *Abbott and Costello Meet Frankenstein*? It's just an excuse to spend time with old friends. Who could resist the one film that shows Bela Lugosi weaving a cinematic spell as Dracula, Lon Chaney, Jr., howling as The Wolf Man and the voice of Vincent Price providing a final reminder of one of the great gentlemen-artists of the horror genre.

Besides, *Abbott and Costello Meet Frankenstein* is the only Universal classic from which I have a complete set of lobby cards. I'd take the cards along, tack them on a nearby tree, and pretend the area was an old theater lobby.

Of course, the first time someone visited the island, I'd sell him the cards, head to shore, stock up on new prints of *Vertigo* (1958), *Horror of Dracula*, *The Day the Earth Stood Still* (1951), *Return of the Dragon* (1972), *The Rocketeer* (1991), *King Kong* and *Them!* (1954). I'd get back in time to heat the popcorn and enjoy a twilight show.

• • • • •

Steve Thornton

Now, let me get this straight. The premise, as I understand it, is that I am stuck on a desert island with none of the creature comforts of modern living. No phone, no car, no CD player—absolutely none of the amenities to which we have all grown attached. And yet, inexplicably, I have access to a fully functioning DVD player and a selection of three movies to satisfy my personal need for viewing entertainment. Now, this is unquestionably a screwy and farfetched scenario (it sounds like a bad 1950' sci-fi movie!), but hey, I can go along with it.

The first entry in my limited collection would be Universal's 1934 shocker, *The Black Cat*. This film works for me on

a number of levels. For starters, you have the classic teaming of Karloff and Lugosi, the sight of whom conjures up warm, nostalgic memories of my initiation into the world of fright films via late night television. Another compelling feature of this movie is its passionate, classically influenced musical soundtrack. With apologies to Franz Waxman and Max Steiner, I find *The Black Cat*'s symphonic backdrop to be the most effective soundtrack music from any 1930s' horror film. (Given the growing interest in classic movie music that we are witnessing today, I am surprised that no one has seen fit to release it on CD.) Finally, there is the film's haunting and perverse aura, perhaps the most oppressive atmosphere present in any Golden Age horror film. Though many of the Universal horrors now strike me as quaint fairy tales, *The Black Cat* stands alone, its characters festering over with vengeance and malignant intent. Long after the film has ended, I find myself mesmerized by the evil Fort Marmaros (almost a metaphor for contemporary society itself), with its ultra modern decor, amoral ambiance and dark, unspeakable secrets.

Poised with stake and mallet, Jack MacGowran and Roman Polanski begin their vampire hunt through the castle.

"THE FEARLESS VAMPIRE KILLERS OR PARDON ME, BUT YOUR TEETH ARE IN MY NECK"

performance is the darkly ironic tone that allows the film to be both morbid and humorous at the same time. Even when taking into account the film's gratuitous gore and strong sexual content, I still find it to be one of the more "fun" horror films I have seen in recent decades, a feeling which does not come along often enough anymore.

Limiting myself to a selection of three is absurdly difficult. Even within the category of genre films, I have so many favorites that the choice becomes thankless and frustrating. But if I must choose, then these are the trio of terrors that I would take along with me. No matter how often I view these films, I always find them to be a pleasant and worthwhile investment of my time.

You know, I could get used to this island lifestyle thing. I would write more, but I have to go now. Ginger and Mary Ann want to play "rub the coconuts" again.

For my second choice on this cinematic fantasy island, I would bring along a copy of Roman Polanski's *The Fearless Vampire Killers* (1967). I discovered this film at a time when I thought I had become "too grown up" to enjoy horror films. But the unexpected combination of slapstick humor, cockeyed Hammer homage and ghastly vampire masked ball reminded me just how entertaining a good horror yarn can be. And by introducing me to the beguiling charms of lovely Sharon Tate, this film also proved that horror cinema could still interest me on an adult level as well (after this, I would never look at wooden bathtubs the same way again). The film also becomes a kind of tribute to the quaint horrors of decades past; given the tongue-in-cheek attitude that Polanski so successfully employed, it was obvious that a modern audience could not take vampires, werewolves and mad scientists of my youth seriously. *The Fearless Vampire Killers*, consequently, is to me a fond farewell to an era destined to pass away but too sublime to be forgotten.

Only one selection left? How about Stuart Gordon's outrageously over-the-top *Re-Animator* (1985). My appreciation for this film is largely due to the colorful performance of Jeffrey Combs, which echoes the flamboyant portrayals of horror stars from an earlier era. Cast in the role of determined Dr. Herbert West, Combs refuses to let conventional, legal or ethical restrictions stand in the way of his peculiar, though ultimately successful, research work. A perfect hero for corporate America! If Oscars were awarded specifically for genre films, my vote for the best actor of the 1980s would go to Combs, besting such worthy contenders as Jack Nicholson in *The Shining* (1980) or Jeff Goldblum in *The Fly* (1986). Accentuating his animated

John E. Parnum

Isolated with only three videos of my choice to watch for the rest of my life? That's a tough one. There's an irresistible 1993 "feel good" movie called *The Sandlot* that captivates me when it appears on television. Each time I watch this David Evans-directed charmer, I laugh and cry and applaud (even though I'm not crazy about baseball). *The Sandlot* has its fantasy elements, too: The spirit of Babe Ruth (Art LaFleur) appears to Benny "The Jet" Rodriguez (Mike Vitar), reminding him that "heroes get remembered, but legends never die." However, I think I'm only good for 10 more reruns of this one.

If "legends never die," then my first choice is Alexander Korda's *The Thief of Bagdad*. This 1940 classic Arabian fantasy captures the joy of innocence ("This is the land of legend," the old patriarch of a world created by men ceasing to be children explains to the little thief Abu, "where everything is possible when seen through the eyes of youth."), just as it also champions the endurance of true love. The limitless boundaries of imagination are stretched in Miles Malleson's screenplay as the djinni (Rex Ingram) transports Abu (Sabu) to the Temple of the Gods on the roof of the world that is "supported by seven pillars; and the seven pillars are set on the shoulders of a djinni whose strength is beyond thought, and the djinni stands on an eagle; and the eagle on a bull; and the bull a fish; and the fish swims in the sea of eternity." I could listen to this poetry, enhanced by Miklos Rozsa's lush score, all day.

While the special effects (magic carpet, flying horse, giant spider, towering djinni) do not compare with today's state-of-the-art accomplishments (which I feel diminish the range of our own imaginations), *The Thief of Bagdad* conjures up memories of a little boy seeing the film's marvels for the first time on a double bill with the 1942 *Jungle Book* (also starring Sabu). It also reminds me of a wonderful afternoon when that same boy took his wife and two daughters to The Museum of Modern Art nearly 40 years later to see an Ansel Adams exhibit, a display of Peter Ellenshaw's special effects (including the spaceship model from *The Black Hole*), and a screening of *The Thief of Bagdad*. As the end credits rolled after Abu sails away on his flying carpet into the rainbow-filled sky, the entire audience broke into applause, still appreciative and unspoiled by the high-tech profuseness of *Star Wars*. The old king of the Land of Legend proclaims to Abu, "We are the remnants of the Golden Age...Whenever the heart of a child returns to us, or comes into

us, we live again." And each time I watch *The Thief of Bagdad*, I too live again in the world of my childhood and in the hearts of my children.

Readers knowing of my interest in horror films, especially my favorite *Bride of Frankenstein*, may be surprised to find this genre missing from my choices. Oddly, my second selection is not a movie, but rather a tape of previews called *'30s and '40s Horror Trailers*. Compiled by George Stover for Cinemacabre Video, I chose this unique tape for the following three reasons. First, trailers usually contain the most exciting scenes of a film, made even more enticing by the highly exaggerated copy lines such as "Come with the Mad Wizard of the Weird, Past the Last Barriers of Life"—*The Devil Commands*, "The Screen's Mightiest Monsters Thrash Out against the Frenzy of the Mob"—*House of Dracula*, and "Dinosaurs! Earthquake! Ripping, Tearing, Nature Goes Mad, Sucking the Earth Underseas!"—*Son of Kong*. It's fascinatingly nostalgic to hear Helen Chandler in *Dracula* confess again, "He opened a vein in his arm and made me drink" or Edward Van Sloan in *The Mummy* warn, "He's going to make her a living mummy like himself."

The second reason that I chose this video is that while I know these films practically by heart, there are scenes whose absence will actually precipitate my recollection of them: The dinosaurs from *King Kong* are missing from the preview and the Monster's mate in *Bride of Frankenstein* remains hidden under bandages. And in *Black Friday*, we are treated to Lugosi actually being hypnotized as part of a promotional stunt. And thirdly, of three films on the trailer that somehow escaped me, *The Man Who Lived Twice*, *Mystery of the White Room* and *Horror Island* (with a startling silhouette of "The Phantom"), I can let my imagination run wild with my own concepts of horrors never experienced.

In Brian W. Aldiss's poetically written short story "Poor Little Warrior," which first appeared in *The Magazine of Fantasy and Science Fiction*, a narrator, nonexistent to the protagonist, comments that "If you had been in charge of creation you would have found some medium less heartbreaking than Time to stage it all in." And so for my third choice to while away the endless hours, I have chosen George Pal's *The Time Machine* (1960), if only because it represents Man's spirit of adventure and perseverance in the face of extreme odds and the ridicule of his associates. The special effects by Gene Warren, Wah Chang and Tim Barr, which send the conscientious time traveler George (Rod Taylor) from his comfortable 1899 Victorian home, with a stop in 1966 where he narrowly escapes nuclear destruction (a slight miscalculation on Pal's part), to the sterile world of 802,701, are clever and precisely detailed. Small bits, perhaps forgotten in previous viewings, are fun to recollect, such as the brass plate on the ornate time machine that reads, "Manufactured by H. George Wells."

The film unleashes the entire gamut of emotions for me: *Fear* (the attack of the cannibalistic Morlocks and the claustrophobia of being buried under a mountain); *desire* (when George meets the lovely and innocent Weena—Yvette Mimieux); *jubilance* (as the time traveler leads the complacent Eloi in revolt against the Morlocks); *humor* (as George trips through time watching the styles rapidly change on the dress shop mannequin across from his home); and *sadness* (when Filby—Alan Young in several remarkable roles—wanting to believe in George's mad dream—realizes he will never see his friend again). All this makes *The Time Machine* worth watching time and time again. And when Filby returns to George's home after the scoffers have staggered away in the snow, he finds the inventor has disappeared into the future of the simple Eloi and to his love Weena. The housekeeper, Mrs. Watchett (Doris Lloyd), notes that three books are missing from the library—*three books that might be significant in rebuilding a civilization.* Filby asks a question of her, as well as of himself and us the audience, "What three books would you have taken?" And that too, of course, will provide me hours of conjecture in passing away the time in my place of isolation during intermission between my three videos.

• • • • • •

Greg Mank

Only three, eh? Well, let's see...

First of all, the two (obligatory) horror movies.

Naturally, being a "Golden Age" devotee, I'd take one from the 1930s, one from the 1940s:

Frankenstein—Yes, I know *Bride of...* is more brilliant and outrageous, but the 1935 sequel is also remarkably bitter and sad—hence hardly desirable as one of my only three desert island films. The original *Frankenstein* still has all its magic for me: The beauty of Karloff's Monster, the anguish of Colin Clive's Frankenstein, the classic support from Edward Van Sloan and Dwight Frye, the spine-tingling (and restored) lake flower game of Boris' Monster and Marilyn Harris' Little Maria...all given raw, poignant, fairy tale poetry by James Whale. That (almost) final shot of the windmill burning in the night atop the mountain, Karloff (supposedly) perishing inside, inspires lump-in-throat and tear-in-eyes (a power my favorite movies seem to wield more and more powerfully as I grow older).

And, in bringing along this tape, I'd have to find safe shelter on the island for three accompanying items: a packet Karloff sent me in 1964 (when I was 13), containing an autographed portrait of himself and a smaller portrait of himself as the Monster; a transcript of my interview with Marilyn ("Little Maria") Harris; and (to sound immodest), a copy of my book, *It's Alive! The Classic Cinema Saga of Frankenstein.*

The Body Snatcher (RKO, 1945)—This is (I think) the greatest horror movie of the 1940s: Karloff's magnificent title role performance, Lugosi's perpetually underrated character work, Henry Daniell's tragic Dr. "Toddy" MacFarlane, that climactic coach ride ("Never get rid of me!…get rid of me!")—all directed with fireworks by Robert Wise and produced with style by the great Val Lewton. It's a film that "wows" no matter how many times I see it; and having had the luck to have interviewed Mr. Wise and supporting players Russel Wade, Robert Clarke and the late Rita Corday, I have a palpable feeling of the fun that must have existed on the set.

And, along with the tape, comes the letter Mr. Wise kindly sent me years ago, full of reminiscences about the filming; and (to sound immodest) a copy of my book, *Karloff and Lugosi*.

Now, for the "Non-Horror" title:

Drums Along the Mohawk (20th Century Fox, 1939)—John Ford's dramatic, moving, Technicolor saga of Claudette Colbert, Henry Fonda and settlers vs. John Carradine, Tories, and Indians has been a favorite of mine for 30 years. It, too, chokes me up every time I watch it (at least once

a year, usually on the 4th of July). And it now reminds me of one day of the 1988 Western trip in which my wonderful wife Barbara (who, I'm assuming, is on this island with me) and our terrific children Jessie and Chris (who, now in their advanced teens, hopefully at least have frequent island visiting privileges) found the location site of the *Drums the Mohawk* shoot in Cedar Breaks National Monument, Utah. Amidst wildflowers and pine trees and streams and vistas, 11,000 feet up in the mountains, I rejoiced ("That must be where they had built the fort! That must be where they had the cabin!" etc.). My wife, daughter, and son all lovingly indulged me. It was a great day.

And, with the tape: an original 20th Century Fox still of John Carradine from the film (strikingly evil in cape, three-cornered hat, eyepatch, etc.) which I bought at Hollywood's Larry Edmunds Bookshop way back in 1967; and our "home movies" video of the aforementioned vacation.

• • • •

Cindy Collins Smith

The Wizard of Oz (1939)—I thought she called it "The Lizard of Oz." And that misperception led to a classic "I know what's best for you" confrontation with my mother. I was five, and mom was busily trying to force me to watch some stupid lizard movie. "I'll be up past my bedtime," I reminded her. But on this night of all nights, she waived the 7:30 bedtime rule, and I was stuck.

Then the movie began. The song, the dance, the comedy, the fantasy and (yes!) the horror enthralled me. It had everything: Witches and Haunted Forests and Flying Monkeys. And it had Dorothy. As I journeyed with her through Oz, I felt the threat to the little girl, and her little dog too. When it all had ended and the wicked witch melted away, I was honestly glad that my mother had, on this occasion, won.

I've seen *The Wizard* at home alone and in crowded rooms with 50 of my closest college friends. I've watched it in wide-eyed wonder and interpreted it through the haze of critical theories. No matter what, though, this film never changes, never ages. *The Wizard of Oz* is not my favorite musical (that honor belongs to *Singin' in the Rain*), but it may well be my favorite film. It holds the power of the child.

The Empire Strikes Back (1980)—In 1977 I had become a high culture snob, with no use for mindless mass media. And then I saw *Star Wars*, a silly little movie that came out of no-where and did things on the screen that I'd never dreamt of before. It blew my mind (as thoroughly as *King Kong* must have blown moviegoers' minds in 1933) and wrecked my snobbery. Quite simply, it was a life-changing, life-saving revelation.

So why choose *Empire* and not *Star Wars*? In *The Empire Strikes Back*, George Lucas takes an entertaining space romp and elevates it into a mythic battle with inner demons, compelling Luke to descend into the "underworld" to learn the painful knowledge of his own identity. *The Empire* is to *Star Wars* what *The Godfather, Part II* is to that trilogy—the best, most thoughtful film of the three.

Empire's effects are better. Its characterizations gain depth. Its battle between Vadar and Skywalker (*all* the Skywalkers) becomes epic, nearly tragic. And Vadar becomes quite nearly a horror monster. It's all the sort of stuff I love. In the final analysis, and despite Peter Cushing's presence in the first film, *The Empire Strikes Back* is *Star Wars* squared.

Reefer Madness (1936)—I may well be the only person in America who watches *Reefer Madness* in order to get scared out of my wits. Yes, it's overacted. Yes, it's overstated. No, the normal teenager will not turn into an ax-wielding psychopath after a single hit of the *killer weed*. But when Dave O'Brien lurches into that courtroom like some zombie movie refugee, I for one know that this 1936 flick is no misguided attempt at realism. This is a symbolic precursor of all those alien-monster-mind-possession movies of the fifties, here featuring marijuana as the alien entity.

When I watch O'Brien freak out in a sequence that would do Dwight Frye proud, when I see him turn from average party-boy into wild-eyed man possessed, I see in his mad face a reflection of the way I felt inside when I gave away my clarinet for $20, only moments after my stash ran out; I see in him the way I felt when I discovered that I could indeed stop getting high...for five, or maybe 10 to 15, minutes at a time.

Though I escaped the alien-monster's clutches in 1978, seeing O'Brien in *Reefer Madness* still reminds me of what it was like to be a young person possessed by a force beyond my control. In the end, O'Brien's unreal mania is far more frightening to me than ten thousand Draculas, or Werewolves, or even Hannibal Lecters. It reflects my life's worst nightmare right back at myself.

Still, if the cardboard cutout good-guys (and especially Jonathan Harker) weren't so annoying in Browning's *Dracula*, I'd drop *Reefer Madness* in a second and take the movie that made me pull the covers up around my neck until well into my college years. But then maybe, on my Desert Island, O'Brien's flickering image will evoke his scenes with Bela in their horrors of Poverty Row. And if my imagination really takes flight, I

may yet glimpse Renfield enter the web at Castle Dracula, and Count Dracula take delight as he comments on the howling of the "children of the night."

• • • • •

Susan Svehla

Cindy really did me a favor in the above paragraph. I was really torn when pondering which of my favorite films to take with me. When discussing with our writer friends which movies we'd take with us to an island, everyone already knew my choices...*The Wizard of Oz, Singin' in the Rain* and *Star Wars*. Nobody hesitated, they never stopped for a moment to consider I *might* surprise them; they just rambled the titles off with an annoyingly cocky attitude (the fact they were 100% correct is beside the point). So I decided I'm either really boring or enthuse too much over my three favorite films (or maybe both). So, on our island I'll just watch Cindy's copies of *The Wizard of Oz* and *Empire Strikes Back* (it's not *Star Wars*, but it'll do) and select several different choices for my viewing pleasure.

Wow, our writers were right, this is really tough. Should I go with heart-rending tearjerkers I watch when I'm depressed and need a good cry—*Dark Victory, A Star is Born*, or *Now Voyager*. Or should I take comedies that never fail to make me chuckle—*The Philadelphia Story, Bringing Up Baby, The Thin Man, Ghost Breakers,* *The Parent Trap, Some Like it Hot*? What about romances, everyone needs a little romance—*Moonlighting, It Happened One Night, Beauty and the Beast?* Or John Wayne films (hate his politics, love the man)—*The Quiet Man, McClintock, The Searchers*? What about frightfests—*Aliens, Terminator 2, The Bride of Frankenstein, The Haunting*? What about baseball movies—I *love* baseball movies, *Pride of the Yankees, Damn Yankees* (as a Baltimore fan I really do mean DAMN Yankees), *Field of Dreams, Angels in the Outfield*? Or *All About Eve, Band Wagon, It's a Wonderful Life, White Christmas, Sands of Iwo Jima, High Noon, Meet John Doe, Cinderella*! Ahhhhhh!

Okay, take a deep breath, this can't be that difficult. Submitted for your approval, my three choices (and if you ultimately decide my taste is crap—you may be right.)

The Rocky Horror Picture Show. What is the attraction of this warped little film that has gained legendary cult status? I have no idea. But I do know whenever I watch this bizarre tribute to classic horror films, it makes me laugh. The songs are a delight, easy to sing to (and dance with—if you have the nerve, but I've found that usually involves the ingestion of a lot of alcohol. "Let's do the Timewarp again!"), Susan Sarandon and Barry Bostwick lend just the right touch of naughty but niceness to the story and Tim Curry steals the show as the cross-dressing bi-sexual pervert's delight as Dr. Frank N. Furter, leader of this grotesque band of lunatics. His grand entrance would put most prima donnas to shame, as his high-heeled glitter encrusted foot taps to the melodic "I'm just a sweet transvestite from transsexual Transylvania," as he bursts forth from his private elevator wearing a black corset and fishnet

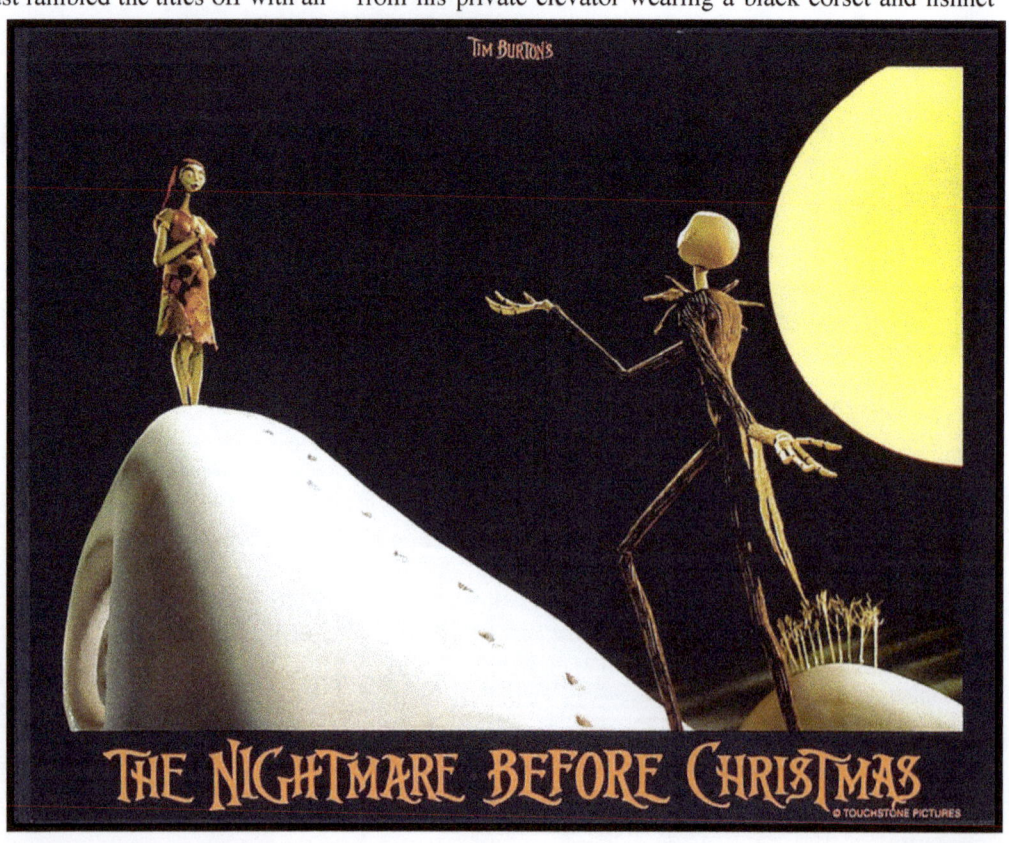

stockings. Curry is hysterical as he chases his new creation, Rocky—a blonde dim-witted hunk—around the lab as his Dr. Frank N. Furter squeals in delight. *Rolling Stone* noted, "It's *Singin' in the Rain* as seen dimly through a quaalude."

The Nightmare Before Christmas (1993). When we first saw this strange Henry Selick-directed stop-motion animated film on the gigantic theater screen, I didn't find it at all enjoyable. However, this amazing film gets better with each successive viewing. The score and songs by Danny Elfman are utterly charming. The weird and wonderful characters grow more engaging with each visit, and you will always discover some new action going on you had never noticed before. Lead character Jack Skellington is Everyman as he searches for meaning in his life. Although he is the most successful Halloween King ever, he feels he is missing something and sets out to find it. Unfortunately, he makes a few disastrous mistakes along the way, before finding the thing he was missing was right under his pointy little skeleton nose.

Singin' in the Rain becomes an almost perfect film from beginning to end. Gene Kelly, Donald O'Connor and Debbie Reynolds (along with screechingly delightful support from Jean Hagen) wrap the viewer in a real Hollywood fable, as our little band sets out to breach the sound barrier and make their first sound picture, *The Dancing Cavalier*. Each musical number is a winner, from Donald O'Connor's hilarious "Make 'Em Laugh" to Kelly and O'Connor's "Moses Supposes." Let's not forget the steamy Cyd Charrise in the "Broadway Ballet" number (she could teach those scream queens a thing or two about sex appeal). But of course the topper is the classic "Singin' in the Rain" number where the incredible Gene Kelly, with just an umbrella and lots of raindrops, creates a cinematic moment that will never be surpassed.

• • • • •

Gary J. Svehla

Preparing for the cruise I suddenly realized a very pertinent bit of information: The best films, even favorite films, are not necessarily those films that demand repeating watchings. As I approach my sixth decade I find it more difficult to watch my favorite films again and again. I love *Bride of Frankenstein*

111

A Christmas Carol, the Alastair Sim version produced in 1951, is my perennial holiday film that always reminds me what it was like to be a kid at Christmas time. It never fails to bring a tear to my eye, and the universally appealing plot, which transcends all ages and cultures, always rings true and reminds me of those important fundamental things in life. That human beings are always too busy to notice the little things around us, that we tend to ignore compassion

and consider it, along with Hammer's *Horror of Dracula*, my favorite horror films, but to be quite honest, I can only take each film at most once a year (*Bride* I've simply seen a few times too many and *Horror of Dracula*'s deliberately slower pacing makes it worth seeing only ocassionally).

But when it comes to movies that can be watched frequently with almost the same amount of passion each time they are viewed, I turn to some quirky choices. At least oddball for a dedicated fan of Golden Age Horrors.

My three choices would be: Alastair Sim's delicious 1951 *A Christmas Carol*; United Artists' 1957 production of *The Vampire*, my favorite B film of the 1950s; and *Aliens* (1986), my favorite adrenaline-paced modern horror classic.

First, my most controversial choice, United Artists' Jules V. Levy/Arthur Gardner's production of *The Vampire,* starring John Beal, Coleen Gray and Kenneth Tobey. The reason this film appeals to my desert island consciousness is complex and difficult to dissect. But this gem occupies a special place in my heart because it left such a wonderful impression when I saw it at the theater with my father in 1957, at the tender young age of seven. Throughout the years, United Artists horror movies of this period became scarce on television, even rarer to find in 16mm collector's prints, so a mystique developed around the title. For some reason, these 1950s' B horror films are generally slow-paced, badly acted or just too juvenile to hold an adult's attention. But *The Vampire*, tautly directed by Paul Landres, blends both science fiction with Jekyll and Hyde horror, allowing John Beal to deliver a truly pathetic hero/villain performance that outshines his peers. Beal, only to appear in this one horror movie, transcends the budget and the low-budget genre to create an involving human being beaming with pathos. The pace is swift, the main plot interesting and the acting is uniformly effective (even right down to Dabbs Greer's supporting performance). Taken for what it is, I can watch *The Vampire* every three months or so and be mesmerized by its budget-minded sense of fun. (My second choice would be *It! The Terror from Beyond Space*.)

and humanity for unfortunates, and that we truly need each other to make our lives meaningful. Sim's characterization of Scrooge is so powerful because he represents the damned humanity in all of us, the person who is too busy to smell the roses, too busy to be kind, too sour to enjoy the simple joys. And in this incredibly stressful world, the reborn Scrooge gives hope to all of us that the spirit of Christmas is still alive (if not well), inside all of us humbugs, just waiting to be recognized to be set free. The movie is uplifting, scary, ghostly, haunting, delightful, energizing and poignant, all at the same time. Emotionally, *A Christmas Carol* pushes all the buttons in such a way that the plot carries the viewer along so effortlessly, that the movie has done a number on us and is over almost as soon as it begins. I could screen this classic at least once every six months. Talk about Christmas in July!

Finally, when it comes to sudden jolts, exhilarating action and tremendous scares, *Aliens* begins (even a decade after its release) to take on the look of a genuine horror classic. For one thing, the monsters are mesmerizing and terrifying at the same time, bogey men from space that are the stuff of which nightmares are made. Sigourney Weaver's performance as Ripley is complex and multi-leveled as the surrogate mother/heroine—notice her vulnerability (her recurring nightmares and regret at having lost her entire family in the blink of an eye), her fear as the horrors slowly mount, her humanity and dignity remaining intact as her life comes crushing down around her and her kick-ass mentality as the female Beowulf of the modern era. And James Cameron's direction is so frenetically paced and exciting that the action sequences can be watched, studied and re-watched almost immediately—and they never loose their intensity. *Bride of Frankenstein* is the better film, but I can watch *Aliens* four times a year and still find something new and be terrified by horrors that never seem to lose their power. Simply because *Aliens* is so modern and film fans have a predisposed notion that classics must be old, it might take another decade or so to realize that Cameron's *Aliens* is a classic-in-the-making and hopefully will hold up for future eras to enjoy time and time again.

What a dream triple feature: A schlocky B feature that never fails to entertain, a superb ghost/fantasy film that both touches the heart and reminds us of our lost humanity and a frenetic action horror picture that blends special effects, fast-paced direction and good performances (from Weaver's starring performance to Bill Paxton's comic relief) to create perhaps the most visceral horror classic of our times. These films I can watch and re-watch continually, hopefully, without growing tired of any of them.

But hopefully, my *full* film library will be available to me for a long time to come, whereby I won't have to choose only three films for eternity. Now that's horror!

• • • • •

We'd like to thank all the writers who contributed to this chapter. Sadly, since this first appeared in Midnight Marquee *magazine, we have lost two of those friends, John Parnum and Joe Guilfoyle.*

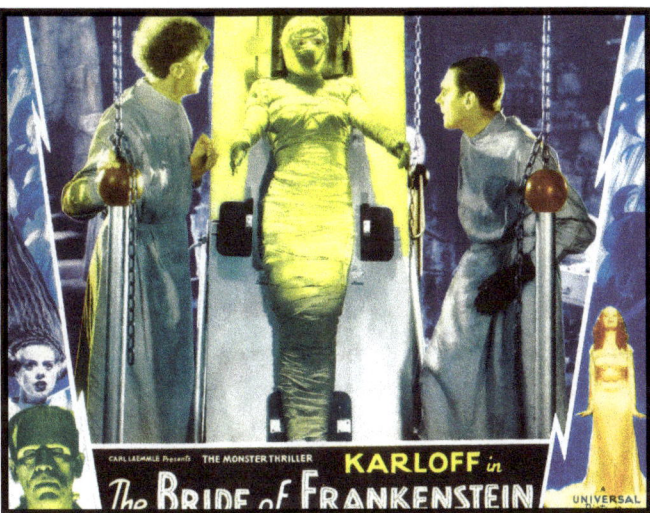

**If you enjoyed this book
please call or write or e-mail for a free catalog**

**Midnight Marquee Press, Inc.
9721 Britinay Lane
Baltimore, MD 21234
410-665-1198 • www.midmar.com**

You may enjoy other MidMar Classic Movie Memories
6x9 paperbacks, $25 each • Popcorn Prozac Sale Price $20! (plus shipping)

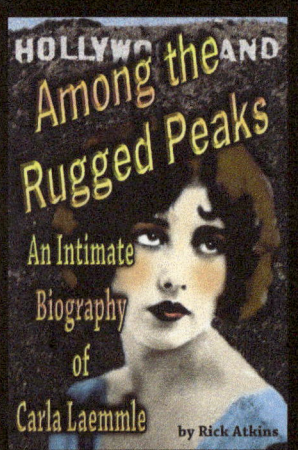

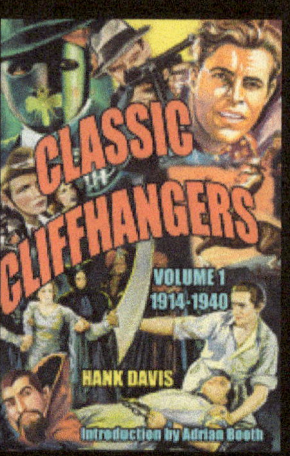

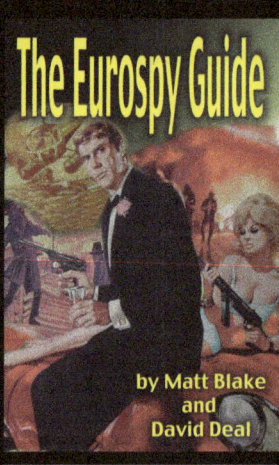
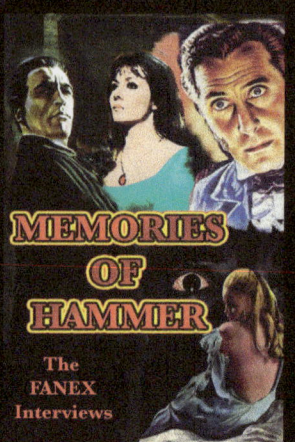

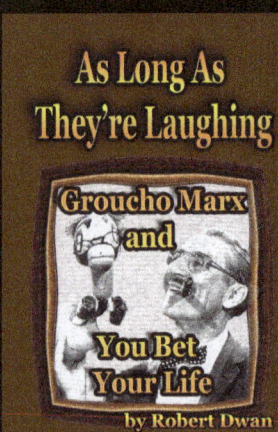
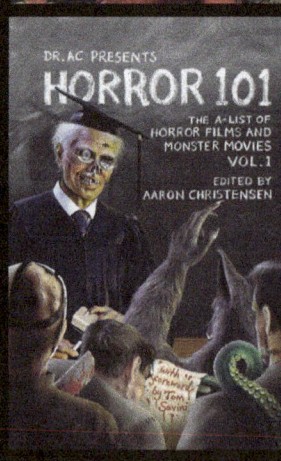

www.ingramcontent.com/pod-product-compliance
Lightning Source LLC
Chambersburg PA
CBHW042026100526
44587CB00029B/4310